.NET Design Patt

Explore the world of .NET design patterns and bring the benefits that the right patterns can offer to your toolkit today

Praseed Pai
Shine Xavier

BIRMINGHAM - MUMBAI

.NET Design Patterns

First published: January 2017

Production reference: 1250117

Published by Packt Publishing Ltd.
Livery Place
35 Livery Street
Birmingham
B3 2PB, UK.
ISBN 978-1-78646-615-0

www.packtpub.com

Credits

Authors

Praseed Pai

Shine Xavier

Reviewers

Soumya Mukherjee

Vidya Vrat Agarwal

Commissioning Editor

Kunal Parikh

Acquisition Editor

Denim Pinto

Content Development Editor

Siddhi Chavan

Technical Editor

Sunith Shetty

Copy Editor

Sonia Mathur

Project Coordinator

Izzat Contractor

Proofreader

Safis Editing

Indexer

Francy Puthiry

Graphics

Jason Monteiro

Production Coordinator

Shraddha Falebhai

Foreword

We are living in an era where most of the things that we do are getting automated through software. Even though, there is definite trend towards pre-packaged software modules and platforms, there is always a place for custom software development and integration projects. In the Enterprise world, .NET and Java EE are the natural platforms of choice for custom software development and deployments. With Agile software development methods, continuous delivery and Domain-Driven Design dominating the scene, there is a need for standardization and communication about software artifacts in a "platform-agnostic" manner. In this context, software design patterns becomes a primary tool for such communications.

You have in your hands a book that encompasses more than four decades of collective wisdom amassed by these two authors, as part of their continuous pursuit of knowledge and excellence, in the software engineering and technology consulting arena. What is more significant is the fact that these knowledge representations are a direct reflection of a practitioner's mindset; some of those have been undertaken for our organization under our supervision! This is more than a reference book and should be looked at as a handbook for developers who are aspiring to take their skills to the next level and design state-of-the-art systems independently. This is undoubtedly a book that helps unfold many underlying principles that further educate and help one appreciate the various programming paradigms that are in vogue, as I write this foreword.

We have been continuously disrupting and pushing computing limits way beyond CPUs and GPUs over the past five decades. It is quite amazing to see the ground the authors have covered, in terms of contemplating the evolution of software design, patterns and idioms, to help developers create scalable and consistent code. More than coverage, their focus has been on certain aspects of design that help you create well structured (leveraging GoF patterns), scalable (through concurrent and parallel programming) and reliable (through functional and reactive programming) code with some of the .NET platform tools that transcend conventional imperative programming techniques.

At the core, the book deals with how pattern-based software development helps one to write better code. The authors have deliberately crafted the book to convey how various development patterns that are part of different catalogues can be put to use in a coordinated manner to write good quality code in .NET. The book covers how one can use GoF, POSA, DDD, POEAA, and EIP catalogue in the C# programming language.

Praseed and Shine are part of UST Global's Technology Consulting group and have been collaborating professionally for the last ten years. They truly complement each other when it comes to software design and development. Their command over computer science first principles, ability to learn new technologies, appetite for challenges, and passion for software design is truly commendable. This makes their technology leadership invaluable to any professional organization.

Leveraging the core platform features (in this case, .NET) in tandem with industry-standard best practices (in this case, proven design pattern catalogues and idioms) is the need of the hour and becomes a clear differentiator when it comes to delivering high quality, scalable, and consistent code. This clearly is any developer's best hedge in the present day's highly volatile technology landscape. I believe the authors have tried their best in articulating this with anecdotes and detailed code samples, and I hope that, after reading this book, you will feel the same way.

Arun Narayanan

COO, UST Global

About the Authors

Praseed Pai is a software engineering/re-engineering professional with good business acumen, technical competency, and software engineering skills. He has presented on various topics in more than two hundred technical events in the last decade and half. His areas of interest include software architecture, design patterns, domain-specific languages, engineering software development, computer graphics, and machine learning. Currently, he is associated with the UST global as a senior solutions architect in their consulting division. He is also the primary force behind the SLANGFORDOTNET compiler infrastructure, which has been ported to VB.NET (CLR), Java (JVM), C++ (LLVM), Python, JavaScript, and Ruby. He lives in the city of Kochi with his wife and two kids.

I would like to start off thanking my co-author Shine Xavier for undertaking this journey along with me. An important acknowledgment goes to my longtime collaborator and friend Shalvin PD, who introduced us to Denim Pinto of Packt. I would like to acknowledge the contributions of Aneesh P Revi, Nikhil Nair, Sarath Soman, Vaisakh Babu, Haridas Nair, John Thomas, Biju Alapat, Joseph Abraham, Shaji P Dayanandan, and members of the Kerala Microsoft Users Group (KMUG) while working on the content of the book. I would like to thank my parents, Mrs. Mohana T Pai and the late K.J. Thrivikrama Pai, who taught me the value of continuous learning. I whole heartedly thank my wife, Sandhya L Kammath, for giving encouragement and taking care of our domestic issues herself, while I was writing this book. Being a developer herself, I could get different perspectives on the content I was writing. Last, but not least, Sidharth Pai and Karthik Pai, my sons, for allowing me to concentrate on the book, by not bothering much with their usual demands! Finally, I thank the wonderful folks at Packt and the two reviewers who helped us to make the book better.

Shine Xavier is a core software engineering practitioner with an extreme passion for designing/building software solutions, application frameworks, and accelerators that help maintain productivity, code quality, performance, and security. His areas of interest include functional programming, interpreters, JavaScript library development, visual programming, algorithms, performance engineering, automation, enterprise mobility, IoT and machine learning. He is currently associated with UST Global as a senior architect, where he continues to provide technical leadership in customer engagements, pre-sales, practice development, product development, innovation, and technology adoption. He lives with his wife and three kids in Thiruvananthapuram, Kerala, India.

I would like to start off thanking my colleague and mentor Praseed Pai for choosing me to co-author this book. It has been a joy and privilege penning this book along with you, my friend! There are others without whom I wouldn't have been able to complete this book. In particular, I would like to thank: the folks at Packt (Denim Pinto, Pooja Mhapsekar, Siddhi Chavan, and Sunith Shetty) who were really patient and inspiring us throughout this journey and the technical reviewers Soumya Mukherjee and Vidya Vrat Agarwal, who really pushed us all along to get this book one knot better. This book has become a lot better and taken its present shape because of you all! My teachers and friends in school and college, mentors (Arun Narayanan and Sunil Balakrishnan), colleagues (Jeenu Mathew, Viby Abraham, Renju Ramadevan, Nikhil Nair, John Thomas, Renjith Ramachandran, Jenson Joseph, Ashok Nair, and Abhilash Ponnachan) and members of the computer science fraternity (many whom I paid my respects to in the book). You all continue to teach, motivate, and inspire me! My parents (Xavier and Grace) without whom I would cease to exist. My wife (Kavitha Jose) and kids (Joel, Sera and Johaan) for their whole-hearted love, support, and understanding in helping me realize this dream.

About the Reviewers

Soumya Mukherjee is very passionate about working on open source projects and has extensive experience in architecting enterprise applications in .NET, JAVA, Ruby, and Python.

He has expertise in implementation of Test Driven and Behavioural Driven development and test automation for large teams. He has developed various tools, one of them is the Quantinuous Agile Framework (QAF) for continuous mobile and web automation.

He is a certified MCAD.NET, Certified Scrum Master (CSM), Certified Professional Selenium Agile Tester, a Trainer, and a seasoned author of couple of books on amazon. He is also a speaker across multiple world renowned conferences, an Agile Practitioner, and loves mentoring team's in Open Source Technologies.

He has extensive experience in Software Test Automation using professional tools, such as QTP, QC, LoadRunner, Jmeter, and Neoload GreenHat, and with Open Source Tools, such as Selenium RC & Web driver with Java, .Net, Python, Ruby, FitNess, JMeter, SoapUI, TestNG, ReportNG, JUnit, Cucumber & Capybara, and Tosca & Perfecto.

An ex-employee of JP Morgan, Merill Lynch, he is currently the co-founder of QAAgility Technologies and AppTestPro. He resides in Mumbai, India, with his wife, Garima.

Vidya Vrat Agarwal is passionate about .NET, a Microsoft MVP, a C# Corner MVP, a TOGAF certified architect, a Certified Scrum Master (CSM), an author, a speaker, a certified MCT, MCPD, MCTS, MCSD.NET, MCAD.NET, and MCSD. He is currently working as a .NET Enterprise Architect and Consultant in USA. He is passionate about .NET technology and loves to contribute to the .NET community. He blogs at `http://www.MyPassionFor.NE T` and can be followed on Twitter, `@DotNetAuthor`. He lives with his wife, Rupali, and two daughters, Pearly and Arshika, in Redmond, WA.

www.PacktPub.com

For support files and downloads related to your book, please visit www.PacktPub.com.

Did you know that Packt offers eBook versions of every book published, with PDF and ePub files available? You can upgrade to the eBook version at www.PacktPub.com and as a print book customer, you are entitled to a discount on the eBook copy. Get in touch with us at service@packtpub.com for more details.

At www.PacktPub.com, you can also read a collection of free technical articles, sign up for a range of free newsletters and receive exclusive discounts and offers on Packt books and eBooks.

https://www.packtpub.com/mapt

Get the most in-demand software skills with Mapt. Mapt gives you full access to all Packt books and video courses, as well as industry-leading tools to help you plan your personal development and advance your career.

Why subscribe?

- Fully searchable across every book published by Packt
- Copy and paste, print, and bookmark content
- On demand and accessible via a web browser

Customer Feedback

Thank you for purchasing this Packt book. We take our commitment to improving our content and products to meet your needs seriously--that's why your feedback is so valuable. Whatever your feelings about your purchase, please consider leaving a review on this book's Amazon page. Not only will this help us, more importantly it will also help others in the community to make an informed decision about the resources that they invest in to learn.

You can also review for us on a regular basis by joining our reviewers' club. **If you're interested in joining, or would like to learn more about the benefits we offer, please contact us**: customerreviews@packtpub.com.

Table of Contents

Preface

Writing modern Enterprise software requires large teams that need close co-ordination to deliver quality products and services. The teams require a common language for communication when dealing with technical solutions and artifacts, in order to work as a cohesive unit for meeting the set objective. The GOF design pattern catalog was a major step in this direction. This was followed by other similar catalogs to empower software engineering teams with a common pool of shared idioms and practices. For all practical purpose, GOF patterns became sine qua non for patterns. But there are other equally important catalogs that you would want to leverage.

There have been attempts to map the pattern catalogs to platforms such as JEE and .NET. The J2EE --design patterns and Microsoft--patterns and practices catalogs were attempts in this direction. The emergence and adoption of functional programming and reactive programming models mandates a fresh look at the patterns, applied to modern .NET software development. That is where this book comes into the picture. This book provides detailed examples written using C#/.NET, which will help developers map different constructs from various pattern catalogs to executable code.

The book you have got in your hand outlines author's perspectives about how design, architecture, and domain patterns can be applied in practice by leveraging the .NET platform. The topics covered deals with various patterns and pattern catalogs, including GOF patterns, concurrent programming, object/functional programming, and functional reactive programming. The final chapter talks about materials which we could not cover in this book, but, which a modern programmer should master to become an effective developer.

Learning, as we all know, is a continuous process. We have made to the best of our ability to impart our learnings on the job so that it benefits any one who is interested. We have leveraged code extensively for illustrating this with very detailed examples. Design illustration in the form of UML and context diagrams accompany the concepts and code. The views and perspectives we have outlined mostly align with the industry references and standards.

What this book covers

Chapter 1, *An Introduction to Patterns and Pattern Catalogs*, deals with the summary of key pattern catalogs and also deals with the evolution of the C# programming language. The chapter deals with the gist of GOF, POSA, DDD, EIP, J2EE, POEAA, and the Arlow and Neustadt pattern catalog.

Chapter 2, *Why We Need Design Patterns?*, provides the rationale for applying patterns in the context of software engineering. The chapter deals with some foundational principles such as SOLID, KISS, YAGNI, DRY/WET and so on, that lay the foundation for pattern oriented software development. A tax computation engine that uses the factory method pattern, the template method pattern, and design by contract is given as a running example.

Chapter 3, *A Logging Library*, implements a logging library which can be used in a multithreaded environment. The implementation leverages the template method pattern, the strategy pattern, and the factory method pattern. A custom Dependency Injection framework loads the classes on the fly.

Chapter 4, *Targeting Multiple Databases*, shows how one can use different persistent technologies (Oracle, SQL Server, SQLite, and so on) without changing a single line of application code. The library leverages ADO.net and uses the abstract factory pattern, the factory pattern, and the adapter pattern.

Chapter 5, *Producing Tabular Reports*, shows how one can create a canonical object model based on the composite pattern and traverse the object model through visitor pattern to generate HTML and PDF documents.

Chapter 6, *Plotting Mathematical Expressions*, deals with a library that uses composite, interpreter, observer, builder, and facade patterns to plot arbitrary mathematical expression on the fly using Windows Presentation Foundation.

Chapter 7, *Patterns in the .NET Base Class Library*, demonstrates how the designers of .NET base class library has leveraged various GOF patterns to give developers a good programing model.

Chapter 8, *Concurrent and Parallel Programming under .NET*, steps into the very important topic of concurrent and parallel programming by leveraging constructs provided by the .NET platform. Topics such as concurrency versus parallelism, fork/join parallelism, producer-consumer model, and so on are dealt at depth.

Chapter 9, *Functional Programming Techniques for Better State Management*, deals with the very important topic of managing state by leveraging closures, lambda, immutability, LINQ and other functional programming techniques.

Chapter 10, *Pattern Implementation Using Object/Functional Programming*, illustrates Map/Reduce, the template method pattern, the iterator pattern, and the strategy pattern by a judicious mix of functional and object-oriented programming constructs.

Chapter 11, *What is Reactive Programming?*, gives you the gist of Functional Reactive programming model and its realization on the .NET platform.

Chapter 12, *Reactive Programming Using .NET Rx Extensions*, carries forward from the previous chapter and shows some concrete examples where Functional Reactive Programming techniques can be put for real world use.

Chapter 13, *Reactive Programming Using RxJS*, gives a very good introduction to the techniques and internals of RxJS for writing web-based responsive UI.

Chapter 14, *A Road Ahead*, sheds light on a learning progression path highlighting the importance of polyglot programming, domain-specific languages, ontology, and antipatterns.

What you need for this book

The reader is supposed to have worked with at least a project with the .NET platform using C# as the primary programming language. A good understanding of basic object oriented programming will help you navigate the territory faster. From a software perspective, a laptop, desktop or a virtual machine with Visual Studio 2012 (or above) to test and play around with the source code.

Who this book is for

The book is useful for any C#/.NET developer to understand how enterprise class applications are designed, developed, and deployed. Rather than studying various patterns in isolation, the book deals with scenarios where patterns are often combined to engineer state of the art applications. Developers who work with Java can also follow the book without much difficulty, as both platforms have lot of things in common.

Conventions

In this book, you will find a number of text styles that distinguish between different kinds of information. Here are some examples of these styles and an explanation of their meaning.

Code words in text, database table names, folder names, filenames, file extensions, pathnames, dummy URLs, user input, and Twitter handles are shown as follows: "An instance of this class needs to be passed to the Sort routine of the List<T> instance."

A block of code is set as follows:

```
class Employee
{
    public String name {get;set;}
    public int age {get;set;}
    public double salary { get; set; }
}
```

When we wish to draw your attention to a particular part of a code block, the relevant lines or items are set in bold:

```
return function () {
  try {
    return fn.apply(null, args.slice(1));
  }
```

Any command-line input or output is written as follows:

```
npm install rx
```

New terms and **important words** are shown in bold. Words that you see on the screen, for example, in menus or dialog boxes, appear in the text like this: "You could simply do this in JSbin by using the **Add library** option shown in the web editor."

Warnings or important notes appear in a box like this.

Tips and tricks appear like this.

Reader feedback

Feedback from our readers is always welcome. Let us know what you think about this book-what you liked or disliked. Reader feedback is important for us as it helps us develop titles that you will really get the most out of. To send us general feedback, simply e-mail `feedback@packtpub.com`, and mention the book's title in the subject of your message. If there is a topic that you have expertise in and you are interested in either writing or contributing to a book, see our author guide at `www.packtpub.com/authors`.

Customer support

Now that you are the proud owner of a Packt book, we have a number of things to help you to get the most from your purchase.

Downloading the example code

You can download the example code files for this book from your account at `http://www.packtpub.com`. If you purchased this book elsewhere, you can visit `http://www.packtpub.com/support` and register to have the files e-mailed directly to you.

You can download the code files by following these steps:

1. Log in or register to our website using your e-mail address and password.
2. Hover the mouse pointer on the **SUPPORT** tab at the top.
3. Click on **Code Downloads & Errata**.
4. Enter the name of the book in the **Search** box.
5. Select the book for which you're looking to download the code files.
6. Choose from the drop-down menu where you purchased this book from.
7. Click on **Code Download**.

Once the file is downloaded, please make sure that you unzip or extract the folder using the latest version of:

- WinRAR / 7-Zip for Windows
- Zipeg / iZip / UnRarX for Mac
- 7-Zip / PeaZip for Linux

The code bundle for the book is also hosted on GitHub at `https://github.com/PacktPublishing/.NET-Design-Patterns`. We also have other code bundles from our rich catalog of books and videos available at `https://github.com/PacktPublishing/`. Check them out!

Errata

Although we have taken every care to ensure the accuracy of our content, mistakes do happen. If you find a mistake in one of our books-maybe a mistake in the text or the code-we would be grateful if you could report this to us. By doing so, you can save other readers from frustration and help us improve subsequent versions of this book. If you find any errata, please report them by visiting http://www.packtpub.com/submit-errata, selecting your book, clicking on the **Errata Submission Form** link, and entering the details of your errata. Once your errata are verified, your submission will be accepted and the errata will be uploaded to our website or added to any list of existing errata under the Errata section of that title.

To view the previously submitted errata, go to https://www.packtpub.com/books/content/support and enter the name of the book in the search field. The required information will appear under the **Errata** section.

Piracy

Piracy of copyrighted material on the Internet is an ongoing problem across all media. At Packt, we take the protection of our copyright and licenses very seriously. If you come across any illegal copies of our works in any form on the Internet, please provide us with the location address or website name immediately so that we can pursue a remedy.

Please contact us at copyright@packtpub.com with a link to the suspected pirated material.

We appreciate your help in protecting our authors and our ability to bring you valuable content.

Questions

If you have a problem with any aspect of this book, you can contact us at questions@packtpub.com, and we will do our best to address the problem.

1
An Introduction to Patterns and Pattern Catalogs

Design patterns have always fascinated software developers, yet true knowledge of their applicability and consequences has eluded many. The various solutions that have been created and applied to solve similar problems have been studied over time by experienced developers and architects. A movement slowly began to catalog such time-tested and successful solutions, which served as a blueprint for software design. The applicability of design patterns exhibited maturity (even though over-engineering was a perceived risk) in solution architecture (in terms of stability, consistency, maintainability, and extensibility), and became a core skill for serious developers and architects. In this introduction to patterns and pattern catalogs, the authors wish to provide a detailed illustration of the movement in the software development industry that led to the discovery and consolidation of the various patterns and pattern catalogs. It is equally important to understand the evolution of patterns, idioms, programming languages, and standards that led to standardization of these technology-agnostic blueprints, which form the basis of enterprise application development today. We will cover the following topics in this regard:

- History of **object-oriented programming** (**OOP**) techniques, idioms, and patterns
- Patterns and pattern movement
- Key patterns and pattern catalogs
- Key C# language features that facilitate implementation of OOP techniques, idioms, and patterns

OOP – A short history

OOP is a programming model that is supposed to combine structure (data) and behavior (methods) to deliver software functionality. This was a marked contrast from the procedural programming model, which was mostly in vogue when the OOP model gained prominence. The primary unit of composition in a procedural programming model is a procedure (mostly a function with side-effects). Data is fed into a series of procedures that constitutes the process or algorithm in a solution context. In the case of OOP, the data and related functions are represented together as a class, which acts as a fundamental unit in the programming model. Schematically it is as follows:

```
Class Test
{
    <------ Static (Class Level) Variables --------------->
    <------ Instance (Object Level) Variables ------------>
    <------ Private Methods ------------------------------>
    <------ Public Methods ------------------------------->
}
```

As a programmer, one can create many instances of a class during the execution of a program. Since class encapsulates data and its associated operations to provide a coherent entity, the problems (or rather side-effects) associated with global variables/data (being used as payload for the procedures) went away all of a sudden. This helped to manage the complexity of developing large software.

OOP revolutionized the way programmers modeled the problem domain, with class compositions leveraging encapsulation, association, inheritance, and polymorphism. Additionally, with the flexibility to model hierarchies (that closely represent the problem domain) with ease, it became natural for developers to think in terms of objects.

 The origin of OOP can be traced back to the Simula programming language created by Kristen Nygaard and Ole-Johan Dahl, released in the year 1965. The advent of the **Smalltalk** system helped the ideas of OOP to percolate to the academia and some consulting circles. Smalltalk was a dynamically typed language, and primarily designed as a message passing system. Later, they added Simula's class-based Object model. Alan Kay, Dan Inaglis, and Adele Goldberg at Xerox PARC designed the language.

The OOP model reached a critical mass in the early 1990s, with the popularity of the C++ programming language. Even though Smalltalk and C++ were OOP languages, Smalltalk was a dynamically typed programming language, and C++ was a statically typed (though weakly enforced) programming language. The C++ programming language was created by Bjarne Stroustrup at the AT&T Bell Laboratories, as an extension of C (for wider adoption). In this regard, C++, as a programming language, has issues in terms of usage because of the compulsion to make it C-compatible. The story of evolution of the language is well chronicled in, *The Design and Evolution of C++*, a book written by Bjarne himself. The book deals with the rationale of designing the language and the design choices available for him to incorporate features such as single inheritance, multiple inheritance, virtual methods, exception handling, templates (Generics), I/O streams, and so on. Any serious C++ developer should not miss this particular book, as it helps to understand the reason why the C++ programming language is the way it is!

There were attempts to make protocol-based development using middleware technologies like Microsoft's **Component Object Model (COM)** and OMG's **Common Object Request Broker Architecture (CORBA)**. Both CORBA and COM were very similar, and both facilitated object interoperability at the binary level. Each protocol had its own binary encoding format, and interoperability between these two standards became a problem. Some enterprising companies made a living by writing COM/CORBA bridge to rectify this problem. Also, COM was mostly available only on Microsoft Windows, making it a platform-specific solution.

Then, in 1996, Sun Microsystems came up with a language which was marketed as a programming language to write applications that are hosted in a browser (Applets). They named it Java. However, due to performance and political reasons, applet development did not took off. The language, along with its associated platform, was soon projected as a server-side programming system. This was a tremendous success, and the Java language made a strong comeback, further popularizing the OOP programming model. The primary architect of the Java language was James Gosling.

In the year 2001, Microsoft released C#, a brand new OOP language for their new virtual machine development platform, known as .NET. Later, Microsoft did add support for generics, lambda, dynamic typing, and LINQ, among others, to make C# one of the most powerful programming languages in the world. The primary architect of the language was Anders Hejlsberg.

Meanwhile, languages such as Ruby and Python made an appearance, and are still relevant in certain areas. Then, there were object-functional languages such as F#, Scala, Groovy, Clojure, and so on. However, the OOP model is symbolized by C++, C#, and Java.

Patterns and pattern movement

Programmers of the early 1990s struggled a lot to understand OOP, and how to effectively use them in large projects. Without a viral medium such as the Internet, it was quite a struggle for them. Early adopters published technical reports, wrote in periodicals/journals, and conducted seminars to popularize OOP techniques. Magazines such as *Dr. Dobbs Journal* and *C++ Report* carried columns featuring OOP.

A need was felt to transfer the wisdom of the experts to the ever-increasing programming community, but this knowledge propagation was not happening. The legendary German mathematician Carl Friedrich Gauss once remarked, *"Always learn from the masters"*. Even though Gauss had mathematics in mind, it is true for any non-trivial human endeavor. However, there were very few masters of the OOP techniques, and the apprenticeship model was not scaling well.

James Coplien published an influential book titled *Advanced C++ Programming Styles and Idioms*, which dealt with low-level patterns (idioms) associated with the usage of the C++ programming language. Despite being not widely cited, authors consider this a notable book towards cataloguing the best practices and techniques of OOP.

- It was during this time that Erich Gamma began his work on a pattern catalog as part of his PhD thesis, inspired by an architect named Christopher Alexander. Christopher Alexander's *A Pattern Language – Towns, Buildings, Construction* was a source of inspiration for Erich Gamma. Then, people with similar ideas, namely Ralph Johnson, John Vlissides, and Richard Helm, joined hands with Erich Gamma to create a catalog of 23 patterns, now popularly known as the **Gang of Four (GoF)** design patterns. Addison Wesley published the book *Design Patterns: Elements of Reusable Object-Oriented Software* in the year 1994. This soon became a great reference for the programmer, and fueled software development based on patterns. The GoF catalog was mostly focused on software design.

- In the year 1996, a group of engineers from Siemens published a book titled *Pattern-Oriented Software Architecture*, which focused mostly on the architectural aspects of building a system. The entire **Pattern-Oriented Software Architecture (POSA)** pattern catalog was documented in five books published by John Wiley and Sons. The group was joined by Douglas Schmidt, the creator of the **Adaptive Communication Environment (ACE)** network programming library and **TAO (The ACE ORB)**. He later became the chair of **Object Management Group (OMG)**, which develops, adopts, and maintains standards such as CORBA and UML.

- Another influential catalog was published by Martin Fowler in a book titled *Patterns of Enterprise Application Architecture* in the year 2001. The book mostly focused on patterns that come up while developing enterprise applications using the JEE and .NET frameworks. Incidentally, most of the code snippets were in Java and C#.

- Gregor Hohpe and Bobby Woolf published a pattern catalog to document the patterns that arise in the enterprise integration scenario. Their catalog titled *Enterprise Integration Patterns*, published as part of the Martin Fowler signature book series, is widely recognized as a source of ideas regarding enterprise integration techniques. The Apache Camel integration library is inspired by this book.

- *Core J2EE Patterns: Best Practices and Design Strategies* (by Deepak Alur et al.), although a platform-specific catalog, is a rich source of ideas regarding the structuring of an enterprise application. The book includes patterns for presentation, data, and service tiers in web application development.

- *Domain-Driven Design*, published by Eric Evans in the year 2003, deals with a technique called **domain-driven design (DDD)**. The book uses GoF and **Patterns of Enterprise Application Architecture (POEAA)** patterns to put forward a design methodology that focuses on building a persistent ignorant domain model. The book also introduces some patterns and idioms for structuring domain logic.

- Jim Arlow and Ila Nuestadt published a book entitled *Enterprise Patterns and MDA*, which catalogued a set of patterns based on the *Jungian Archetypes*. This catalog contains nine top-level archetypes and 168 business archetypes for developing applications.

The following figure illustrates the evolution of design methodologies, programming languages, and pattern catalogs:

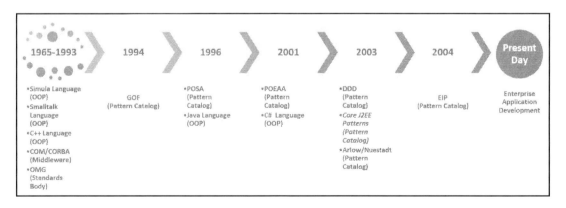

Key pattern catalogs

Patterns are most often catalogued in some kind of pattern repository. Some of them are published as books. The most popular and widely used pattern catalog is GoF, named after the four collaborators that produced them. They are Eric Gama, Ralph Johnson, John Vlissides, and Richard Helm.

GoF patterns

The GoF catalog, named after the four creators of the catalog, started the pattern movement. The creators mostly focused on designing and architecting object-oriented software. The ideas of Christopher Alexander were borrowed to the software engineering discipline, and applied to application architecture, concurrency, security, and so on. The GoF divided the catalog into structural, creational, and behavioral patterns. The original book used C++ and Smalltalk to explain the concepts. These patterns have been ported and leveraged in most of the programming languages that exist today.

Sr. no	Pattern type	Patterns
1	Creational patterns	Abstract factory, builder, factory method, prototype, singleton.
2	Structural patterns	Adapter, bridge, composite, decorator, facade, flyweight, proxy.
3	Behavioral patterns	Chain of responsibility, command, interpreter, iterator, mediator, memento, observer, state, strategy, template method, visitor.

We believe that a good understanding of the GoF patterns is necessary for any programmer. These patterns occur everywhere, regardless of the application domain. GoF patterns help us to communicate and reason about systems in a language-agnostic manner. They are widely implemented in the .NET and Java world.

POSA catalog

POSA Volume 5 is an influential book series, which covers most of the applicable patterns while developing mission-critical systems. An element of bias is seen towards native code programming; perhaps C++ was the prevalent OOP language during the time of research. The catalog, which spanned five published volumes, is listed as follows:

Sr. no	Pattern type	Patterns
1	Architectural	Layers, pipes and filters, blackboard, broker, MVC, presentation-abstraction-control, microkernel, reflection.
2	Design	Whole-part, mater-slave, proxy, command processor, view handler, forwarder-receiver, client-dispatcher-server, publisher-subscriber.
3	Service access and configuration patterns	Wrapper façade, component configurator, interceptor, extension interface.
4	Event handling patterns	Reactor, proactor, asynchronous completion token, acceptor-connector.
5	Synchronization patterns	Scoped locking, strategized locking, thread-safe interface, double-checked locking optimization.
6	Concurrency patterns	Active object, monitor object, half-sync/half-async, leader/followers, thread-specific storage.
7	Resource acquisition patterns	Lookup, lazy acquisition, eager acquisition, partial acquisition.
8	Resource lifecycle	Caching, pooling, coordinator, resource lifecycle manager.
9	Resource release patterns	Leasing, evictor.
10	A pattern language for distributive computing	Consolidation of patterns from different catalogs in the context of distributed programming.
11	On patterns and pattern languages	This last volume gives some meta information about patterns, pattern languages, and their usage.

We believe the POSA catalog is very important (to the extent, one of the author feels, that if someone has not heard about the POSA catalog, he or she does not understand patterns) if one is writing middleware servers and scalable web infrastructure. For some reason, it has not got the kind of traction that it deserves. They are very useful for writing server-class software infrastructure such as web containers, application containers, and other middleware components.

POEAA catalog

Martin Fowler, along with some co-authors, published a book entitled *Patterns of Enterprise Application Architecture*. The book is a treasure trove of patterns, that helps one to structure and organize the design of enterprise applications using .NET and Java. Some of Fowler's pattern has been leveraged in the context of distributed computing by POSA-Volume 4 authors.

Sr. no	Pattern type	Patterns
1	Domain logic	Transaction script, domain model, table module, service layer.
2	Data source architectural patterns	Table data gateway, row data gateway, active record, data mapper.
3	Object-relational behavioral patterns	Unit of work, identity map, lazy load.
4	Object-relational structural patterns	Identity field, foreign key mapping, association table mapping, dependent mapping, embedded value, serialized LOB, single table inheritance, class table inheritance, concrete table inheritance, inheritance mappers.
5	Object-relational metadata mapping patterns	Metadata mapping, query object, repository.
6	Web presentation patterns	Model view controller, page controller, front controller, template view, transform view, two-step view, application controller.
7	Distribution patterns	Remote facade, data transfer object.
8	Offline concurrency patterns	Optimistic offline lock, pessimistic offline lock, coarse grained lock, implicit lock.
9	Session state patterns	Client session state, server session state, database session state.
10	Base patterns	Gateway, mapper, layer supertype, separated interface, registry, value object, money, special case, plugin, service stub, record set.

The POEAA catalog is a rich source of ideas when it comes to enterprise application software development. Some of these patterns are implemented by frameworks such as Spring (including Spring.NET), Nhibernate/Entity Framework, **Windows Communication Foundation** (**WCF**), and **Windows Presentation Foundation** (**WPF**). Awareness about the POEAA catalog helps one to reason about the architecture of pretty much everything happening in the .NET platform.

EIP catalog

A modern day enterprise requires information to flow from one application to another, in real time or while offline. Since applications use different implementation technologies, we require message passing systems to transfer the data. Most often, these communications happen in an asynchronous manner. The **Enterprise Integration Patterns** (**EIP**) catalog deals with time-tested solutions by professionals, who have cut their teeth on integration issues for recurring problems.

Sr. no	Pattern type	Patterns
1	Messaging systems	Message channel, message, pipes and filters, message router, message translator, message endpoint.
2	Messaging channels	Point-to-point channel, publish-subscribe channel, datatype channel, invalid message channel, dead letter channel, guaranteed delivery, channel adapter, messaging bridge, message bus.
3	Message construction	Command message, document message, event message, request-reply, return address, correlation identifier, message sequence, message expiration, format indicator.
4	Message routing	Content-based router, message filter, dynamic router, recipient list, splitter, aggregator, resequencer, composed message processor, scatter-gather, routing slip, process manager, message broker.
5	Message transformation	Envelope wrapper, content enricher, content filter, claim check, normalizer, canonical data model.
6	Messaging endpoints	Messaging gateway, messaging mapper, transactional client, polling consumer, event-driven consumer, competing consumers, message dispatcher, selective consumer, durable subscriber, idempotent receiver, service activator.

7	System management	Control bus, detour, wire tap, message history, message store, smart proxy, test message, channel purger.

The EIP catalog is a very influential one in transferring knowledge about strategies for asynchronous messaging and point-to-point synchronous communication between applications. The Apache Camel library implements most of the commonly occurring patterns, while doing **Enterprise Application Integration (EAI)**. The authors feel that this catalog is worth studying should one embark on a project that requires information/data flow from one system to another, including mobile device communication with backend services (MBAAS) that involves data synchronization and queuing mechanisms.

J2EE design patterns catalog

This is a catalog that captures design experience in the form of a book entitled *Core J2EE Patterns: Best Practices and Design Strategies* by Deepak Alur, John Crupi, and Dan Malks. The book and the associated website deals with common solutions that can be leveraged while writing enterprise web applications. Even though conceived for the J2EE platform, the patterns outlined in the catalog can be used in any context where there is a programming model similar to the J2EE platform. Fortunately, the .NET server-side model is very similar to J2EE.

Sr. no	Pattern class	Patterns
1	Business tier pattern	Business delegate, session facade, service locator, transfer object, composite entity, transfer object, assembler, value list handler, business object, application service.
2	Presentation tier patterns	Intercepting filter, front controller, composite view, view helper, service to worker, dispatcher view, context object, application controller.
3	Integration patterns	Data access object, service activator, domain store, web service broker.

The authors believe that the J2EE catalog has been used extensively in the .NET platform, especially after Microsoft released the ASP.Net MVC programming model. The catalog is a rich source of ideas to structure your enterprise web application.

DDD-based patterns

The book entitled *Domain-Driven Design* by Eric J. Evans, released in the year 2003, is not a book on patterns in itself. The primary goal of the book is to outline a method by which one can create persistent ignorant domain models by leveraging the ubiquitous language used by the stakeholders in a business scenario. The book contains a lot of patterns and idioms for architecture, design, and application integration, in a model-driven manner.

Sr. no	Pattern type	Patterns
1	Patterns for supple design	Intention-revealing interfaces, side-effect-free functions, assertions, conceptual contours, standalone classes, closure of operations, declarative design.
2	Patterns for domain model expression	Associations, entities (reference objects), value objects, services, modules (packages).
3	Patterns for domain model integrity	Bounded context, context map, shared kernel, anticorruption layer, open host service, published language.
4	Patterns for domain model distillation	Core domain, generic subdomains, segregated core, abstract core.

This is one of the most influential books in terms of thought leadership towards creating a methodology that goes along with the Agile development models. The ideas from this book have percolated deep into building the present day software systems.

Arlow/Nuestadt patterns

Jim Arlow and Ila Nuestadt published a book entitled *Enterprise Patterns and MDA*. The book is based on the concept of an archetype borrowed from the works of Carl Gustav Jung. Archetypes are primordial entities that occur time and again in the sociocultural context across cultures. Business archetypes are entities that occur in a business context (where business is a socio-economic activity). The business archetypes covered in the book include party, CRM, product, business rules, order, inventory, units, and so on. Archetypes help model the business problem, and this gives a clear indication of the expected composition and behavior of the solution. Archetypes are a powerful meme that provide direct mapping between the business and solution models, thereby avoiding mismatch during business analysis, design, and implementation. The ideas and schema from the book can be used to write better enterprise software products.

Sr. no	Pattern type	Patterns
1	Party archetype pattern	PartyIdentifier, RegisteredIdentifier, PartySignature, PartyAuthentication, address, person, ISOGender, ethnicity, BodyMetrics, PersonName, organization, company, company names, identifiers for companies, company organizational units, partnerships and sole proprietors, preferences, PartyManager.
2	Party relationship archetype pattern	PartyRole, PartyRoleType, PartyRelationshipType, responsibilities, capabilities.
3	Customer relationship management archetype pattern	Customer, CustomerCommunicationManager, customer communication, CustomerServiceCase.
4	Product archetype pattern	ProductType, ProductInstance, SerialNumber, batch, product specification, ProductCatalog, CatalogEntry, packages, PackageType, package instance, combining ProductTypes, rule-driven package specification, ProductRelationships, price, package pricing, measured products, services, ServiceType and ServiceInstance, product pleomorphs.
5	Inventory archetype pattern	The inventory archetype, ProductInventoryEntry, ServiceInventoryEntry, inventory capacity planning, inventory management, availability, reservations.
6	Order archetype pattern	The order archetype, PurchaseOrder, SalesOrder, OrderLine, PartySummaryRoleInOrder, DeliveryReceiver, ChargeLine, OrderManager, OrderEvents, order status, LifeCycleEvents, AmendEvents, AmendOrderLineEvent, AmendPartySummaryEvent, AmendTermsAndConditionsEvent, DiscountEvent, DespatchEvent, ReceiptEvent, OrderPayment, PaymentEvents, payment strategy, PurchaseOrder process, PurchaseOrder cancellation, process PurchaseOrder, SalesOrder process archetype, SalesOrder process, process SalesOrder, OrderProcess documentation.
7	Quantity archetype pattern	Quantity archetype pattern, metric, units/SystemOfUnits, SIBaseUnit, DerivedUnit, ManHour, quantity, StandardConversion/UnitConverter.
8	Money archetype pattern	Money archetype pattern, currency, locale, ISOCountryCode, ExchangeRate/CurrencyConverter, payment.
9	Rule archetype pattern	Rule archetype pattern, business rules/system rules, RuleElement, RuleContext, rule evaluation, ActivityRule, RuleSet, RuleOverride.

The authors have borrowed ideas from the book, while creating an ontology for realizing a **domain-specific language (DSL)** on a mobile-based healthcare application. If one is embarking on creating a DSL-based system architecture, this book can be a good starting point for rich domain models based on business archetypes.

Should we use all of these?

Pattern catalogs are available to deal with various concerns of software development, be it design, architecture, security, data, and so on. Most applications, or even frameworks, leverage only a fraction of the patterns listed earlier. Understanding the pattern catalogs and their applicability is a rich source of design ideas for any software developer. A developer should be careful to avoid the malady of so-called **pattern diarrhoea**.

Sr. no	Pattern catalog	Primary use-case
1	GoF patterns	These are fundamental patterns which occur time and again, regardless of the domain. These are used in a context agnostic manner.
2	POSA catalog	The areas where these patterns are relevant include concurrency management, distributed programming, middleware software, and so on.
3	POEAA catalog	Enterprise web application development using .NET and JEE platforms.
4	EIP	Application integration in modern enterprises.
5	J2EE design patterns	Writing web applications using .NET and Java.
6	DDD	In fact, this book is a framework for developing rich domain models in a persistent ignorant manner.
7	Arlow/Nuestadt	Very useful when we are writing enterprise applications, and no need to break one's head to create the database schema. Most of the entities are available here as a business archetype.

The C# language and the .NET platform

Microsoft (MS) initially placed their bets on an enterprise architecture strategy called **Windows DNA**, centered on the **Distributed Component Object Model (DCOM)**. The advent and traction of the Java programming model forced Microsoft to rework their strategy, so they decided to create a virtual machine platform called .NET. The .NET platform was released in 2002, and it was monikered Microsoft's Java. The old adage *imitation is the sincerest form of flattery* was echoed by industry pundits. Web development is done using the ASP.Net Web Forms programming model, and desktop development is based on Windows forms. They also created a new language for the new platform, named C#. For platform interoperability, they created .NET remoting architecture, which became the gateway for communication between homogeneous systems (including CLR-managed and unmanaged) via TCP and DCOM protocols. For communication with heterogeneous systems, open standards such as SOAP and WSDL were leveraged by remoting objects, either self-hosted or hosted, within an IIS context.

In 2003, Microsoft released .NET v1.1, which fixed many of the bugs in .NET v1.0. The release of Microsoft .NET 1.1 encouraged people to bet their future on this platform. There was no application server in its offering. This led to some delay in the adoption of the platform. A code snippet in C#, which computes the average of a series of numbers through the command line, is shown as follows:

```
// Chap1_01.cs
using System;
using System.Collections;
class Temp
{
  public static void Main(String [] args) {
  //---- accumulate command line arguments to
  //---- to a list
  ArrayList a = new ArrayList();
  for(int i=0; i< args.Length; ++i)
    a.Add(Convert.ToDouble(args[i]));
  //----- aggregate value to a variable (sum)
  double sum = 0.0;
  foreach(double at in a)
    sum = sum + at;
  //------------ Compute the Average
  double ar = sum/a.Count;
  //------------ Spit value to the console
  //------------ Wait for a Key
  Console.WriteLine(ar);
  Console.Read();
  }
}
```

In 2005, Microsoft added a lot of features to their platform, which included generics and anonymous delegates. With C# 2.0, we can rewrite the average computation program by using generics and anonymous delegates as follows:

```
// -- Chap1_02.cs
using System;
using System.Collections;
using System.Collections.Generic;public delegate double
Del(List<double> pa);
class Temp
{
  public static void Main(String [] args) {
  //----- Use a Generic List (List<T> )
  //----- to accumulate command line arguemnts
  List<double> a = new List<double>();
  for(int i=0; i< args.Length ; ++ i )
  a.Add(Convert.ToDouble(args[i]));
  //--- Define a anonymous delegate and assign
  //--- to the variable temp
  //--- The delegate aggregates value and
  //--- compute average
  Del temp = delegate(List<double> pa ) {
    double sum = 0.0;
    foreach( double at in pa )
      sum = sum + at;
    return sum/pa.Count;
  };
  //---- invoke the delegate
  //---- and wait for the key
  Console.WriteLine(temp(a));
  Console.Read();
  }
}
```

The release of .NET platform 3.0 overcame the shortcomings of the previous releases by introducing WCF, WPF, and **Windows Workflow Foundation** (**WF**), which coincided with the release of the Vista platform.

Microsoft released version 3.5 of the platform with some key features including LINQ, lambda, and anonymous types. They also released the C# 3.0 programming language. Using type inference and lambda expressions, the average computation program is rewritten as follows:

```
//--- Chap1_03.cs
using System;
using System.Collections;
using System.Collections.Generic;
```

[21]

```
using System.Linq;
class Temp {
  public static void Main(String [] args) {
  //---- leverage type inference feature to assign
  //---- a List<T> and accumulate values to that list
  var a = new List<double>();
  for(int i=0; i< args.Length ; ++ i )
    a.Add(Convert.ToDouble(args[i]));
  //----- Define a Lambda function which passes
  //----- through the value.
  Func<double,double> ar2 = (x => x );
  //------- use the Sum function available with List<T>
  //------- to compute the average
  var ar = a.Sum(ar2 )/a.Count;
  //------ Spit the value to the console
  Console.WriteLine(ar);
  Console.Read();
  }
}
```

With Visual Studio 2010, Microsoft released C# 4.0 with support for dynamic programming. The following code snippet demonstrates dynamic typing (based on DynamicObject) and ExpandoObjects. The following code snippet shows how one can create a custom object that can add arbitrary properties and methods:

```
// Chap1_04.cs
using System;
using System.Collections.Generic;
using System.Linq;
using System.Text;
using System.Dynamic;

namespace TestVS
{
  class DynamicClass : DynamicObject
{
  //---- underlying container for storing
  //---- Ibject memebers
  private Dictionary<string, Object> props =
  new Dictionary<string, object>();

  public DynamicClass() { }

  //------- Retrieve value from a member
  public override bool TryGetMember(GetMemberBinder binder,
  out object result){
    string name = binder.Name.ToLower();
    return props.TryGetValue(name, out result);
```

```
      }
      public override bool TrySetMember(SetMemberBinder binder,
      object value){
        props[binder.Name.ToLower()] = value;
        return true;
      }
  }

  class Program{
    static void Main(string[] args){
      dynamic dc = new DynamicClass();
      //--------- Adding a property
      dc.hell = 10;
      //--------read back the property...
      Console.WriteLine(dc.hell);
      //------- Creating an Action delegate...
      Action<int> ts = new Action<int>( delegate(int i ) {
        Console.WriteLine(i.ToString());
      });
      //------------Adding a method....
      dc.rs = ts;
      //----------- invoking a method....
      dc.rs(100);
      Console.Read();
    }
  }
}
```

The following code snippet shows how one can use `ExpandoObject` to add a property to a type we created. We will be leveraging the dynamic feature of C# 4.0:

```
using System;
using System.Collections.Generic;
using System.Linq;
using System.Text;
using System.Dynamic;

namespace TestVS
{
  class Program
{
  static void Main(string[] args){
    dynamic ds = new ExpandoObject();          //---- Adding a property
    ds.val = 20;
    Console.WriteLine(ds.val);
    //---- Assign a new value to the "val" property
    //------This is possible because of dynamic typing
    ds.val = "Hello World...";
```

```
      Console.WriteLine(ds.val);
      //--------------- Wait for the Keyboard input
      Console.Read();
    }
  }
}
```

In 2012, Microsoft released version 5.0 of the C# programming language, which incorporated a declarative concurrency model based on the async/await paradigm. The following C# code demonstrates the usage of async/await:

```
//-- Chap1_05.cs
using System;
using System.IO;
using System.Threading.Tasks;

class Program
{
  static void Main() {
    //--- Create a Task to Start processing
    Task task = new Task(ProcessCountAsync);
    task.Start();    task.Wait();
    Console.ReadLine();
  }

  static async void ProcessCountAsync()
  {
    // Start the HandleFile method.
    Task<int> task = HandleFileAsync(@".\WordCount.txt");
    //
    // -------- One can do some lengthy processing here
    //
    int x = await task;
    Console.WriteLine("Count: " + x);
  }

  static async Task<int> HandleFileAsync(string file)
  {
    int count = 0;
    using (StreamReader reader = new StreamReader(file))
    {
      string v = await reader.ReadToEndAsync();
      count += v.Length;
    }
    return count;
  }
}
```

With Visual Studio 2015, Microsoft released C# 6.0, which mostly contains cosmetic changes to the language. Additionally, C# 7.0 does not add many features to the language. The .NET Core released by Microsoft runs on Windows GNU Linux and MAC OS X, promises to make C# a multiplatform/cross platform language. The acquisition of Xamarin has helped Microsoft to foray into cross-platform, native code-based mobile development.

C# language and the singleton pattern

The authors consider the singleton pattern, the way it was presented in the GoF book, as some kind of anti-pattern. A lot has been written about how to implement it in a multi-core/multi-threaded environment. Constructs such as the double-checked locking pattern have been implemented to incorporate lazy loading while implementing singleton.

The C# programming language has got a nifty feature called a static constructor, which helps to implement the singleton pattern in a thread-safe manner. The static constructor is guaranteed to be called before any method (including the constructor) is called. We believe we can stop cutting down trees in order to write about the singleton pattern, at least in the .NET world.

```csharp
//--Chap1_06.cs
using System;

class SingleInstance
{
  private int value = 10;
  //----- In the case of Singleton Pattern, we make our
  //----- ctor private to avoid instantiating the object using
  //----- the new keyword
  private SingleInstance() { }

  //----- The static method acts as a mechanism to expose
  //------ the internal instance
  public static SingleInstance Instance {
    get {
      return Nested.instance;
    }
  }

  private class Nested
  {
    static Nested() { }
    internal static readonly SingleInstance instance
    = new SingleInstance();
  }
```

```
    public void Increment()
    {
      value++;
    }
    public int Value { get { return value; } }
}

public class SingletonExample
{
    public static void Main(String[] args)
{
    SingleInstance t1 = SingleInstance.Instance;
    SingleInstance t2 = SingleInstance.Instance;
    t1.Increment();
    if (t1.Value == t2.Value)
      Console.WriteLine("SingleTon Object");
  }
}
```

Summary

The pattern movement has revolutionized the way people are developing software. By capturing the wisdom of experts in their respective areas, pattern catalogs can be used for software engineering, library design, and all areas where they are available. The famous GoF pattern book started the whole movement in the year 1994. Some notable catalogs include POSA, POEAA, EIP, J2EE, DDD, and Arlow/Nuestadt. We have also seen how a multi-paradigm language such as C# is well-suited for pattern-based software development, considering the language's evolution in terms of features. We will continue to explore the applicability and consequence of patterns in the following chapters. We will also be looking at the key design principles, and will explain the need for design patterns using an application case study.

2
Why We Need Design Patterns?

In this chapter, we will try to understand the necessity of choosing a pattern-based approach to software development. We start with some principles of software development, that one might find useful while undertaking large projects. The working example in this chapter starts with a requirements specification and progresses toward a preliminary implementation. We will then try to iteratively improve the solution using patterns and idioms, and come up with a good design that supports a well-defined programming Interface. During this process, we will learn about some software development principles that one can adhere to, including the following:

- SOLID principles for OOP
- Three key uses of design patterns
- Arlow/Nuestadt archetype patterns
- Entity, value, and data transfer objects
- Command pattern and factory method pattern
- Design by contract idiom and the template method pattern
- Facade pattern for API
- Leveraging the .NET Reflection API for plugin architecture
- XML processing using LINQ for parsing configuration files
- Deep cloning of CLR objects using extension methods
- Designing stateless classes for better scalability

Some principles of software development

Writing quality production code consistently is not easy without some foundational principles under your belt. The purpose of this section is to whet the developer's appetite, and towards the end, some references are given for detailed study. Detailed coverage of these principles warrants a separate book on its own scale. The authors have tried to assimilate the following key principles of software development, which help one write quality code:

- **KISS**: Keep it simple, stupid

- **DRY**: Don't repeat yourself

- **YAGNI**: You aren't gonna need it

- **Low coupling**: Minimize coupling between classes

- **SOLID principles**: Principles for better OOP

 William of Ockham framed the maxim **Keep it simple, stupid (KISS)**. It is also called the law of parsimony. In programming terms, it can be translated as "writing code in a straightforward manner, focusing on a particular solution that solves the problem at hand".

This maxim is important because, most often, developers fall into the trap of writing code in a generic manner for unwarranted extensibility. Even though it initially looks attractive, things slowly go out of bounds. The accidental complexity introduced in the code base for catering to improbable scenarios, often reduces readability and maintainability. The KISS principle can be applied to every human endeavor. Learn more about the KISS principle by consulting the Web.

 Don't repeat yourself (DRY), a maxim that is often forgotten by programmers while implementing their domain logic. Most often, in a collaborative development scenario, code gets duplicated inadvertently due to a lack of communication and proper design specifications.

This bloats the code base, induces subtle bugs, and makes things really difficult to change. By following the DRY maxim at all stages of development, we can avoid additional effort and make the code consistent. The opposite of DRY is **write everything twice (WET)**.

You aren't gonna need it (YAGNI), a principle that complements the KISS axiom. It serves as a warning for people who try to write code in the most general manner, anticipating changes right from the word go.

Too often, in practice, most of the code which are written in a generic manner, might result in code smells.

 While writing code, one should try to make sure that there are no hard-coded references to concrete classes. It is advisable to program to an interface as opposed to an implementation.

This is a key principle which many patterns use to provide behavior acquisition at runtime. A dependency injection framework could be used to reduce coupling between classes.

SOLID principles are a set of guidelines for writing better object-oriented software. It is a mnemonic acronym that embodies the following five principles:

Sr. no	Principles	Description
1	**Single Responsibility Principle (SRP)**	A class should have only one responsibility. If it is doing more than one unrelated thing, we need to split the class.
2	**Open Close Principle (OCP)**	A class should be open for extension, closed for modification.
3	**Liskov Substitution Principle (LSP)**	Named after Barbara Liskov, a Turing Award laureate, who postulated that a sub-class (derived class) could substitute any super class (base class) references without affecting the functionality. Even though it looks like stating the obvious, most implementations have quirks that violate this principle.
4	**Interface Segregation Principle (ISP)**	It is more desirable to have multiple interfaces for a class (such classes can also be called components) than having one Uber interface that forces implementation of all methods (both relevant and non-relevant to the solution context).

5	**Dependency Inversion (DI)**	This is a principle which is very useful for framework design. In the case of frameworks, the client code will be invoked by server code, as opposed to the usual process of the client invoking the server. The main principle here is that abstraction should not depend upon details; rather, details should depend upon abstraction. This is also called the **Hollywood** principle (Do not call us, we will call you back).

The authors consider the preceding five principles primarily as a verification mechanism. This will be demonstrated by verifying the ensuing case study implementations for violation of these principles.

 Karl Seguin has written an e-book titled *Foundations of Programming – Building Better Software*, which covers most of what has been outlined here. Read his book to gain an in-depth understanding of most of these topics. The SOLID principles are well covered in the Wikipedia page on the subject, which can be retrieved from
`https://en.wikipedia.org/wiki/SOLID_(object-oriented_design`.
Robert Martin's *Agile Principles, Patterns, and Practices in C#* is a definitive book on learning about SOLID, as Robert Martin himself is the creator of these principles, even though Michael Feathers coined the acronym.

Why are patterns required?

According to the authors, the three key advantages of pattern-oriented software development that stand out are as follows:

- A language/platform-agnostic way to communicate about software artifacts
- A tool for refactoring initiatives (targets for refactoring)
- Better API design

With the advent of the pattern movement, the software development community got a canonical language to communicate about software design, architecture, and implementation. Software development is a craft that has got trade-offs attached to each strategy, and there are multiple ways to develop software. The various pattern catalogs brought some conceptual unification for this **cacophony** in software development.

Most developers around the world today who are worth their salt can understand and speak this language. We believe you will be able to do the same by the end of the chapter. Imagine yourself stating the following about your recent implementation:

> For our tax computation example, we have used the command pattern to handle the computation logic. The commands (handlers) are configured using an XML file, and a factory method takes care of the instantiation of classes on the fly using Lazy loading. We cache the commands, and avoid instantiation of more objects by imposing singleton constraints on the invocation. We support the prototype pattern where command objects can be cloned. The command objects have a base implementation, where concrete command objects use the template method pattern to override methods that are necessary. The command objects are implemented using the design by contracts idiom. The whole mechanism is encapsulated using a Facade class, which acts as an API layer for the application logic. The application logic uses entity objects (reference) to store the taxable entities, attributes such as tax parameters are stored as value objects. We use **data transfer object** (**DTO**) to transfer the data from the application layer to the computational layer. The Arlow/Nuestadt-based archetype pattern is the unit of structuring the tax computation logic.

For some developers, the preceding language/platform-independent description of the software being developed is enough to understand the approach taken. This will boost developer productivity (during all phases of SDLC, including development, maintenance, and support) as the developers will be able to get a good mental model of the code base. Without Pattern catalogs, such succinct descriptions of the design or implementation would have been impossible.

In an Agile software development scenario, we develop software in an iterative fashion. Once we reach a certain maturity in a module, developers refactor their code. While refactoring a module, patterns do help in organizing the logic. The case study given next will help you to understand the rationale behind *patterns as refactoring targets*.

APIs based on well-defined patterns are easy to use and impose less cognitive load on programmers. The success of the ASP.NET MVC framework, NHibernate, and APIs for writing HTTP modules and handlers in the ASP.NET pipeline are a few testimonies to the process. You will see how these three key advantages are put into practice in the ensuing chapters and case studies.

A quick foray into the .NET Reflection API

When we write non-trivial software that should go to production, it is mandatory to have the ability to load and execute modules on the fly. This is useful when you are planning to provide user defined extensions as a mechanism to add new features to the existing software. The .NET Reflection API is a nifty mechanism supported by the Microsoft Corporation to help developers to write code that can be loaded dynamically, after the base software has been written. The platform technologies, such as ASP.net, WCF,EF, and WPF, use reflection extensively:

```
public class Test
{
  //---- Only Property this class has
  public int X { get; set; }
  //----- This method will be invoked dynamically
  public void Spit()
  {
    Console.WriteLine(" X is " + X);
  }
}
```

We will write a simple program that will instantiate the object using the new keyword, and after the object instantiation, a property (X) will be set to the value 0xBEEF. The .NET Reflection API will be used to retrieve the property value and invoke a method (Spit) using them:

```
class Program
{
  static void Main(string[] args)
{
  Test a = new Test();
  //------ Set the property
  a.X = 0xBEEF;
  //------ Retrieve the CLR Type
  Type t = a.GetType();
  if (t == null)   return;
  //---- Retrieve the Property Handle
  PropertyInfo np = t.GetProperty("X");
  //---- Retrieve the Property  Value
  Console.WriteLine(np.GetValue(a));
  //------ Retrieve the Method Handle
  MethodInfo mi = t.GetMethod("Spit");
  //------ Invoke the method
  mi.Invoke(a, null);

  Console.Read();
```

```
        }
    }
```

We will be using .NET Reflection API extensively in our programs. A competent programmer should know the .NET Reflection API and its features to write any advanced piece of code. Do consult the Microsoft documentation to understand the features available and the nuances of the API. If you want to be a library or framework designer, you should know Reflection API in depth.

Personal income tax computation – A case study

Rather than explaining the advantages of patterns, the following example will help us to see things in action. Computation of annual income tax is a well-known problem domain across the globe. We have chosen an application domain that is well known for focusing on software development issues.

The application should receive inputs regarding the demographic profile (UID, Name, Age, Sex, Location) of a citizen and the income details (Basic, DA, HRA, CESS, Deductions) to compute their tax liability. The system should have discriminants based on the demographic profile, and have a separate logic for senior citizens, juveniles, disabled people, female senior citizens, and others. By discriminant we mean that demographic parameters such as age, sex, and location should determine the category to which a person belongs and therefore apply category-specific computation for that individual. As a first iteration, we will implement logic for the senior citizen and ordinary citizen categories.

After preliminary discussions, our developer created a prototype screen, as shown in the following image:

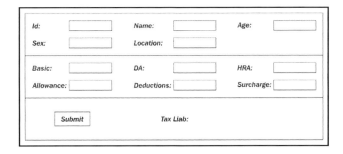

Archetypes and business archetype patterns

The legendary Swiss psychologist, Carl Gustav Jung, created the concept of archetypes to explain fundamental entities that arise from a common repository of human experiences. The concept of archetypes percolated to the software industry from psychology. The Arlow/Nuestadt patterns describe business archetype patterns such as Party, Customer Call, Product, Money, Unit, Inventory, and so on. An example is the Apache Maven archetype, which helps us to generate projects of different natures, such as J2EE apps, Eclipse plugins, OSGI projects, and so on. The Microsoft patterns and practices describe archetypes for targeting builds such as web applications, rich client applications, mobile applications, and services applications. Various domain-specific archetypes can exist in respective contexts as organizing and structuring mechanisms.

In our case, we will define some archetypes that are common in the taxation domain. Some of the key archetypes in this domain are as follows:

Sr.no	Archetype	Description
1	SeniorCitizenFemale	Tax payers who are female, and above the age of 60 years.
2	SeniorCitizen	Tax payers who are male, and above the age of 60 years.
3	OrdinaryCitizen	Tax payers who are male/female, and above 18 years of age.
4	DisabledCitizen	Tax payers who have any disability.
5	MilitaryPersonnel	Tax payers who are military personnel.
6	Juveniles	Tax payers whose age is less than 18 years.

We will use demographic parameters as discriminants to find the archetype that corresponds to the entity. The whole idea of inducing archetypes is to organize the tax computation logic around them. Once we are able to resolve the archetypes, it is easy to locate and delegate the computations corresponding to the archetypes.

Entity, value, and data transfer objects

We are going to create a class that represents a citizen. Since a citizen needs to be uniquely identified, we are going to create an entity object, which is also called a reference object (from the DDD catalog). The **universal identifier** (**UID**) of an entity object is the handle to which an application refers. Entity objects are not identified by their attributes, as there can be two people with the same name. The ID uniquely identifies an entity object. The definition of an entity object is given as follows:

```
public class TaxableEntity
```

```
{
  public int Id { get; set; }
  public string Name { get; set; }
  public int Age { get; set; }
  public char Sex { get; set; }
  public string Location { get; set; }
  public TaxParamVO taxparams { get; set; }
}
```

In the preceding class definition, Id uniquely identifies the entity object. TaxParams is a value object (from the DDD catalog) associated with the entity object. Value objects do not have a conceptual identity. They describe some attributes of things (entities). The definition of TaxParams is given as follows:

```
public class TaxParamVO
{
  public double Basic {get;set;}
  public double DA { get; set; }
  public double HRA { get; set; }
  public double Allowance { get; set; }
  public double Deductions { get; set; }
  public double Cess { get; set; }
  public double TaxLiability { get; set; }
  public bool Computed { get; set; }
}
```

While writing applications ever since Smalltalk, **Model-view-controller** (**MVC**) is the most dominant paradigm for structuring applications. The application is split into a model layer (which mostly deals with data), a view layer (which acts as a display layer), and a controller (to mediate between the two). In the web development scenario, they are physically partitioned across machines. To transfer data between layers, the J2EE pattern catalog identified the DTO. The DTO object is defined as follows:

```
public class TaxDTO
{
  public int id { }
  public TaxParamVO taxparams { }
}
```

If the layering exists within the same process, we can transfer these objects as-is. If layers are partitioned across processes or systems, we can use XML or JSON serialization to transfer objects between the layers.

A computation engine

We need to separate UI processing, input validation, and computation to create a solution that can be extended to handle additional requirements. The computation engine will execute different logic depending upon the command received. The GoF command pattern is leveraged for executing the logic based on the command received.

The command pattern consists of four constituents. They are as follows:

- Command object
- Parameters
- Command Dispatcher
- Client

The command object's interface has an `Execute` method. The parameters to the command objects are passed through a bag. The client invokes the command object by passing the parameters through a bag to be consumed by the Command Dispatcher. The parameters are passed to the command object through the following data structure:

```
public class COMPUTATION_CONTEXT
{
  private Dictionary<String, Object> symbols = new
  Dictionary<String, Object>();
  public void Put(string k, Object value) {
    symbols.Add(k, value);
  }
  public Object Get(string k) { return symbols[k]; }
}
```

The `ComputationCommand` interface, which all the command objects implement, has only one `Execute` method, which is shown next. The `Execute` method takes a bag as a parameter. The `COMPUTATION_CONTEXT` data structure acts as the bag here:

```
Interface ComputationCommand
{
  bool Execute(COMPUTATION_CONTEXT ctx);
}
```

Since we have already implemented a command interface and bag to transfer the parameters, it is time that we implemented a command object. For the sake of simplicity, we will implement two commands where we hardcode the tax liability:

```
public class SeniorCitizenCommand : ComputationCommand
{
  public bool Execute(COMPUTATION_CONTEXT ctx)
```

```
    {
      TaxDTO td = (TaxDTO)ctx.Get("tax_cargo");
      //---- Instead of computation, we are assigning
      //---- constant tax for each archetypes
      td.taxparams.TaxLiability = 1000;
      td.taxparams.Computed = true;
      return true;
    }
}

public class OrdinaryCitizenCommand : ComputationCommand
{
  public bool Execute(COMPUTATION_CONTEXT ctx)
  {
    TaxDTO td = (TaxDTO)ctx.Get("tax_cargo");
    //---- Instead of computation, we are assigning
    //---- constant tax for each archetypes
    td.taxparams.TaxLiability = 1500;
    td.taxparams.Computed = true;
    return true;
  }
}
```

The commands will be invoked by a CommandDispatcher object, which takes an archetype string and a COMPUTATION_CONTEXT object. The CommandDispatcher acts as an API layer for the application:

```
class CommandDispatcher
{
  public static bool Dispatch(string archetype,
  COMPUTATION_CONTEXT ctx)
  {
    if (archetype == "SeniorCitizen")
    {
      SeniorCitizenCommand cmd = new SeniorCitizenCommand();
      return cmd.Execute(ctx);
    }
    else if (archetype == "OrdinaryCitizen")
    {
      OrdinaryCitizenCommand cmd = new OrdinaryCitizenCommand();
      return cmd.Execute(ctx);
    }
    else {
      return false;
    }
  }
}
```

The application to engine communication

The data from the application UI, be it web or desktop, has to flow to the computation engine. The following ViewHandler routine shows how data, retrieved from the application UI, is passed to the engine, via the Command Dispatcher, by a client:

```
public static void ViewHandler(TaxCalcForm tf)
{
  TaxableEntity te = GetEntityFromUI(tf);
  if (te == null){
    ShowError();
    return;
  }
  string archetype = ComputeArchetype(te);
  COMPUTATION_CONTEXT ctx = new COMPUTATION_CONTEXT();
  TaxDTO td = new TaxDTO { id = te.id, taxparams =
  te.taxparams};
  ctx.Put("tax_cargo",td);
  bool rs = CommandDispatcher.Dispatch(archetype, ctx);
  if ( rs ) {
    TaxDTO temp = (TaxDTO)ctx.Get("tax_cargo");
    tf.Liabilitytxt.Text =
    Convert.ToString(temp.taxparams.TaxLiability);
    tf.Refresh();
  }
}
```

At this point, imagine that a change in requirements has been received from the stakeholders. Now we need to support tax computation for new categories.

 Initially, we had different computations for senior citizens and ordinary citizens. Now we need to add new archetypes. At the same time, to make the software extensible (loosely coupled) and maintainable, it would be ideal if we provided the capability to support the new archetypes in a configurable manner, as opposed to recompiling the application for every new archetype owing to concrete references.

The Command Dispatcher object does not scale well to handle additional archetypes. We need to change the assembly whenever a new archetype is included, as the tax computation logic varies for each archetype. We need to create a pluggable architecture to add or remove archetypes at will.

The plugin system to make system extensible

Writing system logic without impacting the application warrants a mechanism–that of loading a class on the fly. Luckily, the .NET Reflection API provides a mechanism for one to load a class during runtime, and invoke methods within it. A developer worth his salt should learn the Reflection API to write systems that change dynamically. In fact, most of the technologies such as ASP.NET, Entity Framework, .NET Remoting, and WCF work because of the availability of Reflection API in the .NET stack.

Henceforth, we will be using an XML configuration file to specify our tax computation logic. A sample XML file is given next:

```xml
<?xml version="1.0"?>
<plugins>
  <plugin archetype ="OrindaryCitizen"
  command="TaxEngine.OrdinaryCitizenCommand"/>  <plugin
  archetype="SeniorCitizen"
  command="TaxEngine.SeniorCitizenCommand"/>
</plugins>
```

The contents of the XML file can be read very easily using LINQ to XML. We will be generating a `Dictionary` object with the following code snippet:

```csharp
private Dictionary<string,string> LoadData(string xmlfile)
{
  return XDocument.Load(xmlfile)
  .Descendants("plugins")
  .Descendants("plugin")
  .ToDictionary(p => p.Attribute("archetype").Value,
  p => p.Attribute("command").Value);
}
```

Factory method pattern and plugins

The factory method (from the GoF catalog) is a pattern that solves the creation of objects through a static method exposed solely for this purpose. The object we create will be based on a particular class or derived class. In our case, we need to create objects that have implemented the `ComputationCommand` interface.

The consumer of the `Factory` class can also indicate whether it requires a singleton or a prototype. The default behavior of the factory method is singleton, and it is supposed to return the same instance whenever a call to the `Factory` (`Get`) method is received. If the prototype option is given, a clone of the object will be created and returned:

```
public class ObjectFactory
{
  //--- A Dictionary to store
  //--- Plugin details (Archetype/commandclass)
  private Dictionary<string, string> plugins = new
  Dictionary<string, string>();
  //--- A Dictionary to cache objects
  //--- archetype/commandclassinstance
  private Dictionary<string, ComputationCommand> commands =
  new Dictionary<string, ComputationCommand>();

  public ObjectFactory(String xmlfile)
  {
    plugins = LoadData(xmlfile);
  }

  private Dictionary<string,string> LoadData(string xmlfile)
  {
    return XDocument.Load(xmlfile)
    .Descendants("plugins")
    .Descendants("plugin")
    .ToDictionary(p => p.Attribute("archetype").Value,
    p => p.Attribute("command").Value);
  }
  //---- Rest of the code omitted
}
```

The consumer of the `ObjectFactory` class will indicate whether it wants a reference to the object to be available in the plugin cache or a clone of the object. We can clone an object using binary serialization. By writing an extension method leveraging generics, we can write an all-purpose clone routine. The following code snippet will help us to achieve that:

```
public static T DeepClone<T>(this T a) {
  using (MemoryStream stream = new MemoryStream()) {
  BinaryFormatter formatter = new BinaryFormatter();
  formatter.Serialize(stream, a);
  stream.Position = 0;
  return (T)formatter.Deserialize(stream);
  }
}
```

Now the implementation of Get becomes a straightforward affair; the full listing of the Get method is given as follows:

```
public ComputationCommand Get(string archetype,
string mode = "singleton")
{
  //---- We can create a new instance, when a
  //---- prototype is asked, otherwise we will
  //---- return the same instance stored in the dictionary
  if (mode != "singleton" && mode != "prototype")
  return null;

  ComputationCommand temp = null;
  //--- if an instance is already found, return
  // it (singleton) or clone (prototype
  if (commands.TryGetValue(archetype, out temp))
  {
    return (mode == "singleton") ? temp :
    temp.DeepClone<ComputationCommand>();
  }

  //---- retrieve the commandclass name
  string classname = plugins[archetype];
  if (classname == null)
  return null;
  //------ retrieve the classname, if it
  //------ is available with CLR
  Type t = Type.GetType(classname);

  if (t == null)
  return null;
  //---- Create a new Instance and store it
  //---- in commandclass instance dictionary
  commands[archetype]=
  (ComputationCommand)Activator.CreateInstance(t);
  return commands[archetype];
}
```

Now that we have got a factory method implementation, let us see how one can consume the code. The Command Dispatcher will get a handle to the instance of a command based on the archetype provided to it. Once the handle to the object is received, the Execute method can be invoked:

```
public class CommandDispatcher
{
  private static ObjectFactory obj =
  new  ObjectFactory("Pluggins.xml");
```

```
public static bool Dispatch(string archetype,
COMPUTATION_CONTEXT ctx)
{
    ComputationCommand cmd = obj.Get(archetype);
    return (cmd == null) ? false : cmd.Execute(ctx);
}
}
```

 The authors of the book feel that command objects should be designed in a stateless manner. In the imperative programming world, this means that there shouldn't be any shared variables between the methods of a class. We should not add class-level variables in order to avoid locks in a multithreaded environment. In effect, parameters become the sole determinant of the results. If you cannot avoid having class-level variables, they should be immutable (read only). If we mutate the state of an object, the prototype created out of that will have an impact because of object references. The Java servlet specification expects the servlets to be stateless, and Spring controllers are also stateless. The Microsoft ASP.NET MVC controllers need not be stateless (not sure why Microsoft chose things that way).

Now, let us revisit our `ViewHandler` routine. The interface does not change here. The real magic happens beneath the Command Dispatcher object:

```
public static void ViewHandler(TaxCalcForm tf)
{
    TaxableEntity te = GetEntityFromUI(tf);
    if (te == null)
    {
        ShowError();
        return;
    }
    string archetype = ComputeArchetype(te);
    COMPUTATION_CONTEXT ctx = new COMPUTATION_CONTEXT();
    TaxDTO td = new TaxDTO { id = te.id, taxparams = te.taxparams};
    ctx.Put("tax_cargo",td);
    bool rs = CommandDispatcher.Dispatch(archetype, ctx);
    if ( rs ) {
        TaxDTO temp = (TaxDTO)ctx.Get("tax_cargo");
        tf.Liabilitytxt.Text =
        Convert.ToString(temp.taxparams.TaxLiability);
        tf.Refresh();
    }
}
```

The view handler routine does the following:

- Retrieves the value from the UI elements to create entity
- Determines the archetype based on demographic parameters
- Creates a DTO and places it in a bag
- Dispatches the method through `CommandDispatcher`
- Updates the UI based on the status

Let's create a new command that will compute taxes for senior citizens who are female:

```
public class SeniorCitizenFemaleCommand : ComputationCommand
{
  public bool Execute(COMPUTATION_CONTEXT ctx)
  {
    TaxDTO td = (TaxDTO)ctx.Get("tax_cargo");
    //---- Compute the Tax for Senior Females
    //---- They belong to different Slabs
    double accum = td.taxparams.Basic +
    td.taxparams.DA + td.taxparams.Allowance +
    td.taxparams.HRA;
    double net = accum - td.taxparams.Deductions -
    td.taxparams.Surcharge;
    //---- Flat 10% Tax
    td.taxparams.TaxLiability = net*0.1;
    td.taxparams.Computed = true;
    return true;
  }
}
```

We have to make some changes to the configuration file. The resulting XML configuration is given as follows:

```
<?xml version="1.0"?>
<plugins>
  <plugin archetype ="OrindaryCitizen"
  command="TaxEngine.OrdinaryCitizenCommand"/>  <plugin
  archetype="SeniorCitizen"
  command="TaxEngine.SeniorCitizenCommand"/>  <plugin
  archetype="SeniorCitizenFemale"
  command="TaxEngine.SeniorCitizenFemaleCommand"/>
</plugins>
```

Finalizing the solution

We started with a solution that solved the problem at hand. After creating a basic pipeline, we created an elaborate pipeline, which made the solution extensible. Now we can add new commands without recompiling the application. This is very important in the case of applications that are governed by amendable laws. To make our code robust, we will add the design by contract strategy to our command objects.

Design by contract and template method pattern

The design by contract idiom, created by Bertrand Meyer (creator of the Eiffel language), extends the ordinary definition of abstract data types with preconditions, post conditions, and invariants. To execute any contract in real life, we need to satisfy some preconditions, followed by execution, and a post execution (verification) phase as listed here:

- Pre-Execute
- Execute
- Post-Execute

At the end of the Post-Execute phase, the invariants are checked to see whether they are violated. The consumer will call `PreExecute` to determine whether there is a context for the execution of the contract. The invocation will proceed only if `PreExecute` returns true. To incorporate design by contract, we extend the interface with two additional methods. The resultant `interface` is given as follows:

```
public interface ComputationCommand
{
  bool PreExecute(COMPUTATION_CONTEXT ctx);
  bool Execute(COMPUTATION_CONTEXT ctx);
  bool PostExecute(COMPUTATION_CONTEXT ctx);
}
```

We will create a `BaseComputationCommand` class, which will stub the methods in the `ComputationCommand` interface. This will help the concrete, derived command classes to override only those methods which have the respective changes. After redefining the interface, we will create a default implementation of the command pattern with methods marked as `virtual`. This helps us to override the implementation in the derived class. This is an instance of the template method pattern:

```
public class BaseComputationCommand : ComputationCommand
{
  public virtual bool PreExecute(COMPUTATION_CONTEXT ctx) { return
```

```
true; } public virtual bool Execute(COMPUTATION_CONTEXT ctx) {
return true; } public virtual bool
PostExecute(COMPUTATION_CONTEXT ctx) { return true; }
}
```

Our commands here will use the template method pattern to override only those methods that are relevant. Otherwise, there is already a fallback in the `BaseComputationCommand`. The template method pattern defines the program skeleton of an algorithm(s) in a method, and they are called template method(s). These template methods are overridden by subclasses, which implement the concrete logic:

```
public class SeniorCitizenCommand : BaseComputationCommand {
  public override bool PreExecute(COMPUTATION_CONTEXT ctx)
  {
    TaxDTO td = (TaxDTO)ctx.Get("tax_cargo");
    //--- Do Some Sanity Checks
    //--- if some problems => return false;
    return base.PreExecute(ctx);
  }
  public override bool Execute(COMPUTATION_CONTEXT ctx)
  {
    TaxDTO td = (TaxDTO)ctx.Get("tax_cargo");
    //---- Compute the Tax for Senior Citizens
    //---- They belong to different Slabs
    td.taxparams.TaxLiability = 1000;
    td.taxparams.Computed = true;
    return true;
  }

  public override bool PostExecute(COMPUTATION_CONTEXT ctx)
  {
    //--- Do the Check on Invariants
    //--- Return false, if there is violation
    return base.PostExecute(ctx);
  }
}
```

We need not override every method, and yet, the whole scheme would still work:

```
public class SeniorCitizenFemaleCommand : BaseComputationCommand
{
  public override bool Execute(COMPUTATION_CONTEXT ctx)
  {
    TaxDTO td = (TaxDTO)ctx.Get("tax_cargo");
    //---- Compute the Tax for Senior Females
    //---- They belong to different Slabs
    double accum = td.taxparams.Basic +
    td.taxparams.DA + td.taxparams.Allowance +
```

```
        td.taxparams.HRA;
        double net = accum - td.taxparams.Deductions -
        td.taxparams.Surcharge;
        //---- Flat 10% Tax
        td.taxparams.TaxLiability = net*0.1;
        return true;
    }
}
```

Now we need to rewrite the command pattern to reflect the implementation of the design by contract idiom in the command classes:

```
public class CommandDispatcher
{
  private static ObjectFactory obj = new
  ObjectFactory("Pluggins.xml");  public static bool
  Dispatch(string archetype,    COMPUTATION_CONTEXT ctx)
  {
    ComputationCommand cmd = obj.Get(archetype);
    if (cmd == null)
    return false;

    if (cmd.PreExecute(ctx))
    {
      bool rs = cmd.Execute(ctx);
      cmd.PostExecute(ctx);
      return rs;
    }
    return false;
  }
}
```

In some implementations, the clients will check the return value to see whether invariants have been violated. In some cases, a compensating transaction will be executed to restore the state to the previous one.

Using the Facade pattern to expose the computation API

Our computation engine contains a lot of classes that coordinate to implement the application logic. Any client who wants to interact with this implementation would prefer a simplified interface to this subsystem. A facade is an object that provides a simple interface to a large body of code in large classes or modules.

The GoF facade pattern is a mechanism that we can use to expose a coarse-grained API:

```
public class TaxComputationFacade
{
    /// <summary>
    ///  A Rule Engine can do Archetype detection
    ///  One can write a small Expression Evaluator Engine
    ///   and GOF terms its Interpreter pattern
    /// </summary>
    /// <param name="te"></param>
    /// <returns></returns>
    private static string ComputeArchetype(TaxableEntity te)
    {
      if ((te.Sex == 'F') && (te.age > 59))
      {
        return "SeniorCitizenFemale";
      }
      else if (te.age<18) {
        return "JuevenileCitizen";
      }

      return (te.age > 60) ? "SeniorCitizen" : "OrdinaryCitizen";
    }

    public static bool Compute(TaxableEntity te)
    {
      string archetype = ComputeArchetype(te);
      COMPUTATION_CONTEXT ctx = new COMPUTATION_CONTEXT();
      TaxDTO td = new TaxDTO { id = te.id, taxparams = te.taxparams
      };
      ctx.Put("tax_cargo", td);
      return CommandDispatcher.Dispatch(archetype, ctx);
    }
}
```

Now the `ViewHandler` has become much simpler, as shown in the following code:

```
public static void ViewHandler(TaxCalcForm tf)
{
  TaxableEntity te = GetEntityFromUI(tf);
  if (te == null)
  {
    ShowError();
    return;
  }
  bool rs = TaxComputationFacade.Compute(te);
  if (rs)
  {
```

```
            tf.Liabilitytxt.Text =
            Convert.ToString(te.taxparams.TaxLiability);
            tf.Refresh();
        }
    }
```

Summary

In this chapter, we have covered quite a lot of ground in understanding why pattern-oriented software development is a good way to develop modern software. We started the chapter by citing some key principles. We progressed further to demonstrate the applicability of these key principles by iteratively skinning an application that is extensible and resilient to changes. Through this journey, we covered concepts such as the command pattern, factory method pattern, facade pattern, design by contract, template method pattern, XML configuration files, LINQ to XML, and so on.

In the next chapter, we will continue our discussion of patterns by implementing a logging library, which can serialize contents into file, database, or remote network.

3
A Logging Library

In this chapter, we will try to create a **logging library** that will enable an application developer to log information to a media (file, network, or database) during program execution. This would be a critical library that the developer would be able to use for audit trail (domain pre-requisite) and code instrumentation (from a debugging and verification stand-point). We will design and implement this library from scratch, and make it available as an API to the end developer for consumption.

During the course of this chapter, as a reader, you will learn to leverage strategy pattern, factory method pattern, template pattern, singleton and prototype patterns to do the following:

- Writing data to a file stream
- Creating a simple **Data Access Layer** (**DAL**) using ADO.NET
- Writing data to an SQLite database
- Writing data to a network stream using the System.Net API
- Handling concurrency
- Threads

Requirements for the library

Before we embark on writing the library, let us scribble down a preliminary requirement statement as shown next:

The logging library should provide a unified interface to handle log entries which are supposed to be persisted in a media (file, remote node, or a database) and target media should be determined during runtime from a configuration file. The API should be target-independent and there should be provision to add new log targets without changing the application logic.

Solutions approach

Before we write the code to implement our library (a Windows assembly), let us enumerate the requirements to get the big picture:

- The data should be written to multiple streams
  - File, network, and DB
- The developer API should be target-agnostic
- The library should maintain its object lifetime
- The library should provide facility for adding new log targets
- The library should be able to handle concurrent writes to log targets

Writing content to a media

To manage the complexity of code isolation, let's declare a C# interface which will manage the idiosyncrasies of multiple log targets:

```
public interface IContentWriter
{
  Task<bool> Write(string content);
}
```

The basic idea here, is that the concrete classes which implement the interface should provide an implementation of this method that writes the log to the respective media. But on closer inspection, we find that it is better to write a base class implementation of this method and its associated semantics in an abstract class. The base class implementation can add a log entry to a queue (that would give concurrency support), flush the queue, and persist to target the media when a threshold (configured) is reached. A method will be marked as abstract which will provide a mechanism for concrete classes to write entries for the respective media.

Since our library is supposed to work in a multi-threaded environment, we need to handle concurrency in a neat manner. While writing to a file or network, we need to be careful that only one thread gets access to the file or socket handle. We will leverage the .NET `async`/`await` declarative programming model to manage background processing tasks. **Model-view-controller (MVC)** is the most dominant paradigm for structuring applications.

Template method pattern and content writers

In the first stage, we plan to flush the log contents to the file, network, and database targets. The bulk of our logic is common for all content writers. To aid separation of concerns and avoid duplication of code, it is best to let the concrete content writer classes manage their target media. Base implementation will take care of concurrency and queue management.

To make the code simple, we will leverage the `ConcurrentQueue` class (data structure introduced with .NET framework version 4) available with the `Systems.Collections.Concurrent` package. In the interest of clarity, we've left out the exception handling code. Please note that the `AggregateException` class should be leveraged for handling exceptions in concurrent execution scenarios.

This class will make sure that only one thread gets to write to the queue at any point of time. We will implement an asynchronous `Flush` method using **Task Parallel Library (TPL)**. This routine will retrieve data from the queue, and delegate the task of persistence (in the media of choice) to the respective concrete classes via an abstract method (`WriteToMedia`):

```
public abstract class BaseContentWriter : IContentWriter
{
  private ConcurrentQueue<string> queue =
  new ConcurrentQueue<string>();
  private Object _lock = new Object();

  public BaseContentWriter() { }
```

```
//---- Write to Media
public abstract bool WriteToMedia(string logcontent);

async Task  Flush()
{
  string content;
  int count = 0;
  while (queue.TryDequeue(out content) && count <= 10)
  {
    //--- Write to Appropriate Media
    //--- Calls the Overriden method
    WriteToMedia(content);
    count++;
  }
}
```

Once the contents of the queue reach a threshold level, a thread will acquire the lock for flushing the data. In our case, we will initiate flushing beyond 10 items in queue:

```
public async Task<bool> Write(string content)
{
  queue.Enqueue(content);
  if (queue.Count <= 10)
  return true;
  lock (_lock){
    Task temp = Task.Run(() => Flush());
    Task.WaitAll(new Task[] { temp });
  }
  return true;
}
```

The concrete classes derived from `BaseContentWriter` will implement the following method to handle the specificities:

```
public abstract bool WriteToMedia(string logcontent);
```

This is an instance of a template method pattern. The template method pattern is a behavioral design pattern where the bulk of logic resides in the base class, and certain steps of a process are implemented by concrete classes. In `BaseContentWriter`, we have the logic for adding elements to and retrieving elements from a concurrent queue. Persistence is taken care of by the sub-classes that implement our template method (`WriteToMedia`).

The following UML class diagram represents the realizations, dependencies, and associations between the various classes. Do observe the annotation that clearly outlines the template method pattern in action:

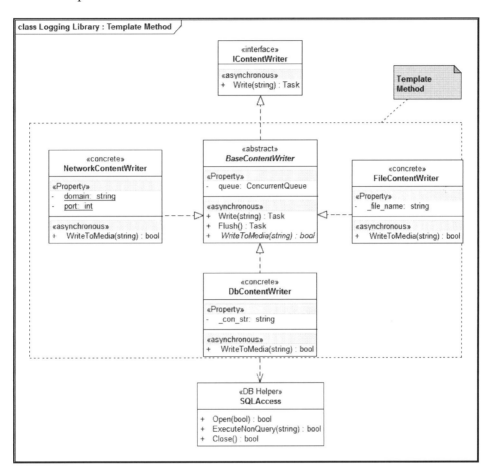

Writing a log entry to a file stream

We will use file streams to write a file. We implement the actual file handling logic in the WriteToMedia template method:

```
public class FileContentWriter : BaseContentWriter
{
  private string _file_name;
  public FileContentWriter(string name){
```

```
    _file_name =  name;
  }
  public override bool WriteToMedia( string content)
  {
    using (FileStream SourceStream =
    File.Open(_file_name, FileMode.Append ))
    {
      byte[] buffer =
      Encoding.UTF8.GetBytes(content+"\r\n");
      SourceStream.Write (buffer, 0, buffer.Length);
    }
    return true;
  }
}
```

Writing a log entry to a database

Some familiarity with ADO.NET is necessary to understand the nitty-gritties of this section. To make the matter simple, we have chosen SQLite as our database of choice to persist the log entries. One can choose MySQL, SQL Server, or Oracle. Because of the ADO.NET library, the code will be more or less the same for every RDBMS offering. We have created a class, SQLAccess, which wraps a subset of the ADO.NET calls to provide a simple interface for SQLite. The class encapsulates and leverages the ADO.NET provider for SQLite to provide an interaction with the SQLite database engine (x86/x64). In case this assembly (System.Data.SQLite) is not available locally, please use nuget to install it via the **Package Manager Console** as PM> Install-Package System.Data.SQLite:

```
public class SQLAccess
{
  private SQLiteConnection _con = null;
  private SQLiteCommand _cmd = null;
  private SQLiteTransaction _cts = null;
  private string _constr;
  public SQLAccess(string constr)
  {
    _constr = constr;
  }
```

The Open method given next instantiates the connection object, and invokes the Open method of the ADO.NET connection object. If we require transaction support, we need to instantiate a transaction context (SQLiteTransaction) object:

```
public bool Open(bool trans = false)
{
  try
```

```
  {
    _con = new SQLiteConnection(_constr);
    _con.Open();
    if (trans)
    _cts = _con.BeginTransaction();
    return true;
  }
  catch( SQLiteException e)
  {
    return false;
  }
}
```

To insert a value or set of values to a database, we instantiate a command object by giving a connection object and a string (containing the SQL statement). ADO.NET has the ExecuteNonQuery method to execute the query:

```
public bool ExecuteNonQuery(string SQL)
{
  try
  {
    _cmd = new SQLiteCommand(SQL, _con);
    _cmd.ExecuteNonQuery();
    _con.Close();
    _con = null;
    return true;
  }
  catch (Exception e)
  {
    _con = null;
    return false;
  }
}
```

We close the connection once we have finished inserting records to the database:

```
public Boolean Close()
{
  if (_con != null)
  {
    if (_cts != null)
    {
      _cts.Commit();
      _cts = null;
    }
    _con.Close();
    _con = null;
    return true;
```

```
    }
    return false;
}
```

Once we have a class which will help us persist data to a relational database, writing the template method (`WriteToMedia`) becomes easy. The whole code listing is given as follows:

```
public class DbContentWriter : BaseContentWriter
{
  private string _con_str =
  @"Data Source=./Logstorage.db";
  public DbContentWriter(){ }
  public override bool WriteToMedia(string logcontent)
  {
    SQLAccess access = new SQLAccess(_con_str);
    if (access.Open())
    {
      string query = "INSERT INTO logs VALUES('" +
      logcontent + "');";
      bool result =  access.ExecuteNonQuery(query);
      access.Close();
      return result;
    }
    return false;
  }
}
```

Writing a log entry to a network stream

We will use the `TCPListener` class under the `System.Net` namespace for writing data to a network stream. For the current implementation, we have hard-coded the domain name (localhost:`127.0.0.1`) and port (`4500`). We can read these values from a configuration file. As usual, the whole action happens within the `WriteToMedia` template method. At the end of the chapter, we have given a simple implementation of a log server for the sake of completeness. The log server receives the entries we write, and prints it to its console:

```
public class NetworkContentWriter : BaseContentWriter
{
  private static string domain = "127.0.0.1";
  private static int port = 4500;
  public NetworkContentWriter(){}
  public override bool WriteToMedia(string content)
  {
    TcpClient _client = new TcpClient();
    if (_client == null){ return false; }
```

```
try{
  _client.Connect(domain, port);
}
catch (Exception) { return false; }

StreamWriter _sWriter =
new StreamWriter(_client.GetStream(), Encoding.ASCII);
_sWriter.WriteLine(content);
_sWriter.Flush();
_sWriter.Close();
_client.Close();
return true;
}
}
```

We have now implemented content writers for file, DB (using ADO.NET), and network streams. With this under our belt, we need to provide an interface for applications to consume these content writers. Depending on the logging strategy chosen by the application, the appropriate content writers are to be connected to the log data streams. This warrants another set of interfaces.

Logging strategy atop the strategy pattern

We will use the GoF strategy pattern to implement the interface for the logging library.

 We can treat the logging of data to different streams as algorithms, and strategy pattern is meant to parameterize the algorithm to be executed.

By having concrete classes for network, file, and DB strategies, we are able to swap the implementation logic:

```
public abstract class LogStrategy
{
  // DoLog is our Template method
  // Concrete classes will override this
  protected abstract bool DoLog(String logitem);
  public bool Log(String app, String key, String cause)
  {
    return DoLog(app + " " + key + " " + cause);
  }
}
```

To test the code, we will write a `NullLogStrategy` class, which prints the log entry to the console. Since we have written the logic for scheduling the execution of the code, our implementation will be much simpler. We implement the template method (`DoLog`) through which we write the log entry in the console:

```
public class NullLogStrategy : LogStrategy
{
  protected override bool DoLog(String logitem)
  {
    // Log into the Console
    Console.WriteLine(logitem+"\r\n");
    return true;
  }
}
```

Since we have taken pains to create the `ContentWriter` classes, our implementation of strategy classes is just a matter of implementing the `DoLog` template method, and delegating the actual work to the respective content writers:

```
public class DbLogStrategy : LogStrategy
{
  BaseContentWriter wt = new DbContentWriter();
  protected override bool DoLog(String logitem)
  {
    return wt.Write(logitem);
  }
}

public class FileLogStrategy : LogStrategy
{
  BaseContentWriter wt = new FileContentWriter(@"log.txt");
  protected override bool DoLog(String logitem)
  {
    // Log into the file
    wt.Write(logitem);
    return true;
  }
}

public class NetLogStrategy : LogStrategy
{
  BaseContentWriter nc = new NetworkContentWriter();
  protected override bool DoLog(String logitem)
  {
    // Log into the Network Socket
    nc.Write(logitem);
    return true;
```

```
    }
  }
```

The following image illustrates the strategy pattern in action:

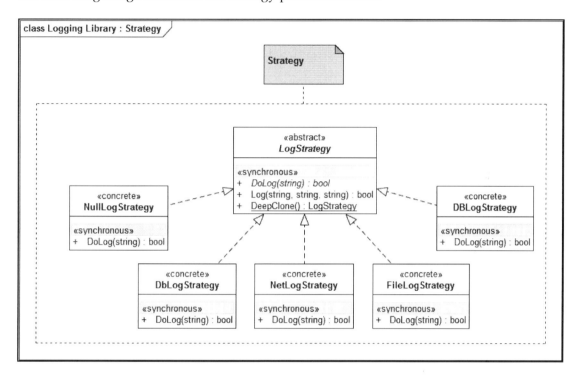

The factory method pattern for instantiation

Now, we should take care of the instantiation of the right object based on the parameter received (often retrieved from a configuration file) to identify the strategy.

We will use the GoF factory method pattern to instantiate the LogStrategy object. By checking the loggertype parameter, the appropriate concrete class will be instantiated.

```
public static LogStrategy CreateLogger(string loggertype)
{
  if (loggertype == "DB")
    return new DbLogStrategy();
  else if (loggertype == "FILE")
```

```
      return new FileLogStrategy();
   else if (loggertype == "NET")
      return new NetLogStrategy();
   else
      return new NullLogStrategy();
}
```

The application developer can also control the logging strategy through a configuration entry. The process of instantiating the `LogStrategy` class is given as follows:

```
string loggertype=read_from_config("loggertype");
LogStrategy lf = LoggerFactory.CreateLogger(loggertype);
//-- somewhere out in the module
lf.Log("APP","KEY","CAUSE");
```

Writing a generic factory method implementation

As discussed in the previous chapter, writing system logic without impacting the application warrants a mechanism – that of loading a class on the fly. We will tweak the factory method (`LogFactory`) implementation to make the system generic. We will use an XML file to provide the metadata that the factory method would use to create the respective log handler (`LogStrategy`) for the requested strategy (by the consumer). The sample XML file (`LogStrategy.xml`) is given as follows:

```
<?xml version="1.0"?>
<entries>
  <entry key ="DB" value="LogLibrary.DbLogStrategy"/>
  <entry key="NET" value="LogLibrary.NetLogStrategy"/>
  <entry key="FILE" value="LogLibrary.FileLogStrategy"/>
  <entry key="NULL" value ="LogLibrary.NullLogStrategy"/>
</entries>
```

The contents of the XML file can be read very easily using LINQ to XML.

Factory method, singleton, and prototype pattern for dynamic class loading

The .NET Reflection API helps us to load a class dynamically and instantiate an object . There is option for cloning an existing object to create a new one. We will use both strategies, for instantiation of objects.

The factory method (from the GoF catalog) is a pattern which solves the creation of objects through a static method exposed solely for this purpose. The object we create will be based on a particular class or derived class. The consumer of the `Factory` class can also indicate whether it requires a singleton or a prototype. The default behavior of the factory method is to create a singleton, and it will return the same instance whenever a call is made to the factory (`Get`) method. If the prototype option is given, a clone of the object will be created and returned. This is a good example that demonstrates how these three patterns compose and work in harmony to give you this desired outcome. Also note the adept usage of the dictionary object to achieve singletons. The constructs for creating an **object pool** is already present in this implementation. That would be a good exercise for any interested reader to uncover and implement.

The consumer of the `ObjectFactory` class would indicate whether it wants a reference to the object available in the cache or a clone of the object. We can clone an object using binary serialization. By writing an extension method leveraging generics, we can create an all-purpose clone routine. The following code snippet achieves that:

```
public static T DeepClone<T>(this T a) {
  using (MemoryStream stream = new MemoryStream()) {
    BinaryFormatter formatter = new BinaryFormatter();
    formatter.Serialize(stream, a);
    stream.Position = 0;
    return (T)formatter.Deserialize(stream);
  }
}
```

However, please note a cloneable interface could be leveraged in case you need custom cloning procedures. Now the implementation of `Get` becomes a straightforward affair; the following is a full listing of the `Get` method:

```
public class ObjectFactory
{
  //----- The Dictionary which maps XML configuration
```

```csharp
//----- Keys (key) to TypeName (value)
private Dictionary<string, string> entries =
new Dictionary<string, string>();
//----- The Dictionary which maps Entry Keys to Objects
//----- already instantiated by the Container
private Dictionary<string, Object> objects =
new Dictionary<string, Object>();

private Dictionary<string, string> LoadData(string str)
{
  //---- We use LINQ lambda syntax to load the contents of the
  //---- XML file.
  return XDocument.Load(str).Descendants("entries").
  Descendants("entry").ToDictionary(p =>
  p.Attribute("key").Value,
  p => p.Attribute("value").Value);
}

public ObjectFactory(String str)
{
  entries = LoadData(str);
}

public Object Get(string key, string mode = "singleton")
{
  //------------ singleton will return the same object
  //------------ every time.
  //------------ prototype will create a clone of the
  //------------ object if already instantiated before
  //------------ Singleton and Protype are the permissible
  //------------ Parameters
  if (mode != "singleton" && mode != "prototype")
    return null;
  Object temp = null;
  if (objects.TryGetValue(key, out temp))
    return (mode == "singleton") ? temp :
  temp.DeepClone<Object>();
  //------ if we could not retrieve an instance of previously
  //------ created object, retrieve the typename from entries
  //------ map

  string classname = null;
  entries.TryGetValue(key, out classname);
  if (classname == null)
    return null;
  string fullpackage = classname;
  //---- use .NET Reflection API to retrieve the CLR type
  //---- of the class name
```

```
      Type t = Type.GetType(fullpackage);
      if (t == null)
        return null;
      //------- Instantiate the object using .NET Reflection API
      objects[key] = (Object)Activator.CreateInstance(t);
      return objects[key];
    }
  }
}
```

We will be using the preceding class and different configuration files for all examples going forward. This will simplify our code, and we would have a terse listing.

Refactoring the code with the generic factory method

Using `ObjectFactory`, our strategy instantiation becomes much cleaner. If we cannot locate a proper implementation of strategy by dictionary lookup (within the factory store), we will instantiate a `NullStrategy` object (fallback option):

```
public class LoggerFactory
{
  private static ObjectFactory of =
  new ObjectFactory("LogStrategy.xml");
  public static LogStrategy CreateLogger(string loggertype)
  {
    LogStrategy sf = (LogStrategy)of.Get(loggertype);
    return (sf != null)?sf: new NullLogStrategy();
  }
}
```

A log server for network logging

An implementation of a server application that can handle incoming streams of data from a remote application is given next. Here we are using System.Net's `TCPListener` class to listen to the incoming connection. Once we receive a connection from the remote process, we will kick-start a thread to handle the log data from that connection. This implementation is given here for the sake of completeness:

```
class LogSocketServer
{
  private TcpListener _server;
```

```
private Boolean _running;
private int port = 4500;

public LogSocketServer()
{
  _server = new TcpListener(IPAddress.Any, port);
  _server.Start();
  _running = true;
  AcceptClients();
}

public void AcceptClients()
{
  while (_running)
  {
    TcpClient newClient = _server.AcceptTcpClient();
    Thread t = new Thread(
    new ParameterizedThreadStart(
    HandleClientData));
    t.Start(newClient);
  }
}

public void HandleClientData(object obj)
{
  TcpClient client = obj as TcpClient;
  StreamReader sReader = new
  StreamReader(client.GetStream(),
  Encoding.ASCII);
  bool bRead = true;
  while (bRead == true)
  {
    String sData = sReader.ReadLine();
    if (sData == null || sData.Length == 0)
    bRead = false;
    Console.WriteLine(sData);
  }
}
}
```

A simple client program to test the library

A simple test harness for the logging library is given next. The program accepts a command-line parameter, which is the log target (NET | FILE | DB). We create the appropriate logging strategy classes using the factory method pattern.

```
class Program
{
  private static bool Table(LogStrategy ls)
  {
    int a = 10;
    int b = 1;
    while (b < 100)
    {
      ls.Log("Table", a.ToString() + " * " +
      b.ToString(), "=" +(a * b).ToString());
      b++;
    }
    return true;
  }
  static void Main(string[] args)
  {
    if (args.Length != 1)
    {
      return;
    }
    string loggertype=args[0];
    LogStrategy lf = LoggerFactory.CreateLogger(loggertype);
    Table(lf);
  }
}
```

The following UML diagram illustrates the key set of patterns in action for the logging API:

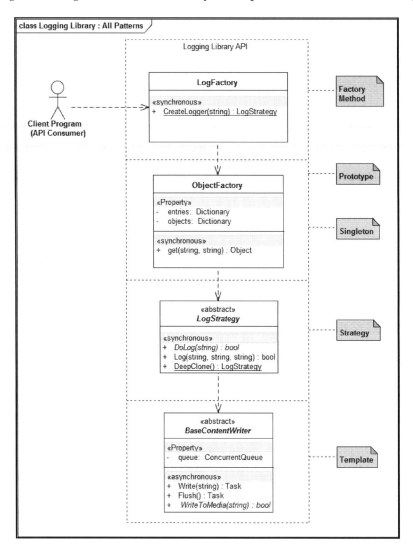

Summary

In this chapter, we covered more ground to gain a good understanding on some of the design patterns. We created a logging library which can log information from multiple threads and handle different targets like file, database, and remote servers. We used strategy pattern to swap the various logger implementations based on a configuration file. Once again, the template method pattern helped us to create an extensible solution for accommodating new log targets. All we needed to do was to override the base implementation with the specifics of the new log targets, as log information processing is handled by the base implementation. We extended our factory method pattern to handle arbitrary objects based on configuration files. We also learned to leverage dictionary objects for generating singletons and prototypes. In the next chapter, we will write a data access layer which can help an application target multiple databases. In the process, you will learn about adapter pattern, factory methods, and so on.

4
Targeting Multiple Databases

In this chapter, we will try to create a library which will help application developers target their applications against SQL Server, SQLite, MySQL, and Oracle. As a result of creating this library, we will be able to write the application code without worrying about the underlying persistence technology. Even though ADO.NET does a wonderful job of abstracting away the nitty-gritties of a **relational database management system (RDBMS)**, we need more than what is available as a stock feature within ADO.NET to write a database-agnostic persistence layer.

During the course of this chapter, as a reader, you will learn to leverage the abstract factory pattern, factory pattern, and the adapter pattern to be able to do the following:

- Interfacing with various ADO.NET providers
- Writing persistence-store agnostic logic
- Writing data to an SQLite database
- Writing data to an SQL Server database
- Writing data to an ODBC data source

Requirements for the library

Before we embark on writing the library, let us scribble down a preliminary requirement statement as follows:

 When we write business applications, our application should be able to persist to relational database engines from different database vendors.

We should be able to support SQL Server, SQLite, Oracle, or any database engine which supports ADO.net. Adding a new DB engine should be a breeze. Likewise, changing the database technology should be seamless for the application developer.

Solutions approach

With the advent of ORM technologies like ADO.NET **Entity Framework (EF)** and **NHibernate**, writing an application which targets multiple database offerings has become easier. The authors believe that ADO.NET EF works in tandem with the Visual Studio environment and its tools, and would be difficult to deal with in a book meant for pattern oriented software development. For people from the Java world, who are accustomed to the Hibernate library, NHibernate flattens the learning curve. Despite its dwindling usage and popularity (reasons unknown) amidst .NET professionals, the authors feel that NHibernate is a viable option to write enterprise grade applications in. In this book, for the sake of simplicity, we will be using the ADO.NET programming model to isolate the database specificities.

The ADO.NET library is based on the following set of interfaces defined in the `System.Data` assembly from Microsoft:

Interface	Definition
`IDbConnection`	Interface for managing database connection specifics.
`IDbCommand`	Interface for issuing SQL commands and queries.
`IDbDataAdapter`	Interface for disconnected data access.
`IDataReader`	Interface for cursor-based access to the database.

There are other interfaces which deal with the management of transactions, stored procedures, and associated parameter handling. We will ignore them in this book for the sake of shortening our code listings. Those can be incorporated into our library without much effort.

Each of the aforementioned Interfaces is implemented by a provider written by the respective database vendor. Microsoft encourages independent vendors to write ADO.NET providers. The SQL Server implementation (`System.Data.SqlClient`) of these interfaces are named as follows:

Class	Definition
SqlConnection	Implementation of `IDbConnection` interface.
SqlCommand	Implementation of `IDbCommand` interface.
SqlDataAdapter	Implementation of `IDbAdapter` interface.
SqlDataReader	Implementation of `IDataReader` interface.

In the case of `System.Data.SQLite`, the scheme is as follows:

Class	Definition
SQLiteConnection	Implementation of `IDbConnection` interface.
SQLiteCommand	Implementation of `IDbCommand` interface.
SQLitelDataAdapter	Implementation of `IDbAdapter` interface.
SQLiteDataReader	Implementation of `IDataReader` interface.

Similar provider classes are implemented by Oracle and MySQL.

 We will be using the GoF catalog's abstract factory methods to instantiate standard ADO.NET-library-specific interfaces for connection, command, data adapter, and reader. The abstract factory pattern is a creational pattern which provides an interface for creating families of related or dependent objects without specifying their concrete classes.

A quick primer on ADO.net

Since we are using ADO.net API for accessing databases, a couple of code snippets will be of help to comprehend the following sections. There are two ways to write code using the ADO.net API. We can directly use the concrete classes to access the database content. The following code snippet shows how one can write code against SQLite using `SQliteConnection`, `SQliteCommand` and `SQliteDataReader` and so on. Similar code can be written for SQL Server, MySQL and Oracle:

```
public static void TestAdoNetSpecificInterface()
{
```

```
string connectionString = @"Data Source=./Logstorage.db";
//----- Create a Connection Object
//----- and open it
SQLiteConnection dbcon=
  new SQLiteConnection(connectionString);
dbcon.Open();
//----------- Create a Command Object
//----------- to issue SQL Query
SQLiteCommand dbcmd = dbcon.CreateCommand();
string sql = "SELECT * from logs";
dbcmd.CommandText = sql;

//----------- Create a Reader Object
//----------- And Iterate through it
SQLiteDataReader reader = dbcmd.ExecuteReader();
while (reader.Read())
{
  string logentry = reader.GetString(0);
  Console.WriteLine(logentry);
}
// clean up
reader.Close();
reader = null;
dbcmd.Dispose();
dbcmd = null;
dbcon.Close();
dbcon = null;
}
```

The above code snippet leverages the concrete classes provided. If we want to write code in a generic manner, we can program against the interfaces like IDbConnection, IDbCommand and IDbDataReader etc. The following code snippet demonstrates the technique:

```
public static void TestAdoNetWithGenericInterface()
{
  string connectionString = @"Data Source=./Logstorage.db";
  //------- Open a connection and assign the connection object
  //------- to the IDbconnection interface. SQliteConnection,
  //------- OracleConnection,SQLConnection etc. implements the
  //------- IDbConnection Interface
  IDbConnection dbcon
    = (IDbConnection)new SQLiteConnection(connectionString);
  dbcon.Open();
  //------------ IDbCommand is the interface for
  //------------ Command Object . Every ADO.net
  //------------ Interface (for Oracle,SQL server etc)
  //------------ supports it
  IDbCommand dbcmd = dbcon.CreateCommand();
```

```
string sql = "SELECT * from logs";
dbcmd.CommandText = sql;
//------- Create a Data Reader and Assign
//------- it to IDataReader Interface
IDataReader reader = dbcmd.ExecuteReader();
while (reader.Read())
{
  string logentry = reader.GetString(0);
  Console.WriteLine(logentry);
}
// clean up
reader.Close();
reader = null;
dbcmd.Dispose();
dbcmd = null;
dbcon.Close();
dbcon = null;
}
```

The abstract factory pattern and object instantiation

In our case, the abstract factory pattern is pertinent, as we are supposed to create a set of related classes based on the ADO.NET defined interfaces. For this very purpose, we will define an abstract class with the following signature:

```
public abstract class DbAbstractFactory
{
  public abstract IDbConnection CreateConnection(string connstr);
  public abstract IDbCommand CreateCommand(IDbConnection con,
  string cmd);
  public abstract IDbDataAdapter CreateDbAdapter(IDbCommand cmd);
  public abstract IDataReader CreateDataReader(IDbCommand cmd);
}
```

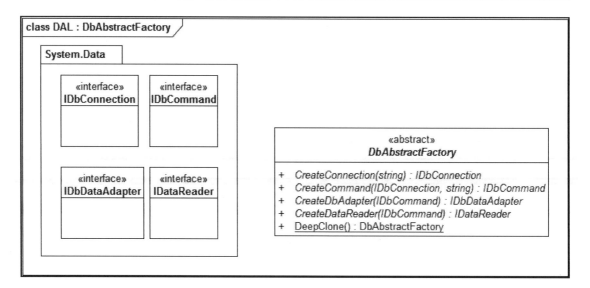

In the preceding interface, we have methods to create connection object, command object, data adapter object, and data reader object. These classes are related, and concrete classes are for each of the database offerings. The concrete classes make calls to the corresponding ADO.NET driver.

The SQL server implementation

The SQL Server implementation of abstract factory uses the default provider given by Microsoft Corporation. We need to include the `System.Data.SqlClient` namespace in our projects to utilize the objects in the provider namespace. Though the code given warrants more robust and defensive programming practices mandated for an industrial strength implementation, it provides clarity and is a good template for such an implementation:

```
[Serializable()]
public class SQLServerDbFactory : DbAbstractFactory,ISerializable
{
  private string drivertype { get; set; }
  public SQLServerDbFactory() { this.drivertype = null; }
  //----------------- Create a Connection Object
  //----------------- returns a reference to
  //----------------- a IDbConnection Interface
  public override IDbConnection CreateConnection(string connstr)
  {
    if (connstr == null || connstr.Length == 0)
      return null;
```

```
      return new SqlConnection(connstr);
    }
    public override IDbCommand CreateCommand(IDbConnection con,
    string cmd)
    {
      if (con == null || cmd == null || cmd.Length == 0)
      return null;
      if (con is SqlConnection)
      return new SqlCommand(cmd,
      (SqlConnection)con);
      return null;
    }
    public override IDbDataAdapter CreateDbAdapter(IDbCommand cmd)
    {
      if (cmd == null) { return null; }
      if (cmd is SqlCommand)
      return new
      SqlDataAdapter((SqlCommand)cmd);
      return null;
    }
    public override IDataReader CreateDataReader(IDbCommand cmd)
    {
      if (cmd == null) { return null; }
      if (cmd is SqlCommand)
        return (SqlDataReader)cmd.ExecuteReader();
      return null;
    }
    public void GetObjectData(SerializationInfo info,
    StreamingContext ctxt)
    {
    }
    protected SQLServerDbFactory(SerializationInfo info,
    StreamingContext context)
    {
    }
  }
```

The SQLite implementation

The SQLite implementation uses the ADO.NET provider maintained by the SQLite implementation team. To include that, we need to download assemblies from the https://system.data.sqlite.org site. We need to also include sqlite3.dll available on the SQLite site.

You could also use nuget to install it via the Package Manager Console as `PM> Install-Package System.Data.SQLite`:

```csharp
[Serializable()]
public class SQLiteDbFactory : DbAbstractFactory,ISerializable
{
  private string drivertype { get; set; }
  public SQLiteDbFactory() { this.drivertype = null; }
  public override IDbConnection CreateConnection(string connstr)
  {
    if (connstr == null || connstr.Length == 0)
    return null;
    return new SQLiteConnection(connstr);
  }

  public override IDbCommand CreateCommand(IDbConnection
  con,string cmd)
  {
    if (con == null || cmd == null || cmd.Length == 0)
    return null;
    if (con is SQLiteConnection )
    return  new SQLiteCommand(cmd,
    (SQLiteConnection)con);
    return null;
  }

  public override IDbDataAdapter CreateDbAdapter(IDbCommand cmd)
  {
    if (cmd == null) { return null; }
    if (cmd is SQLiteCommand)
    return new
    SQLiteDataAdapter((SQLiteCommand)cmd);
    return null;
  }

  public override IDataReader CreateDataReader(IDbCommand cmd)
  {
    if (cmd == null) { return null; }
    if (cmd is SQLiteCommand)
    return (SQLiteDataReader)cmd.ExecuteReader();
    return null;
  }

  public void GetObjectData(SerializationInfo info,
  StreamingContext ctxt)
  {
  }
```

```
    protected SQLiteDbFactory(SerializationInfo info,
    StreamingContext context)
    {
    }
}
```

The Oracle and ODBC implementation

Since Microsoft has deprecated the `System.Data.OracleClient` interface, we need to download ADO.NET providers from the Oracle Corporation site. Incorporating Oracle into the mix is similar to the way we did for SQL Server and SQLite. Since Oracle supports ODBC, we use an ODBC ADO.NET provider through the `System.Data.Oledb` namespace to interact with the other databases. The implementation is available as part of the source code downloads.

The following diagram illustrates the abstract factories in action (though only one has been labeled):

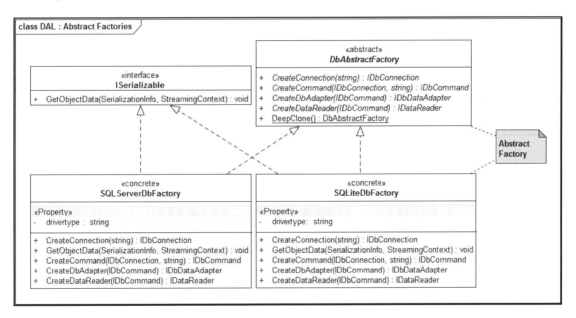

The adapter pattern powered API

The GOF Adapter pattern is useful for us in this context to provide a unified programming model for the consumers of the sub system.

The Adapter pattern is a structural pattern which works as a bridge between different interfaces or different implementations of an interface. In our case, we will use the adapter pattern as a bridge between application developers and various implementations of `DbAstractFactory`.

We need to create an **Application Program Interface (API)** for the application software developer to leverage different implementations based on a configuration entry. We will create a C# interface, which an adapter class needs to implement, to act as an API. At this point in time, we have only one instance of the adapter class. In future, we can have adapters for different scenarios:

```csharp
public interface IDbEngineAdapter
{
  bool Open();
  DataSet Execute(string SQL);
  IDataReader ExecuteQuery(string SQL);
  bool ExecuteNonQuery(string SQL);
  Boolean Close();
}
```

The adapter class Implementation

We will implement an adapter class which will help us to seamlessly integrate multiple database engines with our application. For implementing the adapter class, we will leverage the object factory (`ObjectFactory`) implementation from the previous chapter:

```csharp
public class DbEngineAdapter : IDbEngineAdapter
{
  static  ObjectFactory of = new ObjectFactory("DbDrivers.xml");
  private IDbConnection _con = null;
  private IDbCommand _cmd = null;
  private DbAbastractFactory df = null;
  private string _constr;
  private string _driver;
```

We leverage the factory method infrastructure created in Chapter 3, *A Logging Library* to help instantiate the proper concrete implementation of `DbAstractFactory`. The `DbDrivers.xml` configuration file contains the necessary information to instantiate the concrete classes:

```csharp
public DbEngineAdapter(string constr, string driver)
{
  _constr = constr;
```

```
    _driver = driver;
    //----- Instantiate the correct concrete class
    //----- based on the driver
    df = (DbAbastractFactory)of.Get(driver, "prototype");
}
```

The constructor takes two parameters, that is, connection string and driver name. Using the driver name as the key, the appropriate implementation of ADO.NET will be instantiated:

```
public bool Open()
{
  try
  {
    if (_con != null || df == null || _constr == null)
    {
      return false;
    }
    //------ Create Connection Object
    _con = df.CreateConnection(_constr);
    if (_con == null)
    return false;
    _con.Open();
    return true;
  }
  catch (Exception e)
  {
    e.ToString();
    return false;
  }
}
```

The Open method creates the connection object through the abstract factory concrete implementation. Once the connection object has been created, the ADO.NET connection is opened. The application developer should then make a call to Open method of the current class before calling any other method:

```
public DataSet Execute(string SQL)
{
  try
  {
    if (_con == null || df == null || _cmd != null)
    {
      return null;
    }
    _cmd = df.CreateCommand(_con, SQL);
    IDbDataAdapter da = df.CreateDbAdapter(_cmd);
    if (da == null) { return null; }
    DataSet ds = new DataSet();
```

```
      da.Fill(ds);
      return ds;
    }
    catch (Exception e)
    {
      e.ToString();
      return null;
    }
  }
```

The `Execute` method helps one to dispatch an SQL string to the selected database engine, and returns a dataset. This method is also used for disconnected access where an application wants to retrieve a small set of data to be populated in a user interface:

```
  public IDataReader ExecuteQuery(string SQL)
  {
    try
    {
      if (_con == null || df == null || _cmd != null) { return
      null;}
      _cmd = df.CreateCommand(_con, SQL);
      if (_cmd == null) { return null; }
      IDataReader rs = df.CreateDataReader(_cmd);
      return rs;
    }
    catch (Exception e)
    {
      e.ToString();
      return null;
    }
  }
```

The `ExecuteQuery` method helps one to dispatch an SQL query to a database, and retrieve a data reader object which will help one to navigate one record at a time. This is called cursor-based access, and is suitable for queries which return a large dataset:

```
  public bool ExecuteNonQuery(string SQL)
  {
    try
    {
      if (_con == null || df == null || _cmd != null)
      return false;
      _cmd = df.CreateCommand(_con, SQL);
      if (_cmd == null) { return false; }
      _cmd.ExecuteNonQuery();
      return true;
    }
    catch (Exception e)
```

```
    {
      e.ToString();
      return false;
    }
  }
```

The `ExecuteNonQuery` method is meant to insert, update, or delete records from the table. It does not return any value. In other words, the method is called for mutable operations on a relational database:

```
public Boolean Close()
{
  if (_con != null)
  {
    _con.Close();
    _con = null;
    return true;
  }
  return false;
}
}
```

The `Close` method, as indicated, closes the database connection. The adapter class can be instantiated inside the application code using the following schema. All we need is a connection string and a driver name (`SQLITE`, `SQLSERVER`, and so on) to instantiate the object. Once we have instantiated the object, we can dispatch an arbitrary query against the chosen database engine as indicated in the following code:

```
DbEngineAdapter db =
new DbEngineAdapter(connstr,driver);
if (db.Open())
{
  bool result = db.ExecuteNonQuery(query);
}
db.Close();
```

The adapter configuration

The drivers for the respective database engines are configured via an XML file (`DbDrivers.xml`) as follows:

```
<?xml version="1.0"?>
<entries>
  <entry key ="SQLITE" value="Chapter4_Example.SQLiteDbFactory"/>
  <entry key="SQLSERVER"
```

```
            value="Chapter4_Exanple.SQLServerDbFactory"/>
        <entry key="NULL" value ="Chapter4_Example.NULLDbFactory"/>
    </entries>
```

When we want to target a new database, we need to create a concrete class which implements the abstract factory interface, and add an entry to this configuration file.

The client program

We can write a client program to test this logic. The code for inserting an entry to a database of your choice is given next. We have chosen SQLite initially for the sake of simplicity. Since SQLite is a server-less database engine, we can embed an SQLite DB as part of our project:

```
static void TestInsert(string connstr, string driver)
{
    DbEngineAdapter db =
    new DbEngineAdapter(connstr,driver);
    //----- a Test Log Entry
    string test = "Log value is " + Math.PI * 1999;
    if (db.Open())
    {
        string query = "INSERT INTO logs VALUES('" +
        test + "');";
        bool result = db.ExecuteNonQuery(query);
    }
    db.Close();
    return;
}
```

To retrieve data from a table, we can use either the disconnected recordset model or cursor model. When we are dealing with large datasets, especially for reports, using the cursor model is preferred. For scenarios where we need to edit a small set of data through some control, a disconnected set is preferred. The following code demonstrates how one can use the disconnected recordset for retrieving the data:

```
static void TestDataSet(string connstr, string driver)
{
    IDbEngineAdapter db =
    new DbEngineAdapter(connstr,driver);
    if (db.Open())
    {
        string query = "SELECT * from logs";
        DataSet ds = db.Execute(query);
        DataTable dt = ds.Tables[0];
        int i = 0;
```

```
      int max = dt.Rows.Count;
      while (i < max)
      {
        DataRow dr = dt.Rows[i];
        Console.WriteLine(dr[0]);
        i++;
      }
    }
    db.Close();
    return;
  }
```

The DataReader interface of ADO.NET is meant for cursor-based access to the database. This helps one to iterate through the data which satisfies some criteria. Reporting applications are a typical use case for cursor-based access:

```
static void TestDataReader(string connstr, string driver)
{
  IDbEngineAdapter db =
  new DbEngineAdapter(connstr,driver);
  string query = "select * from logs";
  if (db.Open())
  {
    IDataReader reader = db.ExecuteQuery(query);
    while(reader.Read())
    {
      Console.WriteLine(reader.GetString(1));
    }
  }
  db.Close();
}
```

The Main program which invokes these helper routines is given next. The initial code snippet shows how to use SQLite as a target database:

```
static void Main(string[] args)
{
  TestInsert(@"Data Source=./Logstorage.db", "SQLITE");
  TestDataSet(@"Data Source=./Logstorage.db", "SQLITE");
  TestDataReader(@"Data Source=./Logstorage.db", "SQLITE");
}
```

To use the SQL Server, one needs to make changes to the connection string. Since the connection string is specific to the SQL Server installation (which a reader will have), the general scheme of invoking the program is the following:

```
static void Main(string[] args)
{
   TestInsert(@"sqlserverconnstring", "SQLSERVER");
   TestDataSet(@"sqlserverconnstring", "SQLSERVER");
   TestDataReader(@"sqlserverconnstring", "SQLSERVER");
}
```

The following UML diagram illustrates the key set of patterns in action for the **Database Access Library** (**DAL**) API that we have built:

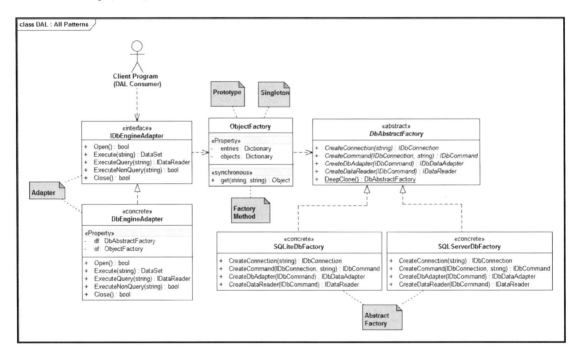

Summary

In this chapter, we created a reusable DAL to target different relational database offerings available for persistence. The library leverages the Microsoft ADO.NET programming model to implement database-agnostic persistence. In the process, you learned about the abstract factory pattern, adapter pattern, and revisited factory method pattern. You also understood the difference between the factory method and the abstract factory pattern. In the next chapter, we will write a document object library which will help one save data contents to different formats like PDF, SVG, and HTML. In that process, you will learn about the composite design pattern and visitor pattern.

5
Producing Tabular Reports

In this chapter, we will create a library that will help application developers to create tabular reports using a custom **Document Object Model (DOM)**, created for this purpose. The tree-structured document object model will be traversed to produce output in the Adobe® **Portable Document Format (PDF)** and HTML format. Support for new target formats would be seamless, with developers writing handlers for those. For PDF output, we plan to use the open source **iTextSharp** library. During the course of this chapter, as a reader, you will learn the following:

- Defining an object model for documents
- The composite pattern for modeling part/whole relationship
- Producing PDF documents by leveraging the iTextSharp library
- The visitor pattern and composite object traversal

Requirements for the library

Before we embark on writing the library, let us scribble down a preliminary requirements statement as follows:

For a large class of business applications, we require tabular reports in various formats. The popular choice for output formats are PDF, HTML, SVG, and so on. We should create a library to produce tabular output in these formats. The library should define a unified programming model, and serve as an API for the developers. The contents of the documents and its tables should be separated from the processing layer to incorporate future output drivers.

Solutions approach

Before writing the code, let us step back a bit to enumerate the details of the requirements. The library which we are planning to write should have the following:

- Support for various output formats like HTML, PDF, and so on
- An object model for storing the contents of the table
- A unified programming model and API for developers
- Separate content and it's processing
- The ability to write new pluggable output processors (drivers)

We will start by creating a hierarchy of elements for storing document contents. A simple hierarchy which has been conceived is as follows:

- *TDocumentElement*
  - *TDocument*
    - *TDocumentTable*
      - *TDocumentTableRow*
        - *TDocumentTableCell*
          - *TDocumentText*

We will encode our content in a tree-structured document model. For the sake of simplicity, we have reduced the number of document elements. In an industrial strength implementation of this library, we will have many more elements. We can create tables within tables in this scheme, as we allow nested tables. Before we get into the implementation of the aforementioned hierarchy, we will look into the specifics of the creation of a PDF document using an open source library.

iTextSharp for the PDF output

To produce the output of a document in the PDF format, we plan to use the .NET version of the open source iText library.

 The library can be downloaded from the iTextSharp website at the following address: `https://www.nuget.org/packages/iTextSharp/`.

A simple program, which produces a PDF document using the library, is given next to make the reader understand the programming model of this library:

```
using iTextSharp;
using iTextSharp.text;
using iTextSharp.text.pdf;
//------some code omitted
FileStream fs = new FileStream(@"D:\ab\fund.pdf",
FileMode.Create);
Document document = new Document(PageSize.A4, 25, 25, 30, 30);
PdfWriter writer = PdfWriter.GetInstance(document, fs);
document.AddAuthor("Praseed Pai");
document.AddCreator("iTextSharp PDF Library");
document.AddTitle("PDF Demo");
document.Open();
PdfPTable table = new PdfPTable(2);
PdfPCell cell = new PdfPCell(new Phrase("A Header which spans
Columns"));
cell.Colspan = 3;
cell.HorizontalAlignment = 1;
table.AddCell(cell);
table.AddCell("Col 1 Row 1");
table.AddCell("Col 2 Row 1");
table.AddCell("Col 3 Row 1");
table.AddCell("Col 1 Row 2");
table.AddCell("Col 2 Row 2");
table.AddCell("Col 3 Row 2");
document.Add(table);
document.Close();
writer.Close();
fs.Close();
```

The preceding code will produce a PDF document with the contents given to the iTextsharp library through the iTextSharp API. Now we will focus on the creation of a DOM for storing our contents.

Composite and visitor pattern – A quick primer

Whenever we deal with hierarchies like W3C DOM, document formats, graphics database or **abstract syntax tree (AST)** of a compiler, we create part/whole relationship. The GoF composite pattern is natural choice for creating hierarchies. Building hierarchies and its processing can be separated using GoF visitor pattern. The visitor pattern visits each node in the hierarchy and perform some action on the node. In a compiler, the tree representation of a program will be processed for type checking, code generation, trans compilation (source to source transformation) and so on. Sometimes people would like to perform additional activities on the tree. It is not feasible to add methods for processing the nodes within a node. Whenever a programmer wants a new method, we are forced to change every node in the hierarchy. A mechanism is necessary for processing to be decoupled from the nodes in a hierarchy. When we use visitor pattern, the nodes within the hierarchy becomes a container for data alone. We will write an expression composite to model a four function calculator to demonstrate the composite and visitor:

```
public enum OPERATOR
{
  //--- supports +,-,*/
  PLUS,MINUS,MUL,DIV
}
/// <summary>
/// Base class for all Expression
/// supports accept method to implement
/// so called "Double Dispatch". Search for
/// "Double Dispatch" and Visitor to understand more
/// about this strategy
/// </summary>
public abstract class Expr
{
  //------ Whenever we start traversal, we will start from
  //------ the topmost node of a hierarchy and
  //--------descends down the heirarchy
  //------ The Visitor will call the accept method of a node
  //------ and node will reflect it back to concrete class
  //------ using Visit method. Thus Visitor dispatches the
  //------ call to a node and node dispatches it back to the
  //--------visit method of the Visitor. This is called a
  //------ a double dispatch
  public abstract double accept(IExprVisitor expr_vis);
}
```

The hierarchy for an expression is

- Expr

    - Number
    - BinaryExpr
    - UnaryExpr

```
/// <summary>
///  Our Visitor Interface. The Purpose of seperating Processing
///  Of Nodes and Data Storage (heirarchy) is for various
///  transformations on the composites created.
/// </summary>
public interface IExprVisitor
{
  double Visit(Number num);
  double Visit(BinaryExpr bin);
  double Visit(UnaryExpr un);
}
```

The following class will store an IEEE 754 double precision floating point value. Our evaluator will handle only constants, as an expression evaluator which supports variables will take additional effort and won't serve our primary purpose of demonstrating the composite and visitor pattern:

```
/// <summary>
///  Class Number stores a IEEE 754 doouble precision
///  floating point
/// </summary>
public class Number : Expr
{
  public double NUM { get; set; }
  public Number(double n) { this.NUM = n; }
  public  override double accept(IExprVisitor expr_vis)
  {
    return expr_vis.Visit(this);
  }
}
```

Now that we have created the `Number` node, we should create a node to compose values through a binary operator. The binary operators supported are +, −, /, * and the class has been named `BinaryExpr`:

```
/// <summary>
///  Class BinaryExpr models a binary expression of
///  the form <Operand> <OPER> <Operand>
/// </summary>
public class BinaryExpr : Expr
{
  public Expr Left { get; set; }
  public Expr Right { get; set; }
  public OPERATOR OP { get; set; }
  public BinaryExpr(Expr l,Expr r,OPERATOR op){
    Left = l; Right = r; OP = op;
  }
  public override double accept(IExprVisitor expr_vis)
  {
    //----- When this method gets invoked by a Concrete
    //----- implementation of Visitor, the call is routed
    //----- back to IExprVisitor.Visit(BinaryExpr )
    return expr_vis.Visit(this);
  }
}
```

The following class implements unary expression node. We support unary operators + and −, in our evaluator:

```
/// <summary>
/// Class UnaryExpr models a unary expression of the form
/// <OPER> <OPERAND>
/// </summary>
public  class UnaryExpr  : Expr {
  public Expr Right;
  public OPERATOR OP;
  public UnaryExpr (Expr r,OPERATOR op) {
    Right = r; OP = op;
  }
  public override double accept(IExprVisitor expr_vis)
  {
    //----- When this method gets invoked by a Concrete
    //----- implementation of a Visitor, the call is routed
    //----- back to IExprVisitor.Visit(UnaryExpr )
    return expr_vis.Visit(this);
  }
}
```

We have defined a expression hierarchy which can be composed to form arithmetical expressions of arbitrary complexity. Our nodes store only data and references to child nodes. The processing of nodes are decoupled from the node proper, using visitor pattern. Let us see couple of examples which we can use to compose arithmetical expression. As an example, let us see how we can store the expression *1+2* using our composites:

```
Expr first = new BinaryExpr(
  new Number(1),
  new Number(2),
  OPERATOR.PLUS);
```

The expression *2+3*4* can be encoded as:

```
Expr r = new BinaryExpr(new Number(2),
new BinaryExpr(
  new Number(3),
  new Number(4),
  OPERATOR.MUL),
OPERATOR.PLUS);
```

We can compose expressions of arbitrary complexity using this method. Now, we will see how we can process these composites using the visitor pattern. As an example, we will write a visitor which generates **Reverse Polish Notation (RPN)** from our expression tree. RPN is also called postfix notation and are used in some calculators and Forth programming language. Read more about RPN from the Internet.

```
/// <summary>
///  A Visitor implementation which converts Infix expression to
///  a Reverse Polish Notation ( RPN)
/// </summary>
public class ReversePolishEvaluator : IExprVisitor
{
  public double Visit(Number num)
  {
    //------ Spit the number to the console
    Console.Write(num.NUM+ " ");
    return 0;
  }
  public double Visit(BinaryExpr bin)
  {
    //------- Traverse the Left Sub Tree followed
    //------ By Right Sub Tree. We follow a Depth
    //------ First Traversal
    bin.Left.accept(this);
    bin.Right.accept(this);
    //----- After Nodes has been processed, spit out
    //----- the Operator
```

```
        if (bin.OP == OPERATOR.PLUS)
          Console.Write(" + ");
        else if (bin.OP == OPERATOR.MUL)
          Console.Write(" * ");
        else if (bin.OP == OPERATOR.DIV)
          Console.Write(" / ");
        else if (bin.OP== OPERATOR.MINUS)
          Console.Write(" - ");
        return Double.NaN;
    }
    public double Visit(UnaryExpr un)
    {
        //-------- In a Unary Expression we have got
        //-------- only a sub tree, Traverse it
        un.Right.accept(this);
        //-------- Spit the operand to the Console.
        if (un.OP == OPERATOR.PLUS)
          Console.Write("  + ");
        else if (un.OP == OPERATOR.MINUS)
          Console.Write("  - ");
        return Double.NaN;
    }
}
```

The above class can be invoked as follows. We will show how one can convert the expression *2+3*4* to *2 3 4 * +*. Let us encode the expression using our expression hierarchy as follows:

```
Expr r = new BinaryExpr(new Number(2),
  new BinaryExpr(
    new Number(3),
    new Number(4),
    OPERATOR.MUL),
  OPERATOR.PLUS);
```

The expression hierarchy composed above can be traversed by `ReversePolishEvaluator` to produce *2 3 4 * +* as follows:

```
IExprVisitor visitor =
  new ReversePolishEvaluator();
second.accept(visitor);
```

The whole purpose of creating an expression tree to evaluate it. We will write a stack based expression evaluator to demonstrate the use of visitor pattern:

```
/// <summary>
/// A Visitor which evaluates the Infix expression using a Stack
///  We will leverage stack implementation available with .NET
```

```csharp
///   collections API
/// </summary>
public class StackEvaluator : IExprVisitor
{
  //------- A stack to store double values
  //------- .NET Framework has got a stack implementation!
  private Stack<double> eval_stack = new Stack<double>();
  //---- return the computed value
  //---- implementation does not do any error check
  public double get_value() { return eval_stack.Pop(); }

  public StackEvaluator() { eval_stack.Clear(); }
  public double Visit(Number num)
  {
    //---- whenever we get an operand
    //---- push it to the stack
    eval_stack.Push(num.NUM);
    return 0;
  }
  public double Visit(BinaryExpr bin)
  {
    bin.Left.accept(this);
    bin.Right.accept(this);
    //--- We have processed left and right sub tree
    //--- Let us pop values, apply the operator
    //--- and push it back
    if (bin.OP == OPERATOR.PLUS)
      eval_stack.Push(eval_stack.Pop() + eval_stack.Pop());
    else if (bin.OP == OPERATOR.MUL)
      eval_stack.Push(eval_stack.Pop() * eval_stack.Pop());
    else if (bin.OP == OPERATOR.DIV)
    {
      double dval = eval_stack.Pop();
      if (dval == 0)
      {
        //--- handle division by zero error
        //--- throw an exception
      }
      eval_stack.Push( eval_stack.Pop()/dval);
    }
    else if (bin.OP == OPERATOR.MINUS)
      eval_stack.Push(eval_stack.Pop() - eval_stack.Pop());
    return Double.NaN;
  }
  public double Visit(UnaryExpr un)
  {
    un.Right.accept(this);
    if (un.OP == OPERATOR.PLUS)
```

```
      eval_stack.Push(eval_stack.Pop());
    else if (un.OP == OPERATOR.MINUS)
      eval_stack.Push(-eval_stack.Pop());
    return Double.NaN;
  }
}
```

The above stack evaluator can be invoked as follows:

```
Expr third = new BinaryExpr(new Number(2),
  new BinaryExpr(
  new Number(3),
  new Number(4),
  OPERATOR.MUL),
OPERATOR.PLUS);

StackEvaluator seval = new StackEvaluator();
third.accept(seval);
Console.WriteLine(seval.get_value());
Console.WriteLine();
```

We have finished our discussion on visitor and composite pattern. In the above example, we defined a small hierarchy to compose mathematical expressions and processed it using visitor classes which traversed the composite to produce RPN expression and evaluate it using a stack. This technique is widely used wherever one is supposed to process a hierarchy. Let us focus on how to create a document hierarchy and process it.

The composite pattern and document composition

While representing part-whole hierarchies (tree-structured), the composite design pattern describes a group of objects to be treated in a uniform manner, as if the leaf node and interior nodes are instances of the same object. A document object can contain multiple tables, and we can nest tables as well. This is an instance of a part-whole hierarchy, and composite design pattern is a natural choice here. To create a composite, we need to declare a base class, and all objects should be derived from this base class:

```
public abstract class TDocumentElement
{
  public List<TDocumentElement> DocumentElements { get; set; }
  //------- The method given below is for implementing Visitor
  Pattern
  public abstract void accept(IDocumentVisitor doc_vis);
  //--- Code Omitted
```

```
    public TDocumentElement()
    {
      DocumentElements = new List<TDocumentElement>(5);
      this.Align = alignment.LEFT;
      this.BackgroundColor = "0xFF000000L";
    }
    //---- Code Omitted
    public void addObject(TDocumentElement value)
    {
      if (value != null)
      DocumentElements.Add(value);
    }
    public Boolean removeObject(TDocumentElement value)
    {
      if (value != null)
      {
        DocumentElements.Remove(value);
        return true;
      }
      return false;
    }
    //----- Code Omitted
}
```

The TDocumentElement class acts as a base class for all the classes in the object model. Please note the following two important things about the TDocumentElement class:

- The first one is the DocumentElements property. Every TDocumentElement has a list of TDocumentElement to store its child objects. This means, we can insert a list of concrete objects which implements TDcoumentElement as a child. Using this technique, we can compose a document hierarchy of arbitrary complexity.
- The second thing is the presence of an abstract method called accept. The accept method is a mechanism by which we will be able to separate the operations on node and the node data structure. We will learn more about the semantics of the accept method in a later section.

The topmost class in the hierarchy is TDocument, which acts as a container for a hierarchical collection of the TDocumentElement derived class. The class will store all the child contents (concrete classes of base type TDocumentElement) to be embedded inside the document.

```
public class TDocument : TDocumentElement
{
  public string Title {get;set;}
  public string BackGroundImage { get; set;}
  public string TextColor { get; set;}
```

```
public string LinkColor {get;set;}
public string Vlink { get; set;}
public string Alink {get;set;}
public  int ColumnCount { get; set;}
public override void accept(IDocumentVisitor doc_vis)
{
  doc_vis.visit(this);
}
public TDocument(int count=1)
{
  this.ColumnCount = count;
  this.Title = "Default Title";
}
}
```

Application developers can leverage the addObject method available in the
TDocumentElement class to add contents to TDocument. In our canned example, the most
obvious choice is a list of tables. The accept method makes a call to the visitor's visit
method with the TDocument instance (this) as a parameter. This will hit the
visit(TDocument) method implemented in a class, which implements the
IDocumentVisitor interface. More on visitor pattern and its implementation is available
in a later section.

The TDocumentTable models a table object, which can be embedded inside a document.
Since the TDocumentTable object inherits from TDocumentElement, we can add any
TDocumentElement derived class as a child. With this technique, we can embed objects of
arbitrary complexity. But, for our library, an Instance of TDocumentTable is the natural
choice as the first child of the TDocument object.

```
public class TDocumentTable : TDocumentElement
{
  public string  Caption {get;set; }
  public int Width { get;set; }
  public int Border { get; set; }
  public int CellSpacing { get;set;}
  public int Cellpadding { get; set; }
  public Boolean PercentageWidth { get;set; }
  public String bgColor {get; set; }

  public int RowCount
  {
    get
    {
      return this.DocumentElements.Count;
    }
  }
}
```

```
public override void accept(IDocumentVisitor doc_vis)
{
  doc_vis.visit(this);
}

public TDocumentTable()
{
}
}
```

Inside a table, we store data as a series of rows, and the class for storing information is appropriately named TDocumentTableRow. We can insert another table as a child as well. One can embed a table within a table. For the sake of brevity, we have not included that feature in the current implementation. If we need to support nested tables, we need to incorporate a data structure called scope tree. The listing of such an implementation cannot be conveniently included in a book.

```
public class TDocumentTableRow : TDocumentElement
{
  public TDocumentTableRow(){}
  public override void accept(IDocumentVisitor doc_vis)
  {
    doc_vis.visit(this);
  }
}
```

A row is a collection of cells, and inside each cell, we can store arbitrary text. It is possible to store an image as well, but, for the sake of brevity, we have limited the cell contents to text. The image or another content type can be incorporated very easily following the schema used for text.

```
public class TDocumentTableCell : TDocumentElement
{
  public int ColumnSpan { get; set; }
  public alignment Horizontal { get; set; }
  public alignment Vertical { get; set; }
  public alignment Type { get; set; }
  public TDocumentTableCell()
  {
    this.ColumnSpan = 1;
    this.Horizontal = alignment.LEFT;
    this.Vertical = alignment.MIDDLE;
    this.Type = alignment.DATA;
  }
  public override void accept(IDocumentVisitor doc_vis)
  {
    doc_vis.visit(this);
```

```
        }
    }
```

Every cell in the table contains a text item for our implementation. We model the text using the `TDocumentText` class. In this class, the `Text` property is used to store and load text.

```
public class TDocumentText : TDocumentElement
{
  public string Text { set;get; }
  public Boolean Bold {get;set;}
  public Boolean Italic {get;set;}
  public Boolean Underline { get; set; }
  public Boolean Center {get;set;}
  public Boolean Preformatted { get; set; }
  public string Color { get; set; }
  public Boolean Font {get;set;}

  public TDocumentText(string value = null)
  {
    this.Text = value;
  }

  public override void accept(IDocumentVisitor doc_vis)
  {
    doc_vis.visit(this);
  }
}
```

Thus, we have defined our DOM. You can see the UML representation of the composite pattern in action in the following diagram:

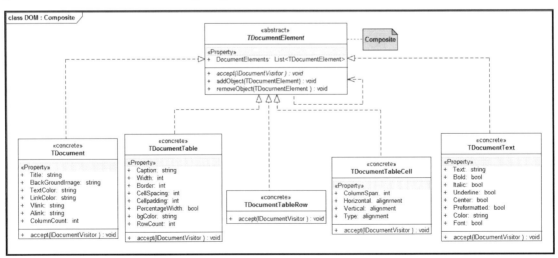

Now we need to create a mechanism to traverse the hierarchy to produce the output of our choice.

Visitor pattern for document traversal

The tree-structured DOM created by us needs to be traversed to produce the content in an output format like HTML, PDF, or SVG.

 The composite tree created by us can be traversed using the GoF visitor pattern. Wherever composite pattern is used for composing an hierarchy of objects, the visitor pattern is a natural choice for the traversal of the tree.

In a visitor pattern implementation, every node in the composite tree will support a method called `accept`, which takes a visitor concrete class as a parameter. The job of the `accept` routine is to reflect the call to the appropriate visit method in the visitor concrete class. We declare an interface named `IDocumentVisitor` with methods for visiting each of the elements in our hierarchy as follows:

```
public interface IDocumentVisitor
{
  void visit(TDocument doc);
  void visit(TDocumentTable table);
  void visit(TDocumentTableRow row);
  void visit(TDocumentTableCell cell);
  void visit(TDocumentText txt);
}
```

The traversal of the tree should start from the top node of the tree. In our case, we start the traversal from the `TDocument` node. For each node in the hierarchy, we will add an `accept` method, which takes an instance of `IDocumentVisitor`. The signature of this function is as follows:

```
public abstract class TDocumentElement
{
  //--- code omitted
  public abstract void accept(IDocumentVisitor doc_vis);
  //--- code omitted
}
```

Each element of the document node which derives from `TDocumentElement` needs to have an implementation of this method. For example, the body of the `TDocument` class is as follows:

```
public class TDocument : TDocumentElement
{
  //----- code omitted
  public override void accept(IDocumentVisitor doc_vis)
  {
    doc_vis.visit(this);
  }
  //------ code omitted
}
```

In the `TDocument` class, the `accept` method will reflect the call to the `IDocumentVisitor` `visit(TDocument)` method implemented by the `Visitor` class. In the `Visitor` class, for each node inserted as a child, a call to the `accept` method of the respective nodes will be triggered. Each time the call gets reflected back to the appropriate visit method of the `Visitor` class. In this manner, the accept/visit pair processes the whole hierarchy.

The traversal starts with the `TDocument` `accept` method, as follows:

```
string filename = @"D:\ab\fund.pdf";
ds.accept(new PDFVisitor(filename));
```

The `ds` object is of type `TDocument`, and the `accept` method takes an instance of the `IDocumentVisitor` interface. In the document object, the call gets reflected to the `IDocumentVisitor` `visit(TDocument)` method.

PDFVisitor for PDF generation

We have defined our object hierarchy and an interface to traverse the hierarchy. Now we need to implement routines to traverse the tree. The `PDFVisitor` class implements the `IDocumentVisitor` interface, as shown in the following code snippet:

```
public class PDFVisitor : IDocumentVisitor
{
  private string file_name = null;
  private PdfWriter writer = null;
  private Document document = null;
  private PdfPTable table_temp = null;
  private FileStream fs = null;
  private int column_count;
```

```
public PDFVisitor(string filename)
{
  file_name - filename;
  fs = new FileStream(file_name, FileMode.Create);
  document = new Document(PageSize.A4, 25, 25, 30, 30);
  writer = PdfWriter.GetInstance(document, fs);
}
```

The visit method, which takes TDocument as a parameter, adds some metadata to the PDF document being created. After this operation, the method inspects all the child elements of TDocument, and issues an accept method call with the current visitor instance. This invokes the accept method of the concrete class of TDocumentElement embedded as a child object:

```
public void visit(TDocument doc)
{
  document.AddAuthor(@"Praseed Pai & Shine Xavier");
  document.AddCreator(@"iTextSharp Library");
  document.AddKeywords(@"Design Patterns Architecture");
  document.AddSubject(@"Book on .NET Design Patterns");
  document.Open();
  column_count = doc.ColumnCount;
  document.AddTitle(doc.Title);

  for (int x = 0; x < doc.DocumentElements.Count; x++)
  {
    try
    {
      doc.DocumentElements[x].accept(this);
    }
    catch (Exception ex)
    {
      Console.Error.WriteLine(ex.Message);
    }
  }
  document.Add(this.table_temp);
  document.Close();
  writer.Close();
  fs.Close();
```

The TDocumentTable object will be handled by the visit method in a similar fashion. Once we have worked with the node, all the children stored in DocumentElements will be processed by invoking the accept method of each of the node element embedded inside the table:

```
public void visit(TDocumentTable table)
{
  this.table_temp = new PdfPTable(column_count);
  PdfPCell cell = new
  PdfPCell(new Phrase("Header spanning 3 columns"));
  cell.Colspan = column_count;
  cell.HorizontalAlignment = 1;
  table_temp.AddCell(cell);
  for (int x = 0; x < table.RowCount; x++)
  {
    try
    {
      table.DocumentElements[x].accept(this);
    }
    catch (Exception ex)
    {
      Console.Error.WriteLine(ex.Message);
    }
  }
}
```

Mostly, an instance of TDocumentTableRow is included as a child of TDocumentTable. For our implementation, we will navigate to all the children of a row object, issuing accept calls to the respective nodes:

A table is a collection of rows, and a row is a collection of cells. Each of the cells contains some text. We can add a collection of text inside a cell as well. Our implementation assumes that we will store only one text.

```
public void visit(TDocumentTableRow row)
{
  for (int I = 0; i < row.DocumentElements.Count; ++i)
  {
    row.DocumentElements[i].accept(this);
  }
}
```

To process TDocumentTableCell, we iterate through all the child elements of a cell, and these elements are instances TDocumentText. For the sake of brevity, we have included an attribute called Text to store the contents of a cell there:

```
public void visit(TDocumentTableCell cell)
{
  for (int i = 0; i < cell.DocumentElements.Count; ++i)
  {
    cell.DocumentElements[i].accept(this);
  }
}
```

The TDocumentText class has a property by the name of Text, where an application developer can store some text. That will be added to the table:

```
public void visit(TDocumentText txt)
{
  table_temp.AddCell(txt.Text);
}
}
```

HTMLVisitor for HTML generation

The HTMLVisitor class produces HTML output by traversing the DOM. The skeleton implementation of HTMLVisitor is as follows:

```
public class HTMLVisitor : IDocumentVisitor
{
  private String file_name = null;
  private StringBuilder document = null;
  public HTMLVisitor(string filename) {
    file_name = filename;
  }
  //--- Code omitted for all methods
  public void visit(TDocument doc){}
  public void visit(TDocumentTable table){}
  public void visit(TDocumentTableRow row) {}
  public void visit(TDocumentTableCell cell) {}
  public void visit(TDocumentText txt) {}
}
```

The HTMLVisitor class can be leveraged as follows:

```
string filename = @"D:\ab\fund.html";
ds.accept(new HTMLVisitor(filename));
```

The client program

A simple program which leverages the DOM is given next. We create a TDocument object as a top-level node, and add the rest of the document contents as child nodes to the respective classes:

```
static void DocumentRender()
{
  TDocument ds = new TDocument(3);
  ds.Title = "Multiplication Table";
  TDocumentTable table = new TDocumentTable();
  table.Border = 1;
  table.Width = 100;
  table.BackgroundColor = "#EFEEEC";
  TDocumentTableRow row = null;
  row = new TDocumentTableRow();

  TDocumentText headtxt = new TDocumentText("Multiplicand");
  headtxt.Font = true;
  headtxt.Color = "#800000";
  TDocumentTableCell cell = null;
  cell = new TDocumentTableCell(alignment.HEADING);
  cell.addObject(headtxt);
  row.addObject(cell);

  headtxt = new TDocumentText("Multiplier");
  headtxt.Color = "#800000";
  cell = new TDocumentTableCell(alignment.HEADING);
  cell.addObject(headtxt);
  row.addObject(cell);
  headtxt = new TDocumentText("Result");
  headtxt.Color = "#800000";
  cell = new TDocumentTableCell(alignment.HEADING);
  cell.addObject(headtxt);
  row.addObject(cell);
  table.addObject(row);

  int a = 16;
  int j = 1;

  while (j <= 12)
  {
    row = new TDocumentTableRow();
    cell = new TDocumentTableCell(alignment.DATA);
    cell.addObject(new TDocumentText(a.ToString()));
    row.addObject(cell);
    cell = new TDocumentTableCell(alignment.DATA);
```

```
        cell.addObject(new TDocumentText(j.ToString()));
        row.addObject(cell);
        cell = new TDocumentTableCell(alignment.DATA);
        int result = a * j;
        cell.addObject(new TDocumentText(result.ToString()));
        row.addObject(cell);
        table.addObject(row);
        j++;
    }
    ds.addObject(table);

    string filename =
    @"D:\ab\fund.pdf";
    ds.accept(new PDFVisitor(filename));

    string filename2 =
    @"D:\ab\fund.html";
    ds.accept(new HTMLVisitor(filename2));
}
```

Summary

In this chapter, we created a library for producing tabular reports in various formats. In the process, we learned about creating arbitrary hierarchies of objects in a tree-structured manner. We leveraged the composite pattern to implement our hierarchy. The composites were processed using the visitor pattern. We dealt with PDF and HTML output by writing `PDFVisitor` and `HTMLVisitor` classes. Incorporating a new output format is just a matter of writing a new visitor (say, `SVGVisitor`), where one needs to map the contents of the document to the appropriate SVG tags. In the next chapter, we will learn about the interpreter pattern and the observer pattern by implementing a library that will help us plot arbitrary expressions as graphs.

6
Plotting Mathematical Expressions

In this chapter, we will create an application which will plot arbitrary mathematical expressions on a **Windows Presentation Foundation** (**WPF**)-based graphical surface. We will be using the GoF observer pattern for wiring expression input control and the rendering surface. In the process, we will develop a library which can evaluate arbitrary arithmetic expressions on the fly. The expression evaluator will support basic arithmetic operators (+, −, *, /, unary +/−), trigonometric functions, and a pseudo variable ($t) which can represent the value of X-axis in a 2D Plane. During the course of this chapter, as a reader, you will learn the following:

- The observer pattern
- Parsing mathematical expressions using recursive descent
- Modeling **abstract syntax tree** (**AST**) as a composite
- The interpreter pattern
- The builder pattern
- Elementary WPF 2D graphics

Requirements for the expressions library and app

Before we embark on writing the library, let us scribble down a preliminary requirement statement, which is as follows:

The ability to plot the result of arbitrary mathematical expressions is a common requirement for business applications. We need to parse an expression to evaluate the resulting tree-structured representation. The process of lexical analysis, parsing, modeling expression nodes, recursive evaluation, and so on should be opaque to the application programmer. The library should support some trigonometric functions and a variable ($t) to pass the information of the current X-coordinate of the graphics surface. The application should evaluate the value of the Y-coordinate for each value of the X-coordinate passed to the expression evaluation engine.

Solutions approach

We will divide the requirement into the two following parts:

- A library for evaluating arbitrary mathematical expressions
- An application which will consume the aforementioned library to plot data

The expression evaluator library requirements can be enumerated as follows:

- Modeling expressions as AST
- Writing a lexical analyzer
- Writing a recursive descent parser
- Depth first walk of the tree
- Supporting trigonometric functions and pseudo variable ($)
- Packaging everything as a facade pattern-based API

The application requirements can be enumerated as follows:

- A screen with a WPF 2D graphics surface
- A prompt for entering expressions
- Implementation of the observer for detecting a new plot request
- Passing the value to the expressions library for change in the X-coordinate value
- Rendering the resulting value

The graph plotter application

The graph plotter application is a simple WPF application with a canvas and a textbox in the frame. The following image gives a snapshot of the screen after the screen has rendered the result of an expression:

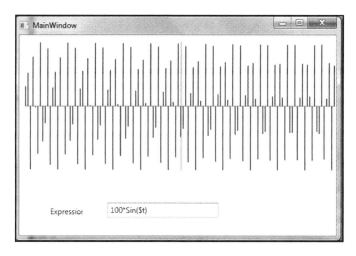

The WPF canvas gets a notification whenever there is a change in the expression textbox. If the expression in the textbox is valid, the graph will be plotted as shown in the preceding image. We will deal with the nuances of implementing an expression evaluation engine in the following sections. The following code snippet shows how the change in text gets handled:

```
public override void
Observer_ExpressionChangedEvent( string expression)
{
  MainWindow mw = this._ctrl as MainWindow;
  mw.Expr = expression;
  ExpressionBuilder builder = new
  ExpressionBuilder(expression);
  Exp expr_tree = builder.GetExpression();

  if ( expr_tree != null )
  mw.Render();
}
```

The observer pattern for UI events

We will use the GoF observer pattern to handle UI events in an automatic fashion. The moment an expression gets changed in the textbox, the window should get a notification about it, and if the expression is valid, the resulting expression will be rendered on the screen.

 While implementing the observer pattern, we have two classes-the Subject class, which represents the event source, and the Observer class, which is a list of observers (observer who are interested in listening to the event. Whenever there is a change in the text, the Subject class which represents the event source sends notification to all the sinks who have subscribed to the event.

We have already mentioned that in the case of the observer pattern, we communicate between the event source and event sinks. The event source is represented using the Subject class, and the event sink is represented using an Observer class. Let us dissect the implementation of the Observer class:

```
public abstract class BaseObserver
{
  protected delegate void
  ExpressionEventHandler(string expression);
  protected ExpressionEventHandler ExpressionChangedEvent;
  protected Control _ctrl = null;
  public abstract void Observer_ExpressionChangedEvent(string
  expression);
```

We declare a delegate which will act as an event handler, and to make the class handle all the WPF controls, we mark the event subscriber as a WPF control. The concrete class can hold any object derived from Control:

```
public BaseObserver(Control ctrl)
{
  this.ExpressionChangedEvent +=
  new ExpressionEventHandler(
  Observer_ExpressionChangedEvent);
  this._ctrl = ctrl;
}
```

In the constructor, we initialize the delegate with an address of an abstract method. This will automatically get wired to the concrete class implementation of the method. We are, effectively, using the GoF template method pattern for the observer implementation. The concrete class is mandated to implement the `Observer_ExpressionChangedEvent` method:

```
private void OnChange(string expression)
{
  if (ExpressionChangedEvent != null)
  ExpressionChangedEvent(expression);
}
public void Update(string expression)
{
  OnChange(expression);
}
}
```

Now, we will try to write the `Subject` class which acts as an event source. The `Subject` class will iterate through the list of observers to dispatch the events which the observers are interested in. Any change in the expression textbox will be relayed to the window object, which acts as a receiver of the events:

```
public class Subject
{
  List<BaseObserver> observers = new List<BaseObserver>();
  private delegate void NotifyHandler(string expression);
  private event NotifyHandler NotifyEvent;

  public Subject(){
    this.NotifyEvent += new NotifyHandler(Notify);
  }

  public void UpdateClient(string expression){
    OnNotify(expression);
  }

  private void OnNotify(string expression){
    if (NotifyEvent != null)
    NotifyEvent(expression);
  }

  private void Notify(string expression){
    foreach (BaseObserver b in observers)
    b.Update(expression);
  }

  public void RegisterClient(BaseObserver obs){
```

```
        observers.Add(obs);
    }
}
```

The `BaseObserver` class given in the preceding code snippet is an abstract class, and we need to create a concrete class which implements `Observer_ExpressionChangedEvent`. The concrete implementation listing is given as follows:

```
class ExpressionObserver : BaseObserver
{
  public ExpressionObserver(Window _win) :
  base(_win){ }

  public override void
  Observer_ExpressionChangedEvent(string expression)
  {
    MainWindow mw = this._ctrl as MainWindow;
    mw.Expr = expression;
    ExpressionBuilder builder = new
    ExpressionBuilder(expression);
    Exp expr_tree = builder.GetExpression();

    if ( expr_tree != null )
      mw.Render();
  }
}
```

Let us see how we can connect the `Subject` and `Observer` class. See the `MainWindow.cs` module in the source code associated with this book. A snippet of the code is given as follows:

```
_observer = new ExpressionObserver(this);
_subject = new Subject();
_subject.RegisterClient(_observer);
```

Whenever there is change in the text, the rendering routine will be notified. The rendering routine uses WPF 2D graphics transformations to plot the equation:

```
private void text_changed(object sender, TextChangedEventArgs e)
{
  if ( _subject != null )
  _subject.UpdateClient(this.ExprText.Text);
}
```

The expression evaluator and interpreter pattern

The authors of this book believe that any programmer worth his salt needs to learn the rudiments of compiler construction for implementing mini-languages or **domain-specific language (DSL)** in his work. A compiler treats expressions as data, and expressions are mostly hierarchical in nature. We use a data structure called AST for representing the nodes of an expression tree. To convert textual expressions into an AST, we need to write a parser to analyze the constituents of an expression. The subsystem which feeds data to the parser is a module called lexical analyzer, which breaks the input stream into a series of tokens.

The definition of a mini language, and writing an evaluator for it, is dealt with by the GoF catalog as interpreter pattern.

In software design, the interpreter pattern is a design pattern that specifies how to evaluate sentences in a (mini) language. The basic idea is to have a class for each symbol (terminal or non-terminal) in a specialized computer language. In our case, we use a mini language with double precision floating point numbers, a symbolic variable ($t), trigonometric functions (sine/cosine), and basic arithmetic operators. The syntax tree of a sentence in the language is an instance of the composite pattern, and is used to evaluate (interpret) the sentence for a client. Some expressions which we handle are *2*3 + SIN($t)*2, $t*100, COS((3.14159/2) – $t)*, and so on.

The abstract syntax tree (AST)

In computer science, an AST, or just syntax tree, is a tree representation of the abstract (simplified) syntactic structure of the source code. Each node of the tree denotes a construct of the programming language under consideration. In our expression evaluator, the nodes are numeric values (IEEE 754 floating points), binary operators, unary operators, trigonometric functions, and a variable.

The syntax is abstract in the sense that it does not represent every detail that appears in the real syntax. For instance, grouping parentheses is implicit in the tree structure, and AST data structure discards parentheses. Before we model the AST, let us see some expressions and its AST representations:

```
// AST for 5*10
Exp e = new BinaryExp(
new NumericConstant(5),
new NumericConstant(10),
OPERATOR.MUL);
```

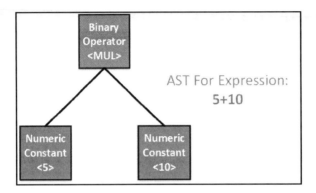

The preceding example uses two node types, that is, `NumericConstant`, `BinaryExp`. Even the simplest expression creates a structure which seems a bit complicated.

Let us look at an expression which has a unary operator as well:

```
// AST for -(10+(30+50))
Exp e = new UnaryExp(
  new BinaryExp(
    new NumericConstant(10),
    new BinaryExp(
      new NumericConstant(30),
      new NumericConstant(50),
    OPERATOR.PLUS),
  OPERATOR.PLUS)
 ,OPERATOR.MINUS);
```

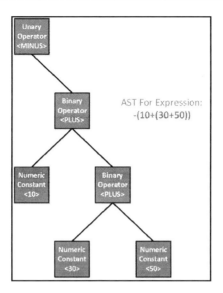

AST For Expression:
-(10+(30+50))

Since our expression evaluator only supports a single variable, we create a context class which will store the variable in question. The class is named RUNTIME_CONTEXT, and the whole listing is given as follows:

```
public class RUNTIME_CONTEXT
{
  private double _t = 0 ;
  public RUNTIME_CONTEXT(){ }
  public double T {
    get { return _t; }
    set { _t = value; }
  }
}
```

In any programming language, expression is what you evaluate for its value. This can be modeled as an abstract class. The numeric value which we support is of the type IEEE 754 double precision floating point:

```
abstract class Exp{
  public abstract double Evaluate(RUNTIME_CONTEXT cont);
}
```

The expression evaluator supports operators like PLUS (+), MINUS (-), DIV (/), and MUL (*). They are modeled using an enumerated type named OPERATOR:

```
public enum OPERATOR{
  ILLEGAL = -1,PLUS, MINUS, DIV, MUL
}
```

We will start by creating a hierarchy of nodes for modeling an expression. We use the composite pattern to compose bigger expressions out of smaller ones:

```
class Exp // Base class for Expression
class NumericConstant // Numeric Value
class BinaryExp // Binary Expression
class UnaryExp // Unary Expression
class SineExp // Trig fn
class SineExp // Trig
class Var // psuedo variable $t
```

The `NumericConstant` class can store an IEEE 754 double precision floating point value in it. This is a leaf node in the AST:

```
public class NumericConstant : Exp
{
  private double _value;
  public NumericConstant(double value){ _value = value; }

  public override double Evaluate(RUNTIME_CONTEXT cont)
  { return _value; }
}
```

The `BinaryExp` class models a binary expression which takes two expressions (`ex1` for the left node and `ex2` for the right node), it applies the operator on both, the left-side value and the right-side value, inside the evaluate routine:

```
public class BinaryExp : Exp
{
  private Exp _ex1, _ex2;
  private OPERATOR _op;

  public BinaryExp(Exp a, Exp b, OPERATOR op)
  { _ex1 = a; _ex2 = b; _op = op; }

  public override double Evaluate(RUNTIME_CONTEXT cont)
  {
    switch (_op)
    {
      case OPERATOR.PLUS:
        return _ex1.Evaluate(cont) + _ex2.Evaluate(cont);
      case OPERATOR.MINUS:
        return _ex1.Evaluate(cont) - _ex2.Evaluate(cont);
      case OPERATOR.DIV:
        return _ex1.Evaluate(cont) / _ex2.Evaluate(cont);
      case OPERATOR.MUL:
        return _ex1.Evaluate(cont) * _ex2.Evaluate(cont);
    }
```

```
      return Double.NaN;
    }
  }
```

In the case of unary expressions, we take an operator and an `Exp` node as a child:

```
public class UnaryExp : Exp
{
  private Exp _ex1;
  private OPERATOR _op;
  public UnaryExp(Exp a, OPERATOR op)
  {_ex1 = a;_op = op }
  public override double Evaluate(RUNTIME_CONTEXT cont)
  {
    switch (_op)
    {
      case OPERATOR.PLUS:
      return _ex1.Evaluate(cont);
      case OPERATOR.MINUS:
      return -_ex1.Evaluate(cont);
    }
    return Double.NaN;
  }
}
```

The sine node takes an expression as a child. We evaluate _ex1, and invoke `Math.Sin` on the resulting value:

```
class SineExp : Exp
{
  private Exp _ex1;
  public SineExp(Exp a)
  { _ex1 = a; }
  public override double Evaluate(RUNTIME_CONTEXT cont){
    double val = _ex1.Evaluate(cont);
    return Math.Sin(val);
  }
}
```

The cosine node takes an expression as a child. We evaluate _ex1, and invoke `Math.Cos` on the resulting value:

```
class CosExp : Exp
{
  private Exp _ex1;
  public CosExp(Exp a)
  { _ex1 = a;}
  public override double Evaluate(RUNTIME_CONTEXT cont){
```

```
      double val = _ex1.Evaluate(cont);
      return Math.Cos(val);
  }
}
```

And finally, the variables ($t) are modeled as follows:

```
class Var : Exp
{
  public Var(){}
  public override double Evaluate(RUNTIME_CONTEXT cont){
    return cont.T;
  }
}
```

The grammar of expressions

The **Backus-Naur Form (BNF)** notation is used to specify the grammar for programming languages. The semantics of BNF can be learned from books, and plenty of material is available. The grammar of the expression evaluator we use is as follows:

```
<Expr> ::= <Term> | Term { + | - } <Expr>
<Term> ::= <Factor> | <Factor> {*|/} <Term>
<Factor>::= <number> | ( <expr> ) | {+|-} <factor> |
            SIN(<expr>) | COS(<expr>) | $t
```

This BNF can be converted to source code very easily.

Lexical analysis

The lexical analyzer groups characters into tokens including '+', '-', '/', '*', SIN, COS, and so on. In the process, the module feeds the parser when a request is made to it. Rather than doing a lexical scan of the entire input, the parser requests the next token from the lexical analyzer. In our expression evaluator, the following tokens are returned by the lexical analyzer upon request for the next token by the parser:

```
public enum TOKEN
{
  ILLEGAL_TOKEN = -1, // Not a Token
  TOK_PLUS = 1, // '+'
  TOK_MUL, // '*'
  TOK_DIV, // '/'
  TOK_SUB, // '-'
```

```
    TOK_OPAREN, // '('
    TOK_CPAREN, // ')'
    TOK_DOUBLE, // '('
    TOK_TPARAM, // $t
    TOK_SIN, // SIN
    TOK_COS, // COS
    TOK_NULL // End of string
}
```

The lexical analyzer module scans through the input, and whenever it finds a token (legal or illegal), it saves the current input pointer and returns the next token. Since the listing is lengthy and code is trivial, it is given as part of the code repository. The following pseudo-code shows the schema of the lexical analyzer:

```
while (<there is input>)
{
  switch(currentchar) {
    case Operands:
      <advance input pointer>
      return TOK_XXXX;
    case '$':
      <Now Look for 't'>
      if found return TOK_TPARAM
        else Error
    case Number:
      <Extract the number(Advance the input)>
      return TOK_DOUBLE;
    case 'S' or 'C':
      <Try to see whether it is SIN/COS>
      Advance the input
      return TOK_SIN Or TOK_COS
    default:
      Error
  }
}
```

The parser module

By using recursive descent parsing, we will arrange the tokens to see whether expressions are valid, and generate the AST out of the input stream with the help of the lexical analyzer.

A recursive descent parser is a top-down parser built from a set of mutually-recursive procedures, where each such procedure usually implements one of the production rules of the grammar. Thus, the structure of the resulting program closely mirrors the grammar that it recognizes:

```
public class RDParser : Lexer
{
  TOKEN Current_Token;
  public RDParser(String str): base(str){}

  public Exp CallExpr()
  {
    Current_Token = GetToken();
    return Expr();
  }
}
```

The constructor of the RDParser class takes the expression string as a parameter, and passes it to the Lexer class. Whenever the parser requires a token, it asks the Lexer class to provide one through the GetToken() method. The whole parsing process starts from the CallExpr() method, and inside it, a token is grabbed by the parser through the Lexer class:

```
//Implementation of <Expr> ::= <Term> | Term { + | - } <Expr>
Grammar
public Exp Expr()
{
  TOKEN l_token;
  Exp RetValue = Term();
  while (Current_Token == TOKEN.TOK_PLUS ||
  Current_Token == TOKEN.TOK_SUB)
  {
    l_token = Current_Token;
    Current_Token = GetToken();
    Exp e1 = Expr();
    RetValue = new BinaryExp(RetValue, e1,
    l_token == TOKEN.TOK_PLUS ?
    OPERATOR.PLUS : OPERATOR.MINUS);
  }
  return RetValue;
}
```

The `Expr()` function descends down to the `Term()` function (which is listed next), and returns the subexpressions from there. As long as there are further operators of the same precedence, it recursively calls the `Expr()` method to retrieve the factors in the form of tree. A `BinaryExp` node is created to represent the subexpressions parsed so far:

```
//Implementation of <Term> ::= <Factor> | <Factor> {*|/} <Term>
Grammar
public Exp Term()
{
  TOKEN l_token;
  Exp RetValue = Factor();
  while (Current_Token == TOKEN.TOK_MUL ||
  Current_Token == TOKEN.TOK_DIV)
  {
    l_token = Current_Token;
    Current_Token = GetToken();
    Exp e1 = Term();
    RetValue = new BinaryExp(RetValue, e1,
    l_token == TOKEN.TOK_MUL ?
    OPERATOR.MUL : OPERATOR.DIV);
  }
  return RetValue;
}
```

The term descends down to the `Factor()` method (shown next) to retrieve a node (which can be an expression itself within the parentheses), and as long as operators of the same precedence are available, it recursively calls itself to generate the terms of the same type:

```
//Implementation of <Factor>::= <number> | ( <expr> ) | {+|-}
<factor> |
//SIN(<expr>) | COS(<expr>) | $t Grammar
public Exp Factor()
{
  TOKEN l_token;
  Exp RetValue = null;

  if (Current_Token == TOKEN.TOK_DOUBLE)
  {
    RetValue = new NumericConstant(GetNumber());
    Current_Token = GetToken();
  }
```

If the parser returns a number, the factor creates a numeric node and returns the same:

```
else if (Current_Token == TOKEN.TOK_TPARAM)
{
  RetValue = new Var();
```

```
        Current_Token = GetToken();
    }
```

If the current token is $t, a `Var` node is returned by the factor method. After instantiating the `Var` object, the parser grabs the next token before returning the expression object instance:

```
    else if ( Current_Token == TOKEN.TOK_SIN ||
    Current_Token == TOKEN.TOK_COS)
    {
      TOKEN old = Current_Token;
      Current_Token = GetToken();
      if (Current_Token != TOKEN.TOK_OPAREN)
      {
        Console.WriteLine("Illegal Token");
        throw new Exception();
      }
      Current_Token = GetToken();
      RetValue = Expr();   // Recurse

      if (Current_Token != TOKEN.TOK_CPAREN)
      {
        Console.WriteLine("Missing Closing Parenthesis\n");
        throw new Exception();
      }

      Retvalue = (old == TOKEN.TOK_COS) ?
      new CosExp(RetValue) :
      new SineExp(RetValue);
      Current_Token = GetToken();
    }
```

If the current token is `SIN` or `COS`, we call `Expr()` recursively to parse the parameters. Once `Expr()` returns, we create the appropriate node:

```
    else if (Current_Token == TOKEN.TOK_OPAREN)
    {
      Current_Token = GetToken();
      RetValue = Expr();   // Recurse
      if (Current_Token != TOKEN.TOK_CPAREN)
      {
        Console.WriteLine("Missing Closing Parenthesis\n");
        throw new Exception();
      }
      Current_Token = GetToken();
    }
```

If we find an opening parenthesis, a call to `Expr()` will go to parse the nested expressions:

```
        else if (Current_Token == TOKEN.TOK_PLUS ||
        Current_Token == TOKEN.TOK_SUB)
        {
          l_token = Current_Token;
          Current_Token = GetToken();
          RetValue = Factor(); // Recurse
          RetValue = new UnaryExp(RetValue,
          l_token == TOKEN.TOK_PLUS ?
          OPERATOR.PLUS : OPERATOR.MINUS);
        }
        else
        {
          Console.WriteLine("Illegal Token");
          throw new Exception();
        }
        return RetValue;
    }
}
```

The preceding code snippet handles unary operators, and if the current token is any other thing which is not supposed to be there, an error will be thrown. The syntax diagrams (also known as railroad diagrams) of the grammar realized are shown next.

Expr is represented with the following syntax diagram. The BNF grammar gives better clarity:

```
        <Expr> ::= <Term> | Term { + | - } <Expr>
```

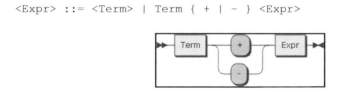

The following syntax diagram represents the **Term.** The BNF grammar is shown for better clarity:

```
        <Term> ::= <Factor> | <Factor> {*|/} <Term>
```

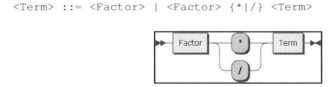

Factor can be represented using the following railroad diagram. The BNF grammar is also shown for the sake of clarity:

```
<Factor>::= <number> | ( <expr> ) | {+|-} <factor> | SIN(<expr>) |
COS(<expr>) | $t
```

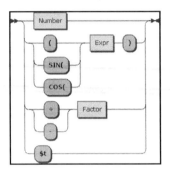

The builder, facade, and expression APIs

The process of interpreting an expression is a complicated process, where a lot of classes work together towards the goal. As an application developer, to focus on the task at hand, we might have to expose an API which abstracts away the complexities of lexical analysis, parsing, and AST generation. We normally use the GoF facade pattern in these contexts. But, we will use the GoF builder pattern here, as this creational pattern is more appropriate in situations where we need to create a composite object. Here, we create expressions which are modeled as composites:

```
public class AbstractBuilder{}

public class ExpressionBuilder : AbstractBuilder
{
  public string _expr_string;
  public ExpressionBuilder(string expr)
  { _expr_string = expr; }

  public Exp GetExpression()
  {
    try
    {
      RDParser p = new RDParser(_expr_string);
      return p.CallExpr();
    }
    catch (Exception)
    {
```

```
        return null;
      }
    }
  }
}
```

The `GetExpression()` method leverages recursive descent parsing and lexical analysis to create an `Exp` object composed of AST nodes. If the parse fails, the routine will return null. The `Builder` class will be used to parse an expression from its textual representation:

```
double t = -x / 2;
double final = x / 2;
ExpressionBuilder bld = new ExpressionBuilder(expr);
Exp e = bld.GetExpression();
if (e == null)
  return false;
```

 We parse the tree once to create the AST. Once the AST has been created, we can evaluate the resulting AST many times over by changing the value in the RUNTIME_CONTEXT object.

```
RUNTIME_CONTEXT context = new RUNTIME_CONTEXT();
context.T = t;
for (; t < final; t += 4)
{
  context.T=t;
  double n = e.Evaluate(context);
  RenderAPixel();
}
```

The expression is parsed once, and an AST is created out of it. Once the tree has been created, it can be evaluated by changing the `context` object. In the preceding loop, `t` is updated and set to the `context` object. Each time you evaluate the tree, you evaluate against a different value of `t`.

Summary

In this chapter, we created an application which plots the result of an arbitrary mathematical expression on a graphics surface. We used WPF for our rendering purpose. We also created an expression evaluator library, which uses the recursive descent parsing technique to parse an expression to a data structure called AST. The AST can be walked depth-first to evaluate the value. This is a good example of the interpreter pattern. We used the observer pattern to automatically relay the changes in the expression input to the canvas object. In the next chapter, you will learn how the .NET framework library leverages patterns to expose a good API for developers.

7
Patterns in the .NET Base Class Library

In this chapter, we will focus on areas where the creators of the .NET Framework library have leveraged GoF design patterns for creating **Application Programming Interfaces (APIs)**. This will give you an enormous insight into the usage of design patterns as a mechanism to expose well-defined software interfaces. Most developers consume design pattern-based software interfaces without knowing much about their underpinnings. This chapter will demystify API design based on patterns. As a reader, you will find real-world application of the following GoF patterns in the .NET Framework library:

- Adapter pattern
- Strategy pattern
- Builder pattern
- Decorator pattern
- Chain of responsibility pattern
- Bridge pattern
- Factory pattern
- Observer pattern
- Composite pattern
- Facade pattern
- Iterator pattern

Adapter pattern in the .NET BCL

The adapter pattern (aka wrapper) translates one interface for a class into a compatible interface expected by the client. This allows objects to work together, which normally wouldn't because of incompatible interfaces.

 This is achieved by providing its cooperating interface to clients while using the original interface to invoke the core functionality provided by the object.

The amount of code necessary to do this is most often small. The adapter is also responsible for transforming data into appropriate forms expected by the library that implements the actual logic. The adapter can be a class adapter or an object adapter. The SQLDataAdapter class in .NET Framework represents a set of data commands (select, update, and delete) and a database connection that is used to fill the DataSet (in the case of select), or update the data source:

```
private static RetrieveRows(
  string connectionString,string queryString)
  {
    using (SqlConnection connection =
    new SqlConnection(connectionString))
    {
      //--- Adapter class here creates a DataSet
      //--- without bothering the developer about
      //--- opening the connections, fetching data
      //--- from the Data Reader and Filling the Data
      //--- to a DataSet
      SqlDataAdapter adapter = new SqlDataAdapter();
      adapter.SelectCommand = new SqlCommand(
      queryString, connection);
      adapter.Fill(dataset);
      return dataset;
    }
  }
```

Strategy pattern in the .NET BCL

The strategy pattern (aka policy pattern) is a design pattern where we can choose algorithms depending upon the context. The pattern is intended to provide a means to define a family of algorithms encapsulated as an object to make them interchangeable. The strategy pattern lets the algorithms vary independently from the clients that use them.

The `Array` and the `ArrayList` classes provide the capability to sort objects contained in them through the `Sort` method. One can use different strategies to sort by leveraging the strategy design pattern-based API provided by the .NET BCL. The designers of .NET Framework have given us the `IComparer<T>` interface to provide a sorting strategy. `Array` and `ArrayList` provide the capability to sort the objects contained in the collection via the `Sort` method. Strategy design pattern is used with `Array` and `Arraylist` to enable sorting using different strategies, without changing any client code, via an `IComparable` interface:

```
class Employee
{
  public String name {get;set;}
  public int age {get;set;}
  public double salary { get; set; }
}
```

To sort an `Employee` list, we need to create a class that implements the `IComparer<T>` interface. An instance of this class needs to be passed to the `Sort` routine of the `List<T>` instance. The `Compare` method of `IComparer<T>` should implement a `SIGNUM` function that returns 1, 0, or −1:

```
class SortByAge : IComparer<Employee>
  {
    public int Compare(Employee a, Employee b)
    {
      return a.age > b.age ? 1 : -1;
    }
  }
```

The following code snippets show how we can change sorting criteria depending on the context:

```
List<Employee> ls = new List<Employee>();
ls.Add(
    new Employee { name = "A", age = 40, salary =  10000 });
ls.Add(
    new Employee { name = "C", age = 20, salary = 6000 });
ls.Add(
    new Employee { name = "B", age = 30, salary = 4000  });
ls.Sort(new SortByAge());
foreach(Employee e in ls)
{
  Console.WriteLine(e.name + " " +
  e.age + " " + e.salary);
}
```

To sort by name, we need to create another object implementing the same interface:

```
class SortByName : IComparer<Employee>
{
  public int Compare(Employee a, Employee b)
  {
    return a.name.CompareTo(b.name);
  }
}
```

We will leverage the `SortByName` class to sort the object based on the lexicographical order. We will also use the `StringBuilder` class to create a string object to be printed on the console. The `StringBuilder` class is an instance where the builder pattern is leveraged by the designers of .NET Framework:

```
ls.Sort(new SortByName());
foreach(Employee e in ls)
{
  StringBuilder strbuilder = new StringBuilder();
  strbuilder.Append(e.name);
  strbuilder.Append(" ");
  strbuilder.Append(e.age);
  strbuilder.Append(" ");
  strbuilder.Append(e.salary);
  Console.WriteLine(strbuilder.ToString());
}
```

Builder pattern in the .NET BCL

The builder pattern is a creational pattern, which separates the construction of a complex object from its representation. Usually, it parses a complex representation to create one or more target objects. Most often, builders create composites. In the `System.Data.SqlClient` namespace, `SqlConnectionStringBuilder` helps one build connection strings for the purpose of connecting to an RDBMS engine:

```
SqlConnectionStringBuilder builder = new
SqlConnectionStringBuilder();
builder["Data Source"] = "(local)";
builder["integrated Security"] = true;
builder["Initial Catalog"] = "AdventureWorks;NewValue=Bad";
Console.WriteLine(builder.ConnectionString);
```

The .NET BCL also contains a class that will help us create a URI by assembling its constituents. The following code snippet creates a secured HTTP (`https`) URL, which sends data to port `3333`:

```
var builder = new UriBuilder(url);
builder.Port = 3333
builder.Scheme = "https";
var result = builder.Uri;
```

Decorator pattern in the .NET BCL

The decorator pattern attaches additional responsibilities to an object dynamically. The inheritance is always not feasible, because it is static and applies to an entire class. Decorators provide a flexible alternative to sub-classing for extending functionality. The pattern helps add behavior or state to individual objects at runtime. The .NET Framework uses decorators in the case of stream processing classes. The hierarchy of stream processing classes are as follows:

- `System.IO.Stream`

  - `System.IO.BufferedStream`
  - `System.IO.FileStream`
  - `System.IO.MemoryStream`
  - `System.Net.Sockets.NetworkStream`
  - `System.Security.Cryptography.CryptoStream`

The following code snippets show how one can use `FileStream` to read contents from an operating system disk file:

```
using (FileStream fs = new FileStream(path, FileMode.Open))
{
  using (StreamReader sr = new StreamReader(fs))
  {
    while (sr.Peek() >= 0)
    {
      Console.WriteLine(sr.ReadLine());
    }
  }
}
```

The `StreamReader` is a decorator object, which uses the additional functionality of buffering the avoid disk access to speed up operation.

Chain of responsibility pattern in ASP.net

The chain of responsibility pattern is a design pattern consisting of a series of processing objects through which we pass a data stream for filtration or modification. Ultimately, the process terminates when the data stream passes the last processing object at the end of the chain. The ASP.NET pipeline is a wonderful example where the chain of responsibility pattern is leveraged to provide an extensible programming model. The ASP.NET infrastructure implements WebForms API, ASMX Web services, WCF, ASP.NET Web API, and ASP.NET MVC using HTTP modules and handlers. Every request in the pipeline passes through a series of modules (a class that implements `IHttpModule`) before it reaches its target handler (a class that implements `IHttpHandler`). Once a module in the pipeline has done its duty, it passes the responsibility of the request processing to the next module in the chain. Finally, it reaches the handler. The following code snippet shows how one can write an object that leverages the chain of responsibility pattern to create a module that filters an incoming request. These filters are configured as chains and will pass the request content to the next filter in the chain by the ASP.net runtime:

```
public class SimpleHttpModule : IHttpModule
{
  public SimpleHttpModule(){}
  public String ModuleName
  {
    get { return "SimpleHttpModule"; }
  }
  public void Init(HttpApplication application)
  {
```

```
    application.BeginRequest +=
    (new EventHandler(this.Application_BeginRequest));
    application.EndRequest |=
    (new EventHandler(this.Application_EndRequest));
  }
  private void Application_BeginRequest(Object source,
  EventArgs e)
  {
    HttpApplication application = (HttpApplication)source;
    HttpContext context = application.Context;
    context.Response.Write(SomeHtmlString);
  }
  private void Application_EndRequest(Object source, EventArgs e)
  {
    HttpApplication application =      (HttpApplication)source;
    HttpContext context = application.Context;
    context.Response.Write(SomeHtmlString);
  }
  public void Dispose(){}
}
```

We can configure the preceding HTTP module in the `Web.config` file as follows:

```
<configuration>
  <system.web>
    <httpModules>
      <add name=" SimpleHttpModule " type=" SimpleHttpModule "/>
    </httpModules>
  </system.web>
</configuration>
```

In the ASP.NET pipeline, a request passes through a series of HTTP modules before it hits a handler. A simple HTTP handler routine is given as follows:

```
public class SimpleHttpHandler: IHttpHandler
{
  public void ProcessRequest(System.Web.HttpContext context){
    context.Response.Write("The page request ->" +
    context.Request.RawUrl.ToString());
  }
  public bool IsReusable
  {
    get{ return true; }
  }
}
```

We can configure the handler as given next. Whenever we create an ASP.NET resource with the `.smp` extension, the handler will be `SimpleHttpHandler`:

```
<system.web>
  <httpHandlers>
    <add verb="*" path="*.smp" type="SimpleHttpHandler"/>
  </httpHandlers>
</system.web>
```

The preceding technique of leveraging the chain of responsibility pattern is available in other web technologies such as Java Servlets (called Servlet filters) and also available in IIS as ISAPI filters.

Bridge pattern in the .NET RCW

The **Component Object Model (COM)** technology solutions packaged as libraries can be consumed through **Runtime Callable Wrapper (RCW)**, available in the .NET platform. By allowing managed classes and COM components to interact, despite their interface disparity, RCWs are an example of bridge pattern (implemented as an adapter!). Please consult the documentation on **Com Callable Wrapper (CCW)** and RCW to understand how the bridge pattern is implemented to interoperate with components written in other languages (mostly C++/ATL). Technically speaking, even ADO.NET API also leverages the bridge pattern, to interact with ODBC and other native drivers implemented by respective database vendors.

Factory pattern in the .NET BCL

The factory design pattern has been used by `System.Data.Common` to create an instance of the provider, connection, command, or adapter objects in order to fetch data from a relational database. The following code snippets demonstrates the idea:

```
DbProviderFactory factory =
DbProviderFactories.GetFactory(providerName);
DbConnection connection = factory.CreateConnection();
connection.ConnectionString = connectionString;
string queryString = "SELECT CategoryName FROM Categories";
DbCommand command = factory.CreateCommand();
command.CommandText = queryString;
command.Connection = connection;
DbDataAdapter adapter = factory.CreateDataAdapter();
adapter.SelectCommand = command;
DataTable table = new DataTable();
```

```
adapter.Fill(table);
```

Observer pattern in the WPF

The `ObservableCollection` can be considered as a data structure, which leverages the observer pattern to provide notifications when items get added or removed, or when the whole list is refreshed:

```
class ObservableDataSource
{
  public ObservableCollection<string> data
  { get; set; }

  public ObservableDataSource()
  {
    data = new ObservableCollection<string>();
    data.CollectionChanged += OnCollectionChanged;
  }
  void OnCollectionChanged(object sender,
  NotifyCollectionChangedEventArgs args)
  {
    Console.WriteLine("The Data got changed ->" +
    args.NewItems[0]);
  }
  public void TearDown()
  {
    data.CollectionChanged -= OnCollectionChanged;
  }
}
```

The following code snippet creates an instance of an `Observableconnection` based `ObservableDataSource` class. When we add items to the class, we get a notification in the `OnCollectionDataChanged` method of the `ObservableDataSource` class:

```
ObservableDataSource obs = new ObservableDataSource();
obs.data.Add("Hello");
obs.data.Add("World");
obs.data.Add("Save");
```

Composite pattern in the .NET Framework

To create complex UI screens, the .NET Framework leverages composite patterns extensively. The WPF, ASP.NET Web Forms, and Winforms are some of the key examples in this regard. In a UI scenario, one can have a frame class, which acts as a container for all the child controls. Typically, developers place panels to divide the physical screen to some kind of logical grouping and child controls are placed inside these panels. The controls like list, grid can embed other controls. Thus, these are wonderful examples of the composite pattern.

Facade pattern in the .NET BCL

The GoF facade pattern is used in scenarios where a lot of work happens in the background and the interfaces to those classes are exposed using a simple API. The XMLSeralizer class in the .NET BCL does quite a bit of its work behind the scenes and access to those routines are given using a very simple interface. The following code snippets create a DataSet to store a multiplication table for the number 42 (remember Douglas Adams!) and the XMLSeralizer class persists the table to a text file:

```
class Program
{
  private static DataSet CreateMultTable()
  {
    DataSet ds = new DataSet("CustomDataSet");
    DataTable tbl = new DataTable("Multiplicationtable");
    DataColumn column_1 = new DataColumn("Multiplicand");
    DataColumn column_2 = new DataColumn("Multiplier");
    DataColumn column_3 = new DataColumn("REsult");
    tbl.Columns.Add(column_1);
    tbl.Columns.Add(column_2);
    tbl.Columns.Add(column_3);

    ds.Tables.Add(tbl);
    int Multiplicand = 42;
    DataRow r;
    for (int i = 0; i < 10; i++)
    {
      r = tbl.NewRow();
      r[0] = Multiplicand;
      r[1] = i;
      r[2] = Multiplicand * i;
      tbl.Rows.Add(r);
    }
```

```
      return ds;
   }
   // The Entrypoint for execution
   // using Serialize method, we can traverse the tree
   // and persist the content to a XML file. Behind the scenes
   // the code to traverse the DataSet structure is getting
   // executed. Using FAÇADE pattern, the .NET framekwork
   // designers have managed to hide the complexity

   static void Main(string[] args)
   {
      XmlSerializer ser = new XmlSerializer(typeof(DataSet));
      DataSet ds = CreateMultTable();
      TextWriter writer = new StreamWriter("mult.xml");
      ser.Serialize(writer, ds);
      writer.Close();
      Console.ReadKey();
   }
}
```

Iterator pattern in the .NET BCL

The iterator pattern is so common that most platforms and frameworks provide a mechanism to support it. The .NET BCL has got IEnumerable and its generic variant , that is, IEnumerable<T> to implement custom iterators. To iterate, we have got the foreach loop construct in C#. Similar constructs are available in Java as well. The following program creates a custom list by leveraging the .NET fixed length array facility:

```
public class CustomList<T> : IEnumerable<T>
{
   //------ A Fixed Length array to
   //------ Example very simple
   T[] _Items = new T[100];
   int next_Index = 0;

   public CustomList(){}

   public void Add(T val)
   {
      // We are adding value without robust
      // error checking
      _Items[next_Index++] = val;
   }

   public IEnumerator<T> GetEnumerator()
```

```
    {
      foreach (T t in _Items)
      {
        //---only reference objects can be populated
        //-- and checked for null
        if (t == null) { break; }
        yield return t;
      }
    }

    System.Collections.IEnumerator
    System.Collections.IEnumerable.GetEnumerator()
    {
      return this.GetEnumerator();
    }
  }
}
// The Entry point function
// creates a Custom List instance and adds entry to the list
// and uses foreach loop to access the iterator implemented
class Program
{
  static void Main(string[] args)
  {
    CustomList<string> lst = new CustomList<string>();
    lst.Add("first");
    lst.Add("second");
    lst.Add("third");
    lst.Add("fourth");

    foreach (string s in lst)
    {
      Console.WriteLine(s);
    }
    Console.ReadKey();
  }
}
```

Summary

In this chapter, we learned how the designers of the .NET BCL leverage design patterns to expose a well-defined programming model and a flexible API for the same. You learned about how some important patterns are put to use by the designers of the .NET Framework. In the next chapter, you will learn about concurrent and parallel programming in the .NET platform.

8
Concurrent and Parallel Programming under .NET

So far, we have been mostly focusing on the GoF design patterns. When the catalog appeared, the computing world was mostly sequential, and the bias was reflected in the catalog. The world has changed a lot since the publication of the catalog in 1994. There was a shift towards language-level concurrency and parallelism due to the arrival of the Java and C# programming languages. The processor designers understood the limits of constructing powerful single-core CPUs, and began focusing on many core CPUs. This brought its own set of complexity in developing software using the existing paradigms. Even a language like C++, which relegated concurrency to libraries, added language-level concurrency features in its latest avatar, C++ 11/14. With the advent of functional programming features into the OOP world, the programming landscape changed drastically. In this chapter, you will learn some techniques for writing concurrent and parallel programs using the C# programming language and .NET platform features. In this chapter, we will cover the following points:

- Factors that influenced evolution of concurrency and parallelization models
- Concurrency versus Parallelism
- .NET Parallel Programming libraries
- Some Parallel/Concurrent memes/idioms
    - Embarrassingly parallel
    - Fork/join parallelism
    - Producer/consumer paradigm

Days of Free Lunch

The celebrated Moore's law went on despite microprocessors hitting the clock-speed limits in terms of heat dissipation and achieving fabrications beyond nano-level. CPU designers found an intelligent workaround for this roadblock–that of leveraging the increased chip densities to scale the computation infrastructure horizontally as opposed to the traditional vertical way. This principle has deep consequences in modern day architecture and design, where application scalability (both vertical and horizontal) inherits natural elasticity with respect to the infrastructure that powers them. What resulted was a new generation of CPU architectures including hyper-threading, multi-core, and many-core. It wasn't too late before the developers realized that the **Free Lunch** (just leveraging the conventional CPU performance gains through clock speed, execution optimization, and cache, with no change in their programs) was over. Herb Sutter wrote an influential article in Dr. Dobb's Journal about this, aptly titled, *The Free Lunch Is Over: A Fundamental Turn toward Concurrency in Software*!

 This realization that software was the gating factor in terms of achieving more with most of what was available was the dawn of a new revolution in software architecture and design.

This new model helped remove many shortcomings in modeling real-world problem scenarios. It seemed though that we (developers) began adding justice to the grand concurrent design that went into modelling this world with interactions to be parallel as opposed to just being sequential and object-oriented. The prevalent parallelization techniques (leveraged mostly by the scientific community for doing embarrassingly parallel computations)–that of explicit threading with an affinity to hardware threads–was primitive and less scalable. Very few people had expertise (or rather felt comfortable) in working with the low-level constructs for leveraging multi-threading in their applications. This state of affairs brought in a strong imperative for creating better abstractions and the needed APIs to write the next generation software that would inherently leverage concurrency and parallelism to achieve more with most of what was available.

Days of Sponsored Lunch

Microsoft's .Net **Common Language Runtime** (CLR) came to the rescue with the managed thread pool (which stabilized around version 2.0), which paved the way for a strong foundation layer on top of which the concurrency and parallelization models subsequently evolved.

The most notable ones include **Asynchronous Programming Model (APM)**, **Concurrency and Coordination Runtime (CCR)**, **Decentralized Software Services (DSS)**, **Parallel LINQ (PLINQ)**, **Task Parallel Library (TPL)**, and the Task-based Async/Await model.

Certain functional constructs and language features like Anonymous Methods, Lambda Expressions, Extension Methods, Anonymous Types, and **Language Integrated Query (LINQ)** were the core catalysts that aided this evolution. Major contributors and SMEs include Erik Meijer for LINQ, Joe Duffy and Jon Skeet for Multithreading in .NET), Stephen Toub, Ade Miller, Colin Campbell, and Ralph Johnson for Parallel Extensions, and Jeffrey Richter and George Chrysanthakopoulos for CCR.

Of the aforementioned notable models, the major ones that matured and are advocated today are the following:

- Task-based async/await model for concurrency
- **Parallel Extensions (PFX)** including PLINQ and TPL for parallelization

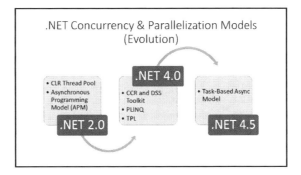

Concurrent versus parallel

These are two key constructs are often confused by developers, and warrant clear demystification. The authors strongly feel that a thorough understanding of this distinction holds the key to effective software design for achieving more by effective utilization of the available infrastructure (processors, cores, hardware, and software threads). Let's start with the classical definition by Rob Pike (inventor of the Go programming language), and try to decode its meaning.

> *Parallelization is doing multiple tasks (related or non-related) at the same time whereas concurrency is about dealing with lots of things at once.*
> *Concurrency is about structure; parallelism is about execution.*
> *Concurrency provides a way to structure a solution to solve a problem that may (but not necessarily) be parallelizable.*
>
> *– Rob Pike*

This clearly articulates the difference between these constructs, and goes further to illustrate how concurrency, as a model, helps to structure a program by breaking it into pieces that can be executed independently. This powerful consequence of a concurrent design model facilitates parallelism depending on the hardware support available for the program's runtime or compiler infrastructure.

 This further means **write-once**, **run-anywhere**.

The days of Free Lunch are back with this model, where a concurrent program can perform better on multiple cores by leveraging parallelization techniques (mostly abstracted or under the hood, and is dependent on the framework library or runtime that executes these programs). This could be understood very clearly as the way an asynchronous programming model works using `async` and `await`. This model helps to structure the program by breaking it into pieces that can be executed independently. These independent pieces become **tasks** (part of the TPL), and are executed simultaneously, leveraging the available hardware (cores and threads). Now you see how parallelism becomes an interesting side-effect of a concurrent model. This is managed (in terms of the degree of parallelism that determines the number of cores to be leveraged for reducing contention) by the TPL API and CLR. So, the developer can focus on the core decomposition (with little or no shared state) of the process into independent tasks as opposed to getting entangled in the low-level constructs (threads and synchronization) for realizing concurrency and parallelization. The APIs have evolved quite intelligently to support this, thus making the code-base quite expressive, declarative, and readable.

On the contrary, if you explicitly try to leverage basic naive parallelism (`Parallel.For` and PLINQ) for executing the decomposed tasks, there is a good chance you would end up blocking your threads, thus curtailing scalability and availability (especially for server-side programs).

> *Don't Block your threads, Make Async I/O work for you*
>
> *– Stephen Toub/Scott Hanselman*

This is the founding principle on which concurrent programming models work. The classic example is Node.js, which has gained prominence as a middleware and backend system with its inherent support for async I/O. Again, one needs to understand that the benefits are seen more in I/O and asynchronous service executions as opposed to long-running CPU-bound tasks (which wouldn't give you the benefit you typically desire, as these tend to block, and, in turn, cause thread starvation). This is a classic scenario, where developers complain that their program takes more time to execute (compared to the serial implementation) when task parallelism is employed with `Parallel.For` loops.

Again, none of these imply that one shouldn't employ high-and low-level constructs for task creation, threading, and parallelism. As long as scalability and availability is not a high priority, task parallelism, with appropriate partitioning strategies, could be very effectively employed. This is because these libraries effectively load balance the work across the CLR threads to minimize contention, and maximize throughput through work stealing.

The consequence of both these models is something to be kept in mind when designing effective algorithms that can leverage the best of what you have, and yet, scale. We will try to illustrate these in the coming sections.

Some common patterns of parallel programming

Now that we understand the power that these two models bring, one needs to be wary of the responsibility that this power brings forth. Typical abuse of concurrency and parallelism in the form of blanket code refactoring are often found counterproductive. Patterns become more pertinent in this paradigm, where developers push the limits of computing hardware.

Issues of races, deadlocks, livelocks, priority inversions, two-step dances, and lock convoys typically have no place in a sequential world, and avoiding such issues makes quality patterns all the more important

– Stephen Toub

The authors wish to put in perspective the modelling/decomposition aspects of the problem, and illustrate the applicability of some of the key patterns, data structures, and synchronization constructs to these so as to aid the programmer to leverage concurrency and parallelism to its full potential. For detailed coverage in terms of patterns and primitive constructs, the authors strongly recommend developers to read *Patterns of Parallel Programming* by Stephen Toub and *Concurrent Programming on Windows* by Joe Duffy.

Embarrassingly or conveniently parallel

This is the foremost pattern we would cover. The candidate programs that can leverage these are ones that can be easily decomposed into tasks/operations which have little or no dependency. This independence makes parallel execution of these tasks/operations very convenient. We will stray a bit from the conventional examples (that of a ray tracer and matrix multiplication), plus instill a sense of adventure and accomplishment in creating an algorithm, which, in turn, is embarrassingly parallel in nature.

We would be articulating this pattern by creating a C# implementation of the *Schönhage-Strassen* algorithm for rapidly multiplying large integers.

Problem statement

As indicated, the problem statement seems straightforward in terms of having an ability to multiply large numbers (let's push ourselves a bit by further stating astronomically large numbers), which cannot even be represented (64-bit computing limit). We have consciously reduced the scope by restricting ourselves to just one operation (multiplication) for outlining the pattern. Nothing prevents any interested reader who is game to go ahead and implement other operations thereby devising their own `BigInteger` version with support for all mathematical operations.

Solutions approach

Let's start by outlining the algorithm to multiply two three-digit sequences (**456** and **789**):

		4	5	6		
	x	7	8	9		
Step1.1		36	45	54		4 5 6 / 9
Step1.2		32	40	48		4 5 6 / 8
Step1.3	28	35	42			4 5 6 / 7
Step2	28	67	118	93	54	<< Acyclic Convolution
Step3	28	67	118	93	54	<< Carrying Operation
RESULT	3	5	9	7	8 4	<< RESULT

Schönhage–Strassen Algorithm

The Schönhage-Strassen algorithm depends fundamentally on the convolution theorem, which provides an efficient way to compute the cyclic convolution of two sequences.

The authors wish to take a disclaimer here: the cyclic convolution computation is not done in the most efficient way here. The prescribed steps include that of taking the **Discrete Fourier Transform** (**DFT**) of each sequence, multiplying the resulting vectors element by element, and then taking the **Inverse Discrete Fourier Transform** (**IDFT**). In contrast to this, we adopt a naïve and computationally intensive algorithmic way. This results in a runtime bit complexity of $O(n^2)$ in Big-O notation for two n digit numbers. The core idea here is to demonstrate the intrinsic parallel nature of the algorithm!

As illustrated, the algorithm to compute the product of two three-digit sequences comprises of three major steps. We will look at the problem decomposition in detail, and interlude the steps with code to see this pattern in action, leveraging some of the core .NET parallelization constructs (specifically, the `For` method of the `Parallel` class in TPL-`Parallel.For`). In this process, you will understand how task decomposition is done effectively, taking into consideration the algorithmic and structural aspects of your application.

Step 1

We will start off multiplying the two numbers 456 (sequence-1) and 789 (sequence-2) using long multiplication with base 10 digits, without performing any carrying. The multiplication involves three further sub-steps as illustrated.

Step 1.1

As part of the long multiplication, we multiply the least significant digit (9) from sequence-2 with all the digits of sequence-1, producing a sequence 36, 45, and 54.

Step 1.2

We multiply the next least significant digit (8) from sequence-2 with all the digits of sequence-1, producing a sequence 32, 40, and 48.

Step 1.3

Finally, we multiply the most significant digit (7) from sequence-2 with all the digits of sequence-1, producing a sequence 28, 35, and 42.

Step 2

Add the respective column elements (again without carrying) to obtain the acyclic/linear convolution sequence (28, 67, 118, 93, 54) of sequence 1 and 2.

Step 3

Perform the final step: that of doing the carrying operation (for example, in the rightmost column, keep the 4 and add the 5 to the column containing 93). In the given example, this yields the correct product, 359,784.

The following is the serial implementation of this algorithm (it faithfully follows the preceding steps for clarity):

```
//----------------------------Abstract Factory
  public interface INumeric
  {
      BigNumOperations Operations ();
  }
//----------------------------Abstract Product
public abstract class BigNumOperations
{
    public abstract string Multiply (string x, string y);
    public virtual string Multiply (
      string x,
```

```
    string y,
    CancellationToken ct,
    BlockingCollection<string> log)
  {
    return this.Multiply(x, y);
  }
```

 In the following `Power` method, we will employ Exponentiation by Squaring Algorithm, which relies on the fact that: $x\char94 y = (x*x)\char94(y/2)$ Using this, we will continuously divide the exponent (in this case y) by two while squaring the base (in this case x). That is, in order to find the result of 2^11, we will do [((2*2)*(2*2))*((2*2)*(2*2))] * [(2*2)] * [(2)] or, to put it simply, we will do 2^8 * 2^2 * 2^1. This algorithm achieves O(log n) efficiency!

```
public string Power (string number, int exponent)
{
    int remainingEvenExp = exponent / 2;
    int remainingOddExp = exponent % 2;
    string result = number;
    if (remainingEvenExp > 0)
    {
        string square = this.Multiply(number, number);
        result = square;
        if (remainingEvenExp > 1)
        {
            if (remainingOddExp == 1)
            {
                result = this.Multiply(
                    this.Power(square, remainingEvenExp),
                    number);
            }
            else
            {
                result = this.Power(square, remainingEvenExp);
            }
        }
        else
        {
            if (remainingOddExp == 1)
            {
                result = this.Multiply(square, number);
            }
        }
    }
    return result;
}
```

```
   // Creates, Initializes and Returns a Jagged Array

  public static int[][] CreateMatrix (int rows, int cols)
  {
      int[][] result = new int[rows][];
      for (int i = 0; i < rows; ++i)
          result[i] = new int[cols];
      return result;
  }
}


// ---------------------------Concrete Product-1

public class BigNumOperations1 : BigNumOperations
{
    /// <summary>
    /// Serial Implementation of Schönhage-Strassen Algorithm
    /// <param name="x">String number Sequence-1</param>
    /// <param name="y">String number Sequence-2</param>
    /// <returns>String Equivalent Product Sequence</returns>
    /// </summary>

    public override string Multiply (string x, string y)
    {
        int n = x.Length;
        int m = y.Length;
        int prodDigits = n + m - 1;
        int[] linearConvolution = new int[prodDigits];
        int[][] longMultiplication = CreateMatrix(m, prodDigits);

        //---------------------------Step-1

        for (int i = m - 1; i >= 0; i--)
        {
            int row = m - 1 - i;
            int col = 0;
            int iProduct;
            for (int j = n - 1; j >= 0; j--)
            {
                col = i + j;
                iProduct = (( int )
                  Char.GetNumericValue(y[i])) *
                  (( int ) Char.GetNumericValue(x[j]));
                longMultiplication[row][col] = iProduct;
            }
        }

        //---------------------------Step-2
```

```
                    for (int j = prodDigits - 1; j >= 0; j--)
                    {
                        int sum = 0;
                        for (int i = 0; i < m; i++)
                        {
                            sum += longMultiplication[i][j];
                        }
                        linearConvolution[j] = sum;
                    }

                    //--------------------------Step-3

                    int nextCarry = 0;
                    int[] product = new int[prodDigits];
                    for (int i = (n + m - 2); i >= 0; i--)
                    {
                        linearConvolution[i] += nextCarry;
                        product[i] = linearConvolution[i] % 10;
                        nextCarry = linearConvolution[i] / 10;
                    }
                    return (nextCarry > 0 ? nextCarry.ToString() : "") +
                      new string
                      (
                          Array.ConvertAll<int, char>
                          (product, c => Convert.ToChar(c + 0x30))
                      );
                }
            }


// Concrete Factory-1

public class BigNumber1 : INumeric
{
  public BigNumOperations Operations()
  {
    return new BigNumOperations1();
  }
}
```

If you closely evaluate the code, Step 1 and Step 2 in our algorithm are embarrassingly, or rather, conveniently parallelizable. Listed next is the equivalent lock-free parallel implementation of the same algorithm. This leverages the TPL `Parallel.For` parallelization construct.

```
// Concrete Product-2

public class BigNumOperations2 : BigNumOperations
{
    public override string Multiply (string x, string y)
    {
      int n = x.Length;
      int m = y.Length;
      int prodDigits = n + m - 1;
      int[] linearConvolution = new int[prodDigits];
      int[][] longMultiplication = CreateMatrix(m, prodDigits);

      //---------------------------Step-1

      Parallel.For(0, m, i =>
      {
          int row = m - 1 - i;
          int col = 0;
          int iProduct;
          for (int j = 0; j < n; j++)
          {
              col = i + j;
              iProduct = (( int ) Char.GetNumericValue(y[i]))
                * (( int ) Char.GetNumericValue(x[j]));
              longMultiplication[row][col] = iProduct;
          }
      });

      //---------------------------Step-2

      Parallel.For(0, prodDigits, j =>
      {
          int sum = 0;
          for (int i = 0; i < m; i++)
          {
              sum += longMultiplication[i][j];
          }
          linearConvolution[j] = sum;
      });

      //---------------------------Step-3
```

```
        //Use code from Concrete Product-1 here...
    }
}

// Concrete Factory-2

public class BigNumber2 : INumeric
{
  public BigNumOperations Operations()
  {
    return new BigNumOperations2();
  }
}
```

 Now, to really understand the leverage we got from the `Parallel.For` parallelization construct, we have to do a CPU-intensive operation, which would be best achieved by computing the power (as opposed to the product) utilizing the multiplication algorithm. Imagine solving the wheat and chess problem, or perhaps more, say, $2^{100,000}$ (to the power of 100,000) in place of 2^{32}. A recursive divide and conquer strategy has been applied to compute the exponential (default implementation of the `Power` method in the abstract class/product `BigNumOperations`, which further uses the overridden, concrete `Multiply` methods of the respective core product implementations).

Can you really compute $2^{100,000}$ (given our limit of 64-bit arithmetic operations)? Well, take a look at the following invocation code and result:

```
public static void Power (string[] args)
{
    var bigN1 = new BigNumber1();
    var bigN2 = new BigNumber2();
    var x = args[0];
    int y = Convert.ToInt32(args[1]);

    var watch = Stopwatch.StartNew();
    var val1 = bigN1.Operations().Power(x, y);

    Console.WriteLine(
      "Serial Computation of {0} ^ {1}: {2} seconds",
        x, y, watch.ElapsedMilliseconds / 1000D);

    watch = Stopwatch.StartNew();
    var val2 = bigN2.Operations().Power(x, y);

    Console.WriteLine(
```

```
        "Parallel Computation of {0} ^ {1}: {2} seconds",
        x, y, watch.ElapsedMilliseconds / 1000D);
    Console.WriteLine("Computed Values are {0}!!!",
        val1.Equals(val2) ? "EQUAL" : "DIFFERENT");
}
```

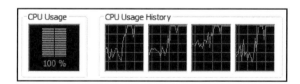

Yes!!! It computed the values, and the parallel implementation took around half the time as compared to the serial one.

> The qualifier here, that of taking half the time, is relative and will depend on the availability of cores and resources; it will also vary with environments.

Also see how the task granularity seems to utilize the CPU (with all its available cores) to the maximum extent possible in the case of parallel execution (towards the right-hand side of the usage spectrum in all of the four cores):

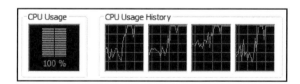

The following is a quick summary of the key applicability of best practices and patterns in this implementation:

- This is a classic case, where data parallelism (applying a single operation to many data elements/inputs) is exploited to the core, and the parallelization construct (`Parallel.For`) we have chosen is best suited for this. We could also leverage the synchronization primitive `Barrier` (`System.Threading.Barrier`), which would enable various sub-tasks to cooperatively work in parallel through multiple phases/tasks. A `Barrier` is recommended when the phases are relatively large in number.

- Choose a lock-free task data structure (here, a two dimensional array has been utilized to capture the product sequences from each iteration in step 1). The operations (reads/writes) are atomic if you examine them closely (including step 2). This makes the parallelization process very effective, as there wouldn't be any synchronization penalties (**locks,** specifically) but a seamless utilization of resources (with the inherent load balancing provided by `Parallel.For`). It is best to leave `Parallel.For` to calibrate the **degree of parallelism** (**DOP**) itself so as to leverage all the available cores, and thereby prevent side-effects because of thread starvation or oversubscription. At best, we could specify `ParallelOptions` of `Parallel.For` to use `Environment.ProcessorCount` so as to explicitly state the usage of one thread per core (a recommended practice in parallelization). The biggest limitation would be in terms of the memory required for array allocation in this case. You would tend to hit the `OutOfMemory` exception beyond powers of 100,000 (again, specific to this algorithm and the associated data structures that it employs).

- Fine-grained partitioning of tasks, as part of the decomposition process, enables throughput (again, it's a balance that needs to be achieved with careful analysis; any attempt to overdo can swing the performance pendulum to the other side).

- Choose the data representation in string format to represent really big numbers. Of course, you do incur the penalty of data conversion (a necessary evil in this case). You could as well create an extension method for string type to support these big number operations (perhaps, with a validation for legal numbers).

- Use of alternate algorithm (reverse long multiplication; that is, reversing steps 1.1 through 1.3) to leverage the parallel loop partition counter, which is forward only (as its purpose is only to partition, unlike that of a step counter in a conventional `for` loop). Restructuring your algorithm is better than tweaking the code that was originally designed to run serially.

- And finally, leverage the abstract factory GoF design pattern to seamlessly support the various implementations (in this case, serial and parallel).

Fork/join or master/worker

This is a pattern that you generally associate with task parallelism. When there are distinct asynchronous operations that can run simultaneously, you can temporarily fork a program's flow of control with tasks that can potentially execute in parallel. You can then wait for these forked tasks to complete.

In the Microsoft® .NET Framework, tasks are implemented by the `Task` class in the `System.Threading.Tasks` namespace. Unlike threads, new tasks that are forked (using the `StartNew` method) don't necessarily begin executing immediately. They are managed internally by a task scheduler, and run based on a FIFO manner (from a work queue) as cores become available. The `Wait` (for task) and `WaitAll` (for task array) method ensures the join operation.

Now, if you try to apply this pattern holistically to our original problem statement (to compute the power of big numbers), you will see the potential to leverage this for executing the tasks within the major phases (Steps 1, 2, and 3) concurrently (by forking off tasks), and have the phases blocking (joining these forked tasks within each phase) to mirror the sequential ordering (steps 1, 2, and 3) as advocated by the algorithm. See the following code that does lock-free parallel implementation of Schönhage-Strassen Algorithm by leveraging the `System.Threading.Tasks` concurrency construct:

```
// Concrete Product-3

public class BigNumOperations3 : BigNumOperations
{
    public override string Multiply (string x, string y,
      CancellationToken ct, BlockingCollection<string> log)
    {
        int n = x.Length;
        int m = y.Length;
        int prodDigits = n + m - 1;
        int[] linearConvolution = new int[prodDigits];
        int[][] longMultiplication = CreateMatrix(m, prodDigits);

        var degreeOfParallelism = Environment.ProcessorCount;
        var tasks = new Task[degreeOfParallelism];

        //---------------------------Step-1

        for (int taskNumber = 0;
          taskNumber < degreeOfParallelism;
            taskNumber++)
        {
          int taskNumberCopy = taskNumber;
          tasks[taskNumber] = Task.Factory.StartNew(
            () =>
            {
                var max =
                    m * (taskNumberCopy + 1) /
                    degreeOfParallelism;
                var min =
                    m * taskNumberCopy /
```

[156]

```
                      degreeOfParallelism;
           for (int i = min; i < max; i++)
           {
               int row = m - 1 - i;
               int col = 0;
               int iProduct;
               for (int j = 0; j < n; j++)
               {
                   col = i + j;
                   iProduct =
                       (( int ) Char
                       .GetNumericValue(y[i])) *
                       (( int ) Char
                       .GetNumericValue(x[j]));
                   longMultiplication[row][col] =
                       iProduct;
               }
           }
        });
}

Task.WaitAll(tasks);        //Blocking Call

//---------------------------Step-2

for (int taskNumber = 0;
    taskNumber < degreeOfParallelism;
    taskNumber++)
{
    int taskNumberCopy = taskNumber;
    tasks[taskNumber] = Task.Factory.StartNew(
        () =>
        {
            var max =
                prodDigits * (taskNumberCopy + 1) /
                degreeOfParallelism;
            var min =
                prodDigits * taskNumberCopy /
                degreeOfParallelism;
            for (int j = min; j < max; j++)
            {
                int sum = 0;
                for (int i = 0; i < m; i++)
                {
                    sum += longMultiplication[i][j];
                }
                linearConvolution[j] = sum;
            }
```

```
                });
        }

        Task.WaitAll(tasks);            //Blocking Call
        //--------------------------Step-3

        //Use code from Concrete Product-1 here...

    }
}

// Concrete Factory-3

public class BigNumber3 : INumeric
{
    public BigNumOperations Operations()
    {
        return new BigNumOperations3();
    }
}
```

The collective sample output along with the preceding code is as follows:

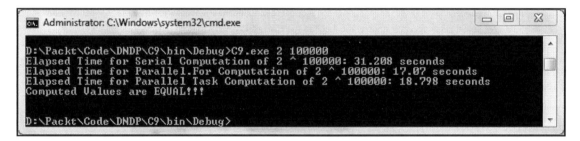

What we have done here in the preceding code is essentially explicit macro-range partitioning with respect to the available cores, and not spinning off in place of micro-range partitioning with respect to the outer loop. This is a strategy which has to be dealt with carefully, as results would vary with the resources available at your disposal. Deliberate calibration can yield much higher throughputs. In this context, we come to the next important pattern.

Speculative execution

Now that we have seen close to three different implementation strategies of the Schönhage-Strassen algorithm, how do we perform deliberate calibration, and decide which is the best strategy (now that we understand that it has a close co-relation with its environment and associated resources)?

 This is where this important pattern really helps us make a decision, when deviations against anticipated results are unavoidable, and need to be smartly addressed.

We would schedule asynchronous tasks for each of these strategies for execution, leverage the `WaitAny` method of the `Task` class to wait for one of the operations to complete (one that finishes first), and attempt to cancel all others. On a smart-learning front, this could be done periodically to continuously calibrate and cache your strategy for mass consumption. It's an aspect of machine learning where the program intelligently adapts to sieve and use effective algorithms. See the following code that incorporates options to cancel tasks upon determination of the winner by working out who is the fastest:

```
// Concrete Product-4

public class BigNumOperations4 : BigNumOperations
{
    /// <summary>
    /// Serial Cancellable Implementation of
    /// Schönhage-Strassen Algorithm
    /// <param name="x">String number Sequence-1</param>
    /// <param name="y">String number Sequence-2</param>
    /// <returns>String Equivalent Product Sequence</returns>
    /// </summary>

    public override string Multiply (
        string x,
        string y,
        CancellationToken ct,
        BlockingCollection<string> log)
    {
        if (ct.IsCancellationRequested == true)
        {
            ct.ThrowIfCancellationRequested();
        }
        //Use code from Concrete Product-1 here...
        //-------------------------Step-1

        for (int i = m - 1; i >= 0; i--)
```

```
        {
        //Use code from Concrete Product-1 here...

            for (int j = n - 1; j >= 0; j--)
            {
                if (ct.IsCancellationRequested)
                {
                    ct.ThrowIfCancellationRequested();
                }

        //Use code from Concrete Product-1 here...

            }
        }

        //---------------------------Step-2

        for (int j = prodDigits - 1; j >= 0; j--)
        {
            if (ct.IsCancellationRequested)
            {
                ct.ThrowIfCancellationRequested();
            }

            //Use code from Concrete Product-1 here...
        }

            //---------------------------Step-3

        for (int i = (n + m - 2); i >= 0; i--)
        {
            if (ct.IsCancellationRequested)
            {
                ct.ThrowIfCancellationRequested();
            }

            //Use code from Concrete Product-1 here...
        }
    }
}
```

 Similarly, concrete products 5 and 6 are created based on constructs employed in products 2 and 3. Please refer the relevant code sections in the companion website for these implementations.

Now that we have executable parallel code that will respond to user interruptions, lets understand how we can do speculative execution.

It's quite interesting, or rather an art, how we can achieve control over these constructs. It's just that you need to see through your algorithm, and determine how the decomposition helps you gain coarser or finer control on execution. You will see areas that pose limitations once you get into the finer intricacies of task parallelization and concurrency. You will also see the power of abstraction that these constructs bring to the table, and better appreciate the instrumentation and hooks that need to go in for aiding you in gaining better control of your program, as opposed to letting **heisenbugs** haunt your programs. Let's observe the output that determined the fastest implementation:

Though the `Parallel.For` construct emerged the winner in all the three trials. This is not a certainty, as the outcome is determined by the available resources and the complexity of the algorithm (in terms of control flow and data flow), depending on input data provided. Something interesting has occurred here, which warrants an explanation, and will, thereby, demystify certain behaviors. Remember, everything ought to have an explanation (unless you are not in control, and have absolutely no idea how your code behaves)!

In case you are wondering why the serial implementation got cancelled, before it started, only once, it's primarily related to the work load in the machine and the precedence/sequence in which the tasks started being executed by the CLR thread pool. Also, the reason why the **Tasks Implementation – Cancelled** message comes only once is because `Console.WriteLine` blocks until the output has been written, as it calls the `Write` method of the underlying stream instance; the ones that don't get blocked appear on the console. You also need to ensure that the token cancellation detection code (`token.IsCancellationRequested`) is set at the required control flow points (forks, joins, and so on) to record near real-time cancellations, and throw `TaskCanceledException` via the `token.ThrowIfCancellationRequested` method (causing the task to transition to the faulted state). Please inspect the highlighted areas in the code to understand this.

The limitation that we noticed in terms of the missing console messages is something that we would need to overcome, as, capturing relevant information during program execution is an important horizontal concern, irrespective of the execution model (synchronous or asynchronous). Ideally, this activity should happen without impacting the normal execution flow, or causing any performance penalties (in terms of blocking calls). Asynchronous I/O is typically a standard option used by logging libraries to capture information (user and system-driven) behind the scenes. We have already dealt with the logging library in `Chapter 3`, *A Logging Library*, and now we will see how to channel data and invoke these libraries asynchronously in the next pattern.

Another relevant GoF pattern that could be leveraged here is the visitor pattern, where new strategic implementation of the algorithms could be declaratively tried out, without flooding consumers with concrete products.

Producer/consumer

This is a natural pattern that one can easily relate to from the moment you start modelling solutions for real-world problems. It is so intuitive that one may fail to appreciate the elegance of it, and yet many times we struggle with implementations associated with it.

A producer producing something which a consumer wants is a common scenario in software modelling. And this can even happen at multiple levels or stages in your data flow. This is a typical pipeline in design parlance, and warrants good synchronization between stages. A seamless interplay between the stages in a pipeline warrants a regulated handshake, where we don't let consumers starve, and at the same time, ensure they are not overfed. Throttling this handshake involves laying down a communication protocol (publish-subscribe model, queue-based, and so on), which requires some of the boiler-plate concurrency constructs (be it data structures or synchronization primitives) to be in place, as opposed to one wiring these on their own. We have concurrent data structure starting with .NET 4.0, including `BlockingCollection<T>`, `ConcurrentBag<T>`, `ConcurrentDictionary(TKey, TValue)`, `ConcurrentQueue<T>`, and `ConcurrentStack<T>`, which help us in this task by abstracting out the synchronization pain-points, and giving us just the adequate blocking features for a seamless integration of concurrent execution scenarios.

If you really look at our big-number multiplication algorithm, it involves a pipeline too, having three stages. The only thing is that our stages aren't concurrent, but serial (this is where, irrespective of the cores you have, you tend to reach the point of diminishing returns that Amdahl's law predicts). Additionally, our data structure (2D Array) gives non-blocking reads/writes for the concurrent producers within each stage.

The performance of a pipeline implementation is purely determined by the performance of its individual stages, and for efficiency, we need a concurrent model for each stage (which was achieved in our case).

Let's look at a producer-consumer model-based implementation for non-blocking or asynchronous logging in the case of speculative execution. We want this primarily to overcome the limitation of blocking, and console-based stream writes (in production you can leverage asynchronous I/O for file or db writes).

The code for the consumer is shown as follows:

```
/// <summary>
/// Adaptive Speculation for determining the best strategy
/// for your environment. Leveraging Task.WaitAny method
/// </summary>
/// <param name="args"></param>

public static void AdaptivePower (string[] args)
{
    var bigN1 = new BigNumber4();
    var bigN2 = new BigNumber5();
    var bigN3 = new BigNumber6();

    var val1 = "";
    var val2 = "";
    var val3 = "";

    var x = args[0];
    int y = Convert.ToInt32(args[1]);

    var tasks = new Task[3];
    var tokenSource = new CancellationTokenSource();
    var token = tokenSource.Token;
    BlockingCollection<string> log = new BlockingCollection<string>();
    Stopwatch watch;

    tasks[0] = Task.Factory.StartNew(() =>
    {
        watch = Stopwatch.StartNew();
        val1 = bigN1.Operations()
          .Power(x, y, token, log);

        Console.WriteLine("Elapsed Time for Serial " +
          "Computation of {0} ^ {1}: {2} seconds " +
            ">> {3}", x, y, watch.ElapsedMilliseconds / 1000D, val1);
    }, token);
```

```
    tasks[1] = Task.Factory.StartNew(() =>
    {
        watch = Stopwatch.StartNew();
        val2 = bigN2.Operations()
          .Power(x, y, token, log);

        Console.WriteLine("Elapsed Time for " +
          "Parallel.For Computation of " +
            "{0} ^ {1}: {2} seconds >> {3}", x, y,
              watch.ElapsedMilliseconds / 1000D, val2);
    }, token);

    tasks[2] = Task.Factory.StartNew(() =>
    {
        watch = Stopwatch.StartNew();
        val3 = bigN3.Operations()
          .Power(x, y, token, log);
        Console.WriteLine("Elapsed Time for Parallel " +
          "Task Computation of {0} ^ {1}: {2} " +
            "seconds >> {3}", x, y,
              watch.ElapsedMilliseconds / 1000D, val3);
    }, token);

    Console.WriteLine("Determining Fastest Algorithm "
      + "Implementation...");
    Task.WaitAny(tasks);     // Wait for fastest task to complete.
    tokenSource.Cancel();    // Cancel all the other slower tasks.
    try
    {
        Task.WaitAll(tasks);
    }
    catch (AggregateException ae)
    {
        ae.Flatten().Handle(e => e is OperationCanceledException);
    }
    finally
    {
        if (tokenSource != null)
            tokenSource.Dispose();
        foreach (string logItem in log)
        {
            Console.WriteLine(logItem);
        }
        Console.WriteLine("Adaptive Speculation Complete!!!");
    }
}
```

Here you can see that we are using a blocking collection to record logs. This needs to be passed as another parameter to the implementation, and, in turn, collects all the log information.

The following is an indicative code for the logger (handled in the respective concrete products):

```
// Concrete Product-4

public class BigNumOperations4 : BigNumOperations
{
  /// <summary>
  /// Serial Cancellable & Loggable Implementation of
  /// Schönhage-Strassen Algorithm
  /// <param name="x">String number Sequence-1</param>
  /// <param name="y">String number Sequence-2</param>
  /// <returns>String Equivalent Product Sequence</returns>
  /// </summary>

  public override string Multiply (string x, string y,
    CancellationToken ct, BlockingCollection<string> log)
  {
    if (ct.IsCancellationRequested == true)
    {
      log.Add("Serial Implementation Task was " +
      "cancelled before it got started!");
      ct.ThrowIfCancellationRequested();
    }
    //Use code from Concrete Product-1 here...
    //--------------------------Step-1

        for (int i = m - 1; i >= 0; i--)
        {
            //Use code from Concrete Product-1 here...

            for (int j = n - 1; j >= 0; j--)
            {
                if (ct.IsCancellationRequested)
                {
                    log.Add("Serial Implementation Step1 " +
                        "was cancelled!");
                    ct.ThrowIfCancellationRequested();
                }

                //Use code from Concrete Product-1 here...

            }
        }
```

```
                //--------------------------Step-2

        for (int j = prodDigits - 1; j >= 0; j--)
        {
            if (ct.IsCancellationRequested)
            {
                log.Add("Serial Implementation Step2 " +
                    "was cancelled!");
                ct.ThrowIfCancellationRequested();
            }

            //Use code from Concrete Product-1 here...
        }

        //--------------------------Step-3

        for (int i = (n + m - 2); i >= 0; i--)
        {
            if (ct.IsCancellationRequested)
            {
                log.Add("Serial Implementation Step3 " +
                    "was cancelled!");
                ct.ThrowIfCancellationRequested();
            }

            //Use code from Concrete Product-1 here...
        }
    }
}
```

So, we have seen some of the key patterns that play a major role in modelling concurrent tasks that could be run in parallel. Though the narration has been primarily based on a single example, we believe that, as a developer, you were able to understand the applicability of these in a real-world problem scenario. In terms of coverage, there is a lot one needs to learn and prototype. Exception handling is a chapter on its own, especially when dealing with concurrent scenarios, and that has been avoided for brevity. A sea of threads awaits you. Bon Voyage!

Summary

In this chapter, we just touched the surface of concurrent and parallel programming under .NET. The topic warrants a book dedicated for itself. Now you have enough background to learn about writing advanced software using features of the C# programming language, like LINQ, lambda, expression trees, extension methods, async/await, and so on. The next chapter will deal with the issue of better state management by leveraging these tools.

9
Functional Programming Techniques for Better State Management

While writing concurrent/parallel code, handling state is difficult in an imperative program (something that you would have seen by now). Modern languages and platforms borrow idioms and practices that enable better state management and facilitate strong concurrency models from the functional programming community. In this chapter, we will see what those are and try to understand, through code samples, how to best leverage some of those features (striving for coverage would stretch this chapter to an entire book) to our advantage. We would also see how C# has evolved as a language to bring the best of both worlds (imperative and functional), and to help you apply functional thinking to model real-world scenarios. This chapter will also cover **Language Integrated Query** (**LINQ**) as a mechanism for writing compositional code. Through this journey, we will uncover some good design practices, leveraging the functional constructs in the language (primarily C#). We hope this chapter serves as a starter kit by providing you with some of the techniques and tools to tackle programming tasks in a functional way. Some of the ideas covered include:

- Being functional
- Referential transparency
- First class functions (also higher order functions)
- Lambda calculus and anonymous functions
- Currying and partial function application
- A brief overview of how LINQ works

Being functional

Functional programming is a programming paradigm that involves algorithm composition, to be dealt on the same lines as mathematical function evaluations. This implies that the output of these functions would purely depend on the inputs provided. Moreover, any applicable data structures that the algorithm would need to create the output would be transient, having a lifetime within the function scope, and thus help in avoiding state mutation. It is also a powerful declarative programming paradigm, which involves leveraging expressions for readable code in place of procedural in-line statements.

Referential transparency

Let's delve a bit deeper to understand the consequences of being functional, as illustrated by the definitions given in the preceding section. Now, when we try to relate functions from both these worlds (mathematical and imperative programming), we see a strong disparity, as the latter mutates state with commands in the source language, thereby bringing in side effects (though desirable from an imperative programming standpoint). This violates one of the fundamental pre-requisites of functional programming – that of referential transparency, that is, the same expressions (when run at different times) yield different values with respect to the executing program's state. This affects the predictability of the program, which is definitely not desirable. On the other hand, pure functions (say f, one without such side effects) in the mathematical world would yield the same result $f(x)$ each time with the same value of x, say $sin(x)$. This characteristic is attributed to idempotency in software behavior (delivers consistency). Now you understand how this characteristic became so fundamental to functional programming.

Let's understand the consequence of this by looking at two functions: one which is referentially opaque (with side effects), and the other which is referentially transparent:

```
public class Counter
{
  private int i = 0;
  public int AddOneRO (int x) //Referentially Opaque
  {
    i += 1;
    return x + i;
  }
  public int AddOneRT (int x) //Referentially Transparent
  {
    return x + 1;
  }
}
```

The function `AddOneRT` is referentially transparent, which means that `AddOneRT (x) = AddOneRT (y)` if x = y. However, we can't say any such thing for `AddOneRO`, because it uses a global variable (`i`) that it modifies.

Now since `AddOneRO (x) <> AddOneRO (y)` if x = y, this further implies `AddOneRO (x) – AddOneRO (x) <> 0`, thus invalidating the fundamental mathematical identity (x – x = 0)!

This has major consequences in terms of code robustness and optimization by means of memorization (caching intermediate results), common subexpression elimination (where the result of a pure expression can be substituted in place of repeated evaluations without affecting the program behavior), lazy evaluation, or parallelization. So, in order to reap the benefits of these consequences from functional computation, one needs to strive to get the functions to be as referentially transparent (that is, free from the side effects of memory and I/O) as a mathematical function. With this, we come to the next important functional programming feature where functions become first-class citizens.

First-class and higher-order functions

Functions are the fundamental processing units in functional programming, and since they can be used like any other value, functions can be stored in variables, properties, objects, and collections. The term first-class function was created by Christopher Strachey.

Higher-order functions are functions that can either take other functions as arguments or return them as results.

C# supports higher-order functions (both named and anonymous), which are treated like ordinary variables with a function type.

Function type

C# provides the capability to define both generic functions and strongly typed delegates. The delegate type carries the method signature of a function prototype, and its instances become function pointers. Thus, you can manipulate a function variable whose function method signature matches with that of the function prototype.

In addition to generic function types, C# 2.0 introduced anonymous methods/delegates and iterators (with the `yield return` statement which lets you create iterator/continuation methods that return sequences based on the caller's demand/pull. That is, you get the benefit of deferred execution without incurring storage allocation overheads for the input and output sequences), which provided more flexibility and compositional capability. We can also use the following three generic function types that C# provides:

- A function that takes multiple type arguments, and returns result of a particular type:

  ```
  Func<T1, T2, . . . , Tn, TReturn>
  ```

- A procedure that takes multiple type arguments, and performs action/s without returning any result:

  ```
  Action<T1, T2, . . . , Tn>
  ```

- A function that takes multiple type arguments, and returns a Boolean result:

  ```
  Predicate<T1, T2, . . . , Tn>
  ```

You can see the preceding function types in action as follows:

```
public static IEnumerable<T> GenerateSequences<T> (
int noOfElements, Func<T> generator)
{
  for ( int i = 0; i < noOfElements; i++ )
  {
    yield return generator();
  }
}

public static IEnumerable<TSource> Where<TSource> (
IEnumerable<TSource> source, Predicate<TSource> predicate)
{
  foreach ( TSource element in source )
  {
    if ( predicate(element) )
      yield return element;
  }
}
```

A client using the anonymous delegate syntax would consume the preceding static methods as follows:

```
int startEven = -2;
int startOdd = -1;
int increment = 2;

//To Generate first 1000 even numbers
IEnumerable<int> evenSequences = GenerateSequences<int> (
  1000, () => startEven += increment);

//To Generate first 1000 odd numbers
IEnumerable<int> oddSequences = GenerateSequences<int> (
  1000, () => startOdd += increment);
```

 As you can see, this deferred execution model makes your algorithms use less storage space and compose better than traditional imperative methods. More importantly, with functional purity you'll be able to leverage parallelism by assigning different operations to different CPU cores, thereby improving throughput.

Now it's time to look at a core functional programming concept which was adopted in C# 3.0, that is, lambda expressions that facilitated wide adoption of functional programming practices (with little or no knowledge on it's consequences) in the imperative world.

Lambda (λ) calculus

λ-calculus is a mathematical formalism for denoting computation in an abstract form using functions. This brings forth a formal notation and transformation rules for representation (function abstraction) and manipulation (function application) of lambda terms. The key to this formalism is variable binding and substitution. **Alonzo Church** created lambda calculus in an attempt to prove mathematical logic.

The λ-calculus provides a simple semantics for computation using computable functions based on **Church-Turing** thesis (readers are urged to take a look at the history of lambda calculus, its motivation, and mathematical implications at a little deeper level to better appreciate this formalism and its consequences, as opposed to just being sheer consumers) by incorporating the following simplifications and concepts:

Anonymous functions

This involves treating functions as anonymous, without giving them explicit names. For example, take this simple `static` method:

```
public static int AddOperation (int x, int y)
{
   return x + y;
}
```

If you rewrite the preceding static method, the equivalent representation as an anonymous delegate would be what is highlighted in the following code:

```
Func<int, int, int> AddOperation = delegate(int x, int y)
{
   return x + y;
};
```

Now, the corresponding lambda expression would be the one highlighted in this code:

```
Func<int, int, int> AddOperation = (x, y) => x + y;
```

Another lambda expression that follows the same function signature, yet bringing in a polymorphic behavior, is as follows:

```
Func<string, string, string> ConcatOperation = (x, y) => x + y;
```

Now you can see the formal syntax that lambda expressions obey, as stated in the definitions given earlier, which denotes that variables x and y are bound to the lambda term $x + y$. You just witnessed the lambda abstraction for the function $f(x, y) = x + y$. The function definitions (`AddOperation` and `ConcatOperation`) with this lambda abstraction just sets up the function without invocation. An application in lambda calculus parlance, with respect to the preceding example, would signify applying inputs x and y to the function f.

Function application in lambda calculus is achieved through **beta reduction** (a continuous reduction process involving substitution of bound variables to the lambda terms till no applications remain for reduction). A function application in lambda calculus is analogous to method invocation in the imperative world, except that the consequences are totally different, which you would have understood by now.

Closures

As mentioned earlier, the key to formalism is variable binding and substitution. Bound variables are the ones that fall within the scope of an abstraction. The remaining variables are said to be free (from the context of that specific abstraction). A closed lambda expression is one with no free variables.

Something to note here is that a variable is bound by its nearest abstraction, which means that a free variable, with respect to an abstraction, would eventually be bound to higher abstractions in the hierarchy. And this free or unbound variable (with its associated references and values), which gets captured in the context of an abstraction (that is, the lexical Scope), constitutes a closure (again pertaining to that abstraction).

```
public static Func<int, Func<int, int>> sum =
x => y => x + y;
```

The preceding code clearly shows a closure in action. Here, the closure object (which constitutes of variable x and its target method) helps to share data between the functions. The use of this higher-order `sum` function (where new functions are composed and returned) is illustrated clearly in the following code snippet:

```
var add10 = sum(10); //Returns closure with 10
var add50 = sum(50); //Returns closure with 50

Console.WriteLine(add10(90));   //Returns 100
Console.WriteLine(add10(190));  //Returns 200
Console.WriteLine(add50(70));   //Returns 120
```

Currying and partial application

Partial application and currying are two distinct techniques, yet loosely depicted. It is facilitated by the capability of higher-order functions, wherein their partial application (against one or multiple arguments) returns new functions (that accept the remaining arguments) with lesser arity (compared to the original function).

Let's now understand the difference between currying and partial application.

 Currying is a natural consequence of lambda calculus, where functions employ only a single input. This technique primarily involves conversion of a function evaluation that accepts multiple arguments (as in any practical function) into a series of function evaluations that accept one argument at a time. Currying got its name from Haskell Curry, who developed it following the work of Gottlob Frege and Moses Schönfinkel.

Without much ado, let's see these in action.

Currying

Let's go back to our old example here:

```
public static int AddOperation (int x, int y)
{
    return x + y;
}
```

Now this is a simple and practical function we employ mostly. Let's see how this is deftly curried to generate functions that accept one argument at a time, and yet leverage the core function for function application:

```
public static Func<T1, Func<T2, TReturn>> Curry<T1, T2, TReturn>
(Func<T1, T2, TReturn> f)
{
    return a => b => f(a, b);
}
```

Any client would leverage the curried function this way:

```
var curriedSum = Curry<int, int, int>(AddOperation);

Console.WriteLine( "Sum: {0}", curriedSum(10)(90));
//Prints Sum: 100
```

There's another interesting way to curry functions; as a matter of fact, we can curry any arbitrary function using the function definition (delegate in our case). Here we leverage extension methods (a language feature introduced in version 3.0) to provide innate currying capability to a generic function definition: Func<T1, T2, TReturn>. This means you can apply currying to any function that has this method signature. See the following code:

```
public static Func<T1, Func<T2, TReturn>> Curry<T1, T2, TReturn>
(this Func<T1, T2, TReturn> f)
{
    return a => b => f(a, b);
}
```

The keyword this in the highlighted code enables the extension method magic for you (which essentially decorates the generic delegate type Func<T1, T2, TReturn) with the curry function. Voila! We finally have imparted innate currying capability to any function that conforms to this definition. Take a look at the following code:

```
Func<int, int, int> op = AddOperation;
var curriedSum = op.Curry<int, int, int>();

Console.WriteLine(
    "Sum: {0}",
    curriedSum1(10)(90)
);
//Prints Sum: 100
```

Now to replicate the same thing in the polymorphic function below:

```
public static string ConcatOperation (string x, string y)
{
    return x + y;
}

Func<string, string, string> op2 = ConcatOperation;
var curriedConcat = op2.Curry<string, string, string>();

Console.WriteLine(
    "Concatenation: {0}",
    curriedConcat("Currying ")("Rocks!!!")
);
//Prints "Concatenation: Currying Rocks!!!"
```

You could continue (as shown in the next code) to create more curry function overloads to support additional function definitions (that has more than two input parameters):

```
//Currying Extension Method that Supports 3 Input Parameters

public static Func<T1, Func<T2, Func<T3, TReturn>>>
Curry<T1, T2, T3, TReturn>
(this Func<T1, T2, T3, TReturn> f)
{
   return a => b => c => f(a, b, c);
}
// Currying Extension Method that Supports 4 Input Parameters

public static Func<T1, Func<T2, Func<T3, Func<T4, TReturn>>>>
   Curry<T1, T2, T3, T4, TReturn>
   (this Func<T1, T2, T3, T4, TReturn> f)
   {
      return a => b => c => d => f(a, b, c, d);
   }
```

Partial application

Now let's look at partial application which is distinctively different from currying, though highly confusing to many programmers.

Partial application (or partial function application) is yet another consequence of lambda calculus where functions employ a fixed set of inputs. This technique primarily involves conversion of a function evaluation that accepts multiple arguments (as in any practical function) into a function that accepts a fixed number of arguments, which in turn yields yet another function that accepts the remaining arguments.

The following code says it all:

```
public static string ConcatOperation(string a, string b, string c,
string d)
{
   return a + b + c + d;
}


//Partial Application in functions that have 3 Input Parameters
public static Func<T2, T3, TReturn>
PartialApply<T1, T2, T3, TReturn>
(this Func<T1, T2, T3, TReturn> f, T1 arg1)
{
   return (arg2, arg3) => f(arg1, arg2, arg3);
```

```
}

//Partial Application in functions that have 4 Input Parameters

public static Func<T2, T3, T4, TReturn>
PartialApply<T1, T2, T3, T4, TReturn>
(this Func<T1, T2, T3, T4, TReturn> f, T1 arg1)
{
   return (arg2, arg3, arg4) => f(arg1, arg2, arg3, arg4);
}

//Sample code that illustrates usage

Func<string, string, string, string, string> op3 = ConcatOperation;

var partiallyAppliedConcat = op3.
PartialApply<string, string, string, string, string>
("Partial ");
Console.WriteLine(
   "Concatenation: {0}",
   partiallyAppliedConcat(
      "Function ",
      "Application ",
      "Rocks!!!")
   );
//Prints "Concatenation: Partial Function Application Rocks!!!"
```

Applying currying and partial application

Let's see these two in action in a real programming scenario. The scenario we would look at is a classic mathematical conundrum – that of determining the Pythagorean Triples within a given range. As the name suggests, the Pythagorean triple constitutes the set of numbers that satisfy the Pythagorean theorem ($a^2 + b^2 = c^2$). The conventional method to find the triples is shown in the following code:

```
//The formula that confirms a Pythagorean Triplet

public static bool IsPythagoreanTriplet (int x, int y, int z)
{
   return (x * x + y * y) == (z * z);
}

//Function that generates the triples within a given range based
//on the above formula.

public static IEnumerable<IEnumerable<int>>
```

```
PythagoreanTriples (int range)
{
  Func<int, int, int, bool> formula = IsPythagoreanTriplet;
  HashSet<string> capturedTriplets = new HashSet<string>();

  for (int a = 1; a < range; a++)
  {
    for (int b = 1; b < range; b++)
    {
      for (int c = 1; c < range; c++)
      {
        if (formula(a, b, c))        //Direct Evaluation
        {
          string keyPart1 = a.ToString();
          string keyPart2 = b.ToString();
          //This check filters the duplicate triplets
          if (!capturedTriplets
          .Contains(keyPart1 + ":" + keyPart2)
          &&
          !capturedTriplets
          .Contains(keyPart2 + ":" + keyPart1)
          )
          {
            capturedTriplets
            .Add(keyPart1 + ":" + keyPart2);
            yield return new List<int>() { a, b, c };
          }
        }
      }
    }
  }
}
```

This preceding code continuously yields the triplets as and when it is discovered. Another interesting thing about the brute force approach here is that it returns duplicates (for example-[3, 4, 5] and [4, 3, 5], [6, 8, 10] and [8, 6, 10], and so on. The filter (highlighted code), in conjunction with the HashSet, helps eliminate these duplicates.

Now let's see the same code leveraging curried functions:

```
public static IEnumerable<IEnumerable<int>>
PythagoreanTriplesCurried (int range)
{
  Func<int, int, int, bool> formula = IsPythagoreanTriplet;
  var cFormula = formula.Curry<int, int, int, bool>();
  HashSet<string> capturedTriplets = new HashSet<string>();

  for (int a = 1; a < range; a++)
```

```
      {
        for (int b = 1; b < range; b++)
        {
          for (int c = 1; c < range; c++)
          {
            if (cFormula(a)(b)(c))      //Curried Evaluation
            {
              // Use same code from PythagoreanTriples function
            }
          }
        }
      }
    }
```

In this case the curried function is created, based on the formula that proves the Pythagorean theorem, which would accept a valid input for a, b, and c consecutively, and final evaluation is done when the last argument is received.

Now let's check out partial application usage in this same scenario:

```
    public static IEnumerable<IEnumerable<int>>
    PythagoreanTriplesPartiallyApplied (int range)
    {
      Func<int, int, int, bool> formula = IsPythagoreanTriplet;
      HashSet<string> capturedTriplets = new HashSet<string>();

      for (int a = 1; a < range; a++)
      {
        var paFormula = formula
        .PartialApply<int, int, int, bool>(a);
        for (int b = 1; b < range; b++)
        {
          for (int c = 1; c < range; c++)
          {
            //Final Evaluation with remaining arguments
            if (paFormula(b, c))
            {
              // Use same code from PythagoreanTriples function
            }
          }
        }
      }
    }
```

Now, you can clearly see the distinction between currying and partial application. The result yielded by partial application becomes a closure (gets captured) for reuse in place of function captures in the currying approach. This early evaluation (a^2 and b^2) in the case of partial application would give an advantage for reuse in subsequent iterations in place of repeated deferred evaluations with respect to currying. The real use of currying and partial application is seen when inputs are generated asynchronously for consumption by a grand computation function. You could capture or partially compute as and when these inputs are generated, and trigger the final evaluation on obtaining the last input. Another thing to note is that partial application can accept more than one arguments (unlike the example shown here where it accepts one as in currying). A typical consumer client would be as follows:

```
Console.WriteLine("PythagoreanTriples within 50....");

foreach (var triplets in PythagoreanTriplesPartiallyApplied(50))
{
    Console.WriteLine(string.Join(",", triplets.ToArray()));
}
Console.ReadLine();
```

So, we guess no more confusions on these two concepts from now on! Another adventure (if you're game; yes, we dare you) is to do the following:

- Optimize this algorithm (now you know there are *range3* iterations and the performance impact is huge when you go beyond the range of 1,000).
- Making the filter operation lazily evaluated as part of the LINQ consumer query which would yield duplicates (without the HashSet in the first place). And again, nothing actually stops you from figuring out a way to generate triplets without duplicates!
- Figure out a way to generate triples forever as they are detected (without the limitation of a range, loop, or any computation limits (such as reaching the max value for a 64-bit signed integer).

Expression trees

By now you have seen how to create delegates from a lambda expression (anonymous function). You can also opt to create expression tree types. Expression trees are analogous to **Abstract Syntax Tree (AST)** in the compiler construction realm, and they embody code in a tree data structure, where each node is represented as an expression. Using expression trees, you can compile and run code, thereby gaining powerful ability to dynamically modify executable code.

Expression trees are also used in the Dynamic Language Runtime (DLR) to provide interoperability between dynamic languages and the .NET Framework and to enable compiler writers to emit expression trees instead of Microsoft Intermediate language (MSIL).

- MSDN

Expression trees are inherently immutable. All that we need to get the compiler emit the code for an expression tree is to assign the lambda expression to a variable of type `Expression<TDelegate>`. The .NET framework provides a rich API (expression class under **System.Linq.Expressions Namespace**) for parsing, creation, and manipulation (of course recreating with appropriate tree visitors). The API supports most of the language grammar.

Altogether, this becomes a very powerful construct that can be leveraged for code/dependency injection, **Domain-Specific Language** (**DSL**) creation, and associated language translations (all you would need to do in such a case is to let your dynamic language lexer and parser to generate the **Abstract Syntax Tree** (**AST**), which in our case is the expression tree itself, and DLR would do the rest. Don't think twice before embarking on your next DSL adventure. There is inherent platform support!)You finally understand how a lambda expression (an anonymous function) can be used to create delegates or expression tree types. By using lambda expressions, you can write local functions that can be passed as arguments or returned as the value of function calls.

Recursion

Recursions are no alien feature to any programmer worth his salt. Recursions are leveraged in functional programming to accomplish iteration/looping. Recursive functions invoke themselves, performing an operation repeatedly till the base case is reached. Tail call-based recursions are a common phenomenon. Recursion typically involves adding stack frames to the call stack, thus growing the stack. You can run out of stack space during deep recursions. The compiler does its own share of optimizations (predominantly tail call optimization/elimination) to conserve stack space and improve throughput. But the functional world (with its first-class and higher-order functions) gives us more flexibility to wire such optimizations in our recursive functions. Let's see how this is achieved with the following factorial example:

```
//Regular Recursion

Func<int, int> factorial = (n) =>
{
    Func<int, int> fIterator = null; //Work-around for "use of
```

```
        unassigned variable" error!
    fIterator = (m) =>
        (m < 2) ? 1 : m * fIterator(m - 1);
    return fIterator(n);
};
```

Unlike the classical example, you see how recursion is put to work by lambda expressions as well, which makes you use these anonymous functions as higher order functions (where they are dynamically created or passed as arguments). You can also notice the use of a wrapper function (factorial in this case), which is directly called, but does not recurse itself, and instead, leverages an auxiliary function (fIterator in this case) to do the actual recursion.

> The wrapper function becomes handy for performing parameter validations, error handling, memorization, and so forth.

In order to conserve stack space, we can opt for a tail call elimination technique known as tail recursion as follows:

```
//Tail Call Elimination with Tail Recursion

Func<int, int> factorial = (n) =>
{
    Func<int, int, int> fIterator = null;
    fIterator = (product, i) =>
        (i < 2) ? product : fIterator(product * i, i - 1);
    return fIterator(1, n);
};
```

In this case, no state, except for the calling function's address, needs to be saved either on the stack or on the heap, and the call stack frame for fIterator is reused for storage of the intermediate results. Another thing to note is the addition of an accumulator argument (product in this case).

Tail recursion can be achieved by another technique called **trampolining**, where functions are called by a trampoline function as opposed to functions calling each other directly. All the needed payload (function pointer and arguments) for the function call is provided to the trampoline function, which then places the call on the caller's behalf. This ensures that the stack does not grow and iteration can continue indefinitely:

```
//Tail Recursion with Trampolining

Func<int, int> factorial = (n) =>
```

```
{
  Func<int, int, int> trampoline = null;
  Func<int, int, int> fIterator = (product, i) =>
    (i < 2) ? product : trampoline(product * i, i - 1);
  trampoline = (product, i) =>
    fIterator(product * i, i - 1);
  return trampoline(1, n);
};
```

The following image depicts the supporting language constructs that have evolved to make these functional programming features available for consumption:

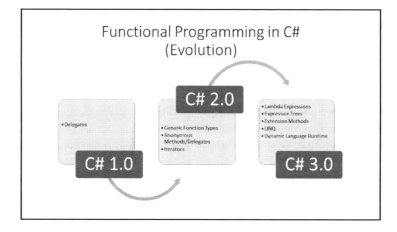

Sample programs

Now that we have taken a detailed look at the core functional programming constructs, it's time to indulge in power play (with code of course). Let's learn to play the game with some hardcore sample programs.

Spell checker

This was inspired by Peter Norvig's (former Research Director at Google) technical blog on *How to Write a Spelling Corrector*. What is interesting is the way the solution has been envisaged. The solution employs the probability theory at its core to find all possible corrections for a word of length n, by accounting for user errors in the form of typos arising because of omissions (deletes), characters misplaced (replaces and transposes), and inserted (inserts).

You can refer to this technical blog on *How to Write a Spelling Corrector* by Peter Norvig for the following:

> For a word of length *n*, there will be *n* deletions, *n-1* transpositions, *26n* replacements, and *26(n+1)* insertions.

To have fair shot at determining the corrections, we do find all possible corrections that are 1 (`edits1` function) and 2 (`edits2` function) distance away. You would be able to see the function compositions in the code given next using LINQ queries that yield these possible corrections in a breeze. This demonstrates the expressive and declarative power of lambda expressions.

What is most important, and to ensure the right filtering of this huge set (for meaningful corrections), is to determine what are the known or meaningful words. For this a dictionary is either fed or created (in our case) from a corpus of free text from Project Gutenberg, and lists of the most frequent words from Wiktionary and the British National Corpus. The text is extracted, concatenated, and provided in the text file `NSC_Training_Model.txt` (you could also directly obtain this from `http://norvig.com/big.txt`). The `known` function does this filtering for you.

Now, to determine the list of corrections in the order of recommendation, we employ the probability of occurrence of the known corrections in the dictionary created out of the corpus (as it becomes a good indication of common usage). Now you know how personalized spelling correctors work on your mobile device! (Yes, you guessed it right, it certainly is based on the probability of the list of possible corrections in the order of your usage of words).

The authors encourage the readers to visit the site (`http://norvig.com/spell-correct.html`), and take a look at the detailed explanation of the solution. One of the authors has his JavaScript implementation published on the site as well.

The function `NorvigSpellChecker` shown below returns a list of potential corrections based on the word and count (maximum items in list) specified:

```
public static IEnumerable<string> NorvigSpellChecker
(string word, int count)
{
  var alphabets = @"abcdefghijklmnopqrstuvwxyz";
  var WORDS = new ConcurrentDictionary<string, int>();
  var trainingFile = @"D:\Packt\Code\NSC_Training_Model.txt";
  //Training Model Creation
```

```
var Train = Task.Factory.StartNew(() =>
{
  foreach (var line in File
    .ReadLines(trainingFile)
    .AsParallel())      //Parallel read
  {
    foreach (Match match in
    Regex.Matches(
      line,
      @"([a-z]+)",       //Word detection
      RegexOptions.IgnoreCase
    )
    .AsParallel())
    {
      WORDS.AddOrUpdate(     //Add detected word to dictionary
        match.Value,
        0,
        (k, v) => v + 1);   //Increment word count
    }
  }
});

//All edits that are 1 edit away from word

Func<string, Task<IEnumerable<string>>> edits1 =
(tWord) => Task.Factory.StartNew(() =>
{
  return from i in Enumerable.Range(0, tWord.Length)
  select new
  {
    part1 = tWord.Substring(0, i),
    part2 = tWord.Substring(i)
  }; //splits
})
.ContinueWith(ant =>
{
  return (from splits in ant.Result
  where splits.part2 != ""
  select splits.part1 +
  splits.part2
  .Substring(1))                 //deletes
  .Union(from splits in ant.Result
  where splits.part2.Length > 1
  select splits.part1 +
  splits.part2[1] +
  splits.part2[0] +
  splits.part2
  .Substring(2))                 //transposes
```

[185]

```
    .Union(from splits in ant.Result
    from c in alphabets
    where splits.part2 != ""
    select splits.part1 + c + splits.part2.Substring(1)) //replaces
    .Union(from splits in ant.Result
    from c in alphabets
    select splits.part1 + c + splits.part2);          //inserts
});

//All edits that are 2 edits away from word

Func<string, Task<IEnumerable<string>>> edits2 =
(tWord) => Task.Factory.StartNew(() =>
{
  return (from e1 in edits1(tWord).Result
  from e2 in edits1(e1).Result
  where WORDS.ContainsKey(e2)
  select e2);
});

//Returns the subset of words that appear in the
//dictionary of WORDS

Func<IEnumerable<string>, Task<IEnumerable<string>>> known =
(tWords) => Task.Factory.StartNew(() =>
{
  return (from e1 in tWords
  where WORDS.ContainsKey(e1)
  select e1);
});

//Generate all possible spelling corrections for word

Func<string, Task<IEnumerable<string>>> candidates =
(tWord) => Task.Factory.StartNew(() =>
{
  List<string> tWords = new List<string>();
  tWords.Add(word);
  return ((from e1 in known(tWords).Result
  select e1)
  .Union(from e2
  in known(edits1(tWord).Result).Result
  select e2)
  .Union(from e3
  in known(edits2(tWord).Result).Result
  select e3)
  .Union(from e4
  in tWords
```

```
    select e4))
     .Distinct();
  });

  //Returns most probable spelling correction for word in the
  //order of their probability of occurrence in the corpus

  Func<string, Task<IEnumerable<string>>> corrections =
  (tWord) => Task.Factory.StartNew(() =>
  {
    var N = (from x in WORDS
    select x.Value)
    .Sum();
    List<string> tWords = new List<string>();
    return (from e1 in candidates(tWord).Result
      .OrderByDescending(
        e1 => WORDS.ContainsKey(e1) ?
        (float) WORDS[e1] / (float) N : 0)
        select e1)
    .Take(count);
  });
  Task.WaitAll(Train);            //Ensures Training Model is Created!
  return corrections(word).Result;
}
```

A declarative style of coding with lambda expressions has been employed fluidly in realizing this spell checker. You could see how the algorithm is composed using LINQ expressions. Closures, concurrency, and parallelism (in the form of PLINQ) has been employed in realizing this function. A typical consumer of this spell checker would be the following:

```
static void SpellCheckerClient ()
{
  var corrections = NorvigSpellChecker("somthing", 10);

  foreach (var correction in corrections)
  {
    Console.WriteLine(correction);
  }
  Console.WriteLine("Training Model Creation Complete! {0}",
  corrections.Count());
}
```

We urge interested developers to explore options to further parallelize the algorithm/steps, and see the results (at least from a performance standpoint). It would be a worthwhile journey to understand that the parallelization constructs at your disposal (especially PLINQ and TPL) are not mere silver bullets!

Subset generation

This problem has a classical implication on a variety of NP-complete problems that we are exposed to in daily life. The procedural and generic serial implementation is shown as follows:

```
public static IEnumerable<IEnumerable<T>>
Subsets<T> (IEnumerable<T> inputSet)
{
  T[] _input = inputSet.ToArray<T>();
  int _bitcount = _input.Length;
  int _mask = Convert.ToInt32(Math.Pow(2.0d, _bitcount));
  int i = 0;
  while (i < _mask)
  {
    List<T> _output = new List<T>();
    int j = 0;
    while (j < _bitcount)
    {
      if ((i & (1 << j)) > 0)
      {
        _output.Add(_input[j]);
      }
      j++;
    }
    yield return _output.ToArray<T>();
    i++;
  }
}
```

As you see, the preceding algorithm leverages Boolean logic to determine the unique sets. The possible *ON (1)* states of the gates determine the sets, and we just need to determine the index of the element in the array (that has the complete list of elements whose sets need to be determined) that yields a state of 1.

The declarative equivalent of the preceding implementation has been realized with PLINQ as follows:

```
string[] names = { "a", "b", "c", "d", "e", "f" };

var result = from i in Enumerable
.Range(0, Convert.ToInt32(Math.Pow(2.0d, names.Length)))
.AsParallel()
from j in Enumerable
.Range(0, names.Length)
.AsParallel()
let k = new
```

```
{
    a = i,
    b = names[j]
}
where ((i & (1 << j)) > 0)
orderby k.a
group k.b by k.a;
```

Now, to take this to the next level, since this has a limit (9,223,372,036,854,775,807 – max value for a 64-bit signed integer) on the _mask, that is, computing the total possible combinations, we would have to trade this algorithm for another which can continuously generate subsets, that too, forever. This is the power of deferred execution and continuation methods (supported by the `yield return` keyword). Let's see this algorithm (again optimized for some amount of parallelism which becomes significant for large set generation). This also employs Boolean logic but in a different way. It computes 1- bit addition forever, in this case using the full adder logic (as the resulting bits directly represent the set):

$$S = A \oplus B \oplus C_{in}$$

$$C_{out} = (A \cdot B) + (C_{in} \cdot (A \oplus B))$$

The parallelization done here is to chunk the binary additions for each `overFlow` (as the code indicates). For example, say there are three elements namely, 10, 20, and 30. The process of determining the sets (including chunking) would happen as follows:

Bits	Chunks	Resulting set
0 – 0 – 1	1	[30]
0 – 1 – 0	2	[20]
0 – 1 – 1	2	[20, 30]
1 – 0 – 0	3	[10]
1 – 0 – 1	3	[10, 30]
1 – 1 – 0	3	[10, 20]
1 – 1 – 1	3	[10, 20, 30]

The initial set of bit (*0-0-0*) which yields an empty set is ignored here. The overflows are indicated by the high-lighted rows, and the bits that shift are represented as bold. The throughput was observed to be ~three times faster than the serial implementation on a quad-Core computer! In case you're wondering why parallelization has been restricted to one level, the authors urge you to find out the effect of parallelizing/optimizing further. This is a NP-complete problem that would demand *2n* cores for the ultimate parallelization! It would be interesting to see how these sets could be applied for packing algorithms:

```
public static IEnumerable<IEnumerable<T>>
BigSubsetsP<T> (IEnumerable<T> inputSet)
{
  T[] _input = inputSet.ToArray<T>();
  BlockingCollection<IEnumerable<T>> output = new
  BlockingCollection<IEnumerable<T>>(boundedCapacity: 20);
  int _bitcount = _input.Length;
  BitArray bits = new BitArray(_bitcount);
  BitArray _bitsIncrement = new BitArray(_bitcount);
  _bitsIncrement.Set(0, true);

  //Stage#1 [GENERATE]

  var generate = Task.Factory.StartNew(() =>
  {
    try
    {
      Parallel.For(0, _bitcount,
      (chunkIndex) =>
      {
        BitArray _bits = new BitArray(_bitcount);
        bool overFlow = false;
        _bits.Set(chunkIndex, true);
        output.Add(new[] { _input[chunkIndex] });
        while (!overFlow)
        {
          List<T> _output = new List<T>();
          int j = 0;
          bool a;
          bool b;
          bool cIN = false;
          bool cOUT = false;
          bool bSUM = false;
          while (j <= chunkIndex) //Full-Adder Addition
          {
            a = _bits[j];
            b = _bitsIncrement[j];
            bSUM = a ^ b ^ cIN;
            cOUT = (a & b) | (cIN & (a ^ b));
```

```
            _bits.Set(j, bSUM);
            if (bSUM)
            {
              _output.Add(_input[j]);
            }
            cIN = cOUT;
            j++;
          }
          overFlow = cIN;
          if (_output.Count > 0)
          {
            output.Add(_output.ToArray<T>());
          }
          _output.Clear();
          _output = null;
        }
        _bits = null;
      });
    }
    finally
    {
      output.CompleteAdding();
    }
  });

  //Stage#2 [CONCURRENT READ]

  foreach (var subset in
  output.GetConsumingEnumerable().AsParallel())
  {
    yield return subset;
  }
  generate.Wait();
}
```

Just in case you are wondering how this could help in solving packing problems (of course with smaller sets), see this client given next, which generates the various ways in which the following packages (having weights 3, 1, 1, 2, 2, and 1 kg) could be packed in boxes that can accommodate 5 kg. We believe this opens up a window of possibilities for any interested developer:

```
static void GenerateBoxingCombinations ()
{
  Console.WriteLine("All possible packages:");
  var watch = Stopwatch.StartNew();
  var resultSet = from subset in
  Program4.BigSubsetsP<int>(
    new List<int>() { 3, 1, 1, 2, 2, 1 })
```

```
  .AsParallel()
  where subset.Sum() == 5
  select subset;
  foreach (var set in resultSet)
  {
    Console.WriteLine(
      "SET >> {0} :: SUM >> {1}",
      string.Join(",", set),
      set.Sum());
  }
  Console.WriteLine(
    "Elapsed Time for Package set Generation : {0} seconds",
    watch.ElapsedMilliseconds / 1000D);
}
```

How does LINQ work?

Before we conclude this chapter, we would like to give you a rough idea about how **Language Integrated Query** (**LINQ**) works under the hood, in a schematic manner. As we know, LINQ is a declarative language embedded inside a multi-paradigm language. The primary advantage of LINQ is the alignment to the rich type system of C#. Syntactically, LINQ is very similar to SQL language and the evaluation model is very similar to an SQL engine. As an example, let us explore a LINQ query which retrieves information regarding a set of employees by querying `Employee` and `Department` table. The query returns an anonymous type consisting of employee name, department name and location of the employee. We are using the comprehension syntax in this particular example:

```
var empInfo = from emp in db.Employee
join dept in db.Department
on emp.deptid equals dept.nid
select new
{
  emp.Name,
  dept.Name,
  emp.Location
};
```

While evaluating this LINQ statement, even though documentation states about outer sequence and inner sequence, schematically speaking, a cartesian product (aka cross join in database parlance) will be performed between `Employee` and `Department` table. The resulting data set will be filtered based on the join clause (on `emp.deptid` equals `dept.nid`), resulting in yet another data set.

Then, a project operation will be performed (`select new { <data> }`) to create an instance of new anonymous type, to add into a collection. The anonymous type will be synthesized by the C# compiler during the compile time. The above example uses comprehension style syntax and it will be transformed into a lambda expression syntax by the C# compiler, before generating the code. When we evaluate comprehension queries or mixed mode queries, the C# compiler transforms everything to lambda syntax before generating the code. The core algorithm for evaluation of LINQ queries are:

- Cartesian product (of data sets involved)
- Restrict or filter (where predicate)
- Order by
- Group operations
- Projection (technical name for selecting subsets of fields, in a result)

To understand more about the query evaluation process, one can consult a book which deals with relational database theory, as this topics warrants another book! The LINQ was introduced with C# with version 3.0 of the language and the designers of language introduced the following features to the language to facilitate the implementation of LINQ. They are:

- **Lambda expressions and functions**: To facilitate the passing of predicates and transformations as parameters to LINQ operator functions
- **Extension methods**: To avoid the syntactic clutter while nesting LINQ operators (transformation of nested queries to fluent interface style)
- **Anonymous types**: To allow developers to project the contents of a data set to types which are not declared ahead of time by the developers
- **Type inference**: This feature was mandated because of the difficulty for programmers to identify the type of result from a LINQ operations

Try to understand in detail what has been covered in this section. If you are able to comprehend what has been dealt here tersely, it can help improve the competence as a developer.

Summary

Functional programming model and its idioms help a programmer to write better code in the many-core architecture of the modern CPUs. C# programming language and the .NET platform has incorporated FP constructs into the language to help write certain kind of code in a functional manner. The mastery of lambda expressions and functions, type inference, expression trees, LINQ, and so on helps structure our code better if used judiciously by mixing the OOP and FP codes. Mixing of OOP and FP to write code is termed as object/functional programming, and most modern day languages like C#, Scala, Java (after version 8), Ruby, and so on support this idiom. In the next chapter, we will implement some GoF design patterns using object/functional programming, and also pick up some OOP/FP programming idioms such as map/reduce.

10
Pattern Implementation Using Object/Functional Programming

Most modern programming languages (partially or completely) support **Functional Programming** (**FP**) constructs these days. As outlined in the previous chapters, the advent of many-core computing is a factor in this progressive evolution. In some cases, we can encode a solution using OOP, and there can be a functional version of the solution as well. The most pragmatic use of the FP constructs can be undertaken by judiciously mixing them with OOP code. This is also called object/functional programming, and is becoming a dominant paradigm in languages such as F#, Scala, Ruby, and so on. The C# programming language is not an exception. There are instances where programmers abuse FP constructs to make themselves appear modern, often resulting in unreadable code. Programming being a social activity (in addition to its intellectual appeal), the readability of code is as important as its elegance and performance. In this chapter, we will take a closer look at this popular paradigm by applying it in the context of GoF patterns.

We will cover the following topics in this chapter:

- A strategy pattern implementation using FP/OOP
- A fresh look at the iterator pattern using FP/OOP
- MapReduce programming idiom
- A new spin on the template method pattern using FP/OOP

A strategy pattern implementation using FP/OOP

To focus on the programming model aspect, let us write a bubble sort routine to sort an array of the int, double, or float types. In a sort routine, we need to compare adjacent elements to decide whether one should swap the position of the elements. In computer science literature, this is called a **comparator**. Since we are using generic programming techniques, we can write a generic comparator interface to model the comparison action that would need to be performed while sorting is happening, and we will apply the strategy pattern to provide comparators based on types.

```
interface IComparatorStrategy<T>
{ int Execute(T a, T b); }
```

Even though we can use a single generic implementation for comparing elements, in real life we might need concrete classes that are specific to the types. We will implement two concrete classes for the comparison of integers and doubles.

```
class IntComparator : IComparatorStrategy<int> {
  public int Execute(int a, int b) {
    return a > b ? 1 : (b > a ) ? -1 : 0;
  }
}

class DoubleComparator : IComparatorStrategy<double> {
  public int Execute(double a, double b){
    return a > b ? 1 : (b > a) ? -1 : 0;
  }
}
```

Armed with the comparison classes, we can write a generic sort routine by parameterizing the comparison classes, as follows:

```
private static void BSort<T>(this T[] arr,
IComparatorStrategy<T> test) where T : struct
{
  int n = arr.Length;
  for(int i = 0; i<n; ++i)
  for (int j = 0; j < n-i-1; j++)
  if (test.Execute(arr[j],arr[j + 1]) > 0){
    T temp = arr[j]; arr[j] = arr[j + 1];
    arr[j + 1] = temp;
  }
}
```

The following code snippets show how the bubble sort routine can be invoked for sorting integers:

```
int [] s= {  -19,20,41, 23, -6};
s.BSort(new IntComparator());
foreach( var n in s )
Console.WriteLine(n);
```

The equivalent version for sorting doubles is given next:

```
double[] s2 = { -19.3, 20.5, 41.0, 23.6, -6.0 };
s2.BSort(new DoubleComparator());
foreach (var n in s2)
Console.WriteLine(n);
```

The OOP version of the code is simple and intuitive. But we need to resort to interface declaration and its implementation to write our code.

In most cases, the comparison logic can be given at the call site, using lambda.

Using FP constructs to make the code better

Lambda functions can be used to write a comparison strategy routine in a much terser and intuitive manner. We can leverage the C# function type `Func<TIn, TResult>` construct to do this. Let's rewrite the sort routine to leverage this idiom. We could also impart this sort capability to the array types using extension methods.

```
private static void BSort2<T>(this T[] arr,
Func<T,T,int> test) where T : struct
{
  int n = arr.Length;
  for (int i = 0; i < n; ++i)
  for (int j = 0; j < n - i - 1; j++)
  if (test(arr[j], arr[j + 1]) > 0) {
    T temp = arr[j]; arr[j] = arr[j + 1];
    arr[j + 1] = temp;
  }
}
```

We can invoke the routine by explicitly defining a `Func<T1, T2, TReturn>` method to do the comparison. The following code snippet demonstrates this method:

```
int[] s3 = { -19, 20, 41, 23, -6 };
Func<int ,int ,int> fn = (int a, int b ) => {
  return (a > b) ? 1 : -1;
};
s3.BSort2(fn);
foreach (var n in s3)
Console.WriteLine(n);
```

We can also invoke the routine by writing a call site lambda, as follows:

```
s3.BSort2( (int a, int b ) =>  (a > b ) ? 1 : -1);
```

If you want to sort a double array, the following code snippet will do the trick:

```
s4.BSort2( (double  a, double  b ) =>  (a > b ) ? 1 : -1);
```

The strategy routine, implemented as lambda expressions, made the code much terse and readable as well.

A fresh look at the iterator pattern using FP/OOP

The C# programming language has built-in support for the iterator pattern using the `foreach` loop construct. Any programmer worth his salt might have written code to iterate over a collection and apply some kind of transformation. To get things in perspective, let's globally write some code to compute the arithmetic mean (average) of a set of numbers.

```
double[] arr = { 2, 4, 4, 4 ,5, 5, 7, 9};
List<double> arrlist = arr.ToList();
double nsum = 0;
foreach (var n in arr) {
  nsum += n;
}
double avg = nsum / arrlist.Count;
Console.WriteLine(avg);
```

The preceding imperative code does the job really well, and it is quite readable. Let us explore whether we can improve the situation further. If you take a closer look, the code iterates through a collection, and applies some logic which is context-dependent. If we want to calculate the product of numbers, we need to write the same code by slightly changing the operation. While computing the geometric mean, we compute the product of the numbers. To parametrize the computation, we will use a lambda expression or function.

Let us write an aggregator function, which will iterate through an array of numbers and perform an operation we specify at the call site. We will use the function to compute the arithmetic sum (called **sigma**) or the multiplicative sum (called **PI**) by passing the transformer function as a parameter:

```
private static double Aggregate( double [] p ,
double init,Func<double,double,double> fn)
{
  double temp = init;
  foreach (var n in p)
  temp =   fn(n,temp);
  return temp;
}
```

Let us see how we can write the arithmetic mean function using our aggregator function. The following code uses a lambda expression to specify the computation:

```
private static double AMEAN(double[] p)
{
  return Aggregate(p, 0, (double a, double b) =>
  { return b += a; }) / p.Length;
}
```

The geometric mean can be computed in the following way (for brevity, we have ignored robustness concerns such as the presence of a zero, empty, or null array):

```
private static double GMEAN(double[] p)
{
  double pi = Aggregate(p, 1,
  (double a, double accum) => { return accum *= a; });
  return Math.Exp(Math.Log(pi)*(1 / p.Length));
}
```

To put everything together, we will write a standard deviation (STD) method to compute the standard deviation of the elements in an array:

```
private static double STD(double[] p)
{
  double avg = Aggregate(p, 0,(double a, double b) =>
  { return b += a; }) / p.Length;
```

```
        double var = Aggregate(p, 0, (double a, double b) =>
        { return b += ((a - avg)*(a-avg)); }) / p.Length;
        return Math.Sqrt(var);
    }
```

The STD method takes the average of the list of numbers as a first step, and uses the value (avg) to compute the variance. For variance computation, the average is subtracted from each number and squared to make the resulting value positive, before accumulating it to a running sum (b) variable. Finally, the square root function is invoked to compute the standard deviation. The resulting code is readable, and can be used as a basis for other transformations on the list.

MapReduce programming idiom

In the FP world, **MapReduce** is considered as a programming idiom.

 The process of mapping can be described as the application of a function or computation on each element of a sequence to produce a new sequence. Reduction gathers computed elements to produce the result of a process, algorithm, or a functional transformation.

In 2003, two Google engineers (Sanjay Ghemawat and Jeff Dean) published a paper about how the company used the MapReduce programming model to simplify their distributed programming tasks. The paper entitled *MapReduce: Simplified Data Processing on Large Clusters* is available on the public domain. This particular paper was very influential, and the Hadoop distributed programming model was based on the ideas outlined in the paper. You can search the Internet to find the details of the paper and the origin of the Hadoop data operating system.

To reduce the complexity, we are going to implement a MapReduce function to apply the computation on an array of doubles. The following Map function applies a lambda on each element of the array, and returns another array; this actually transforms the original array without mutating it. For large arrays, in order to speed up the operation, we can leverage the Parallel.For construct in the code.

```
public static double [] Map( double [] src,
Func<double,double> fnapply)
{
    double[] ret = new double[src.Length];
    Parallel.For(0,ret.Length,
    new ParallelOptions {
        MaxDegreeOfParallelism =Environment.ProcessorCount },
        (i) => { ret[i] = fnapply(src[i]);
```

```
    });
    return ret;
}
```

The MapReduce model can also be considered as the scatter/gather model of computation. In the last example, we leveraged parallel programming techniques to scatter the computation into different tasks, which would be scheduled in different threads. This way, computation for large arrays can be made faster. In the distributed version scenario, we scatter the computation to different machines. In the reduce scenario, we accumulate or aggregate the result of computation that occurred at the map stage. The following code shows the use of a serial operation in aggregating the value to an accumulator:

```
public static double Reduce( double[] arr,
Func<double,double,double> reducer,double init)
{
    double accum = init;
    for(int i=0; i< arr.Length; ++i)
    accum = reducer(arr[i], accum);
    return accum;
}
```

The preceding two functions can be used to compute standard deviation as follows:

```
double[] arr = { 2, 4, 4, 4 ,5,5,7,9};
double avg = Reduce( Map(arr,(double a) => {return a;}),
(double a, double b) =>
{return b +=a;},0)/arr.Length;
double var = Reduce(Map(arr, (double a) =>
{return (a-avg)*(a-avg); }),
(double a, double b) =>
{return b += a; }, 1) / arr.Length;
Console.WriteLine(Math.Sqrt(var));
```

For the time being, we are parking our discussion on the MapReduce programming model. It is a very vast topic, at least in the context of distributed computing environments. The Microsoft Azure platform offers a MapReduce implementation as part of its services. To be a modern developer, one should understand the MapReduce programming model and its stream processing counterparts available as part of various offerings.

A new spin on the template method pattern using FP/OOP

In this section, we will demonstrate how the template method pattern can be implemented using imperative programming techniques, and we will refactor the code to write an FP one. As a concrete example, we plan to use the computation of **Internal rate of return** (IRR) as a running example.

To focus on the essentials, let us quickly hack an engine to compute the IRR, given a series of payments (List<double>), the rate, and the period. As a first step, we need to compute the present value of a series of payments by using the technique of discounting. The following routine computes the present value of the series of payments:

```
public static double CashFlowPVDiscreteAnnual(
List<double> arr, double rate, double period)
{
  int len = arr.Count;
  double PV = 0.0;
  for (int i = 0; i < len; ++i)
  PV += arr[i] / Math.Pow((1+rate/100), i);
  return PV;
}
```

 The definition of IRR goes as follows:

An IRR is a computation that maps a series of payments that are supposed to accrue to the present value by finding the rate at which the series of payments has to be discounted to make the future value equivalent to the present value.

The following routine has been ported from the book, *Financial Numerical Recipes in C++*, Bernt Arne Odegard. For details, one can consult section 3.2.1 (material on IRR) of the book available on the Internet.

```
public static double CashFlow_IRR_Annual(List<double> arr,
double rate,double period)
{
  const double ACCURACY = 1.0e-5;
  const int MAX_ITERATIONS = 50;
  const double ERROR = -1e30;
  double x1 = 0.0;
  double x2 = 20.0;
  // create an initial bracket,
  // with a root somewhere between bot,top
  double f1 = CashFlowPVDiscreteAnnual(arr,x1,period);
```

```
double f2 = CashFlowPVDiscreteAnnual(arr,x2,period);

for (int j = 0; j < MAX_ITERATIONS; ++j)
{
  if ( (f1*f2) < 0.0)  {break; }

  if (Math.Abs(f1) < Math.Abs(f2))
    f1 = CashFlowPVDiscreteAnnual(arr,
    x1+= 1.06*(x1-x2),period );
  else
    f2 = CashFlowPVDiscreteAnnual(arr,
    x2+=1.06*(x2-x1),period);
  if (f2*f1>0.0)
    return ERROR;
}
double f = CashFlowPVDiscreteAnnual(arr,x1,period);
double rtb;
double dx=0;
if (f<0.0) {
  rtb = x1;dx=x2-x1;
}
else {
  rtb = x2; dx = x1-x2;
}
for (int i=0;i<MAX_ITERATIONS;i++)
{
  dx *= 0.5;
  double x_mid = rtb+dx;
  double f_mid = CashFlowPVDiscreteAnnual(arr,x_mid,period);
  if (f_mid<=0.0) { rtb = x_mid; }
  if ( (Math.Abs(f_mid)<ACCURACY) ||
  (Math.Abs(dx)<ACCURACY) )
  return x_mid;
}
return ERROR; // error.
}
```

With the routine under our belt, we can create an IRR calculation class that will use the template method pattern to receive the input for the computation of IRR, based on the series of future payments.

Let us create a class for the purpose of specifying inputs to the IRR computation sub system:

```
public class IRR_PARAMS
{
  public List<double> revenue { get; set; }
  public double rate { get; set; }
  public double period { get; set; }
```

```
    }
```

In the template method pattern implementation, we define an `abstract` base class, which does the bulk of the computation, and an `abstract` method, which the concrete class has to override to create an object out of it:

```
public abstract class IRRComputationEngine
{
  public abstract IRR_PARAMS Compute();
  public double Evaluate()
  {
    IRR_PARAMS par = Compute();
    if (par == null) return -1;
    return CashFlow_IRR_Annual(par.revenue,
    par.rate, par.period);
  }
  private static double CashFlow_IRR_Annual(
  List<double> arr,double rate,double period)
  { //----- Code Omitted }
}
}
```

Since the compute method is flagged as abstract, we cannot instantiate an object. The main thing which we can do is override the class and provide the content of the `abstract` method.

```
public class BridgeIRR :IRRComputationEngine {
  IRR_PARAMS ps = new IRR_PARAMS();
  public BridgeIRR(List<double> rev, double period, double rate){
    ps.period = period; ps.rate = rate; ps.revenue = rev;
  }
  public override IRR_PARAMS Compute() { return ps;}
}
```

We can use the preceding class as follows:

```
double[] ns = { 10, 12, 13, 14, 20 };
BridgeIRR test = new BridgeIRR(ns.ToList(),10,5);
double irr = test.Evaluate();
Console.WriteLine(irr);
```

Using FP for the template method pattern implementation

We will use lambda functions to simplify the template method pattern implementation. Instead of overriding a method after sub-classing the abstract class, we will use anonymous delegates to achieve the same objective. The resulting code, given next, is very simple and easy to understand:

```
public class IRRComputationEngine2
{
  public delegate IRR_PARAMS Compute();
  public Compute comp{get;set;}

  public double Evaluate()
  {
    if (comp == null) return -1;
    IRR_PARAMS par = comp();
    return CashFlow_IRR_Annual(par.revenue,
    par.rate, par.period);
  }
  private static double CashFlow_IRR_Annual(
    List<double> arr,double rate,double period)
  { //--- Code Omitted }
}
```

The class can be leveraged as follows:

```
IRRComputationEngine2 n = new IRRComputationEngine2();
double[] ns = { 10, 12, 13, 14, 20 };
n.comp = () => {
  IRR_PARAMS par = new IRR_PARAMS();
  par.revenue = ns.ToList();
  par.rate = 10; par.period = 5;
  return par;
};
double r = n.Evaluate();
Console.WriteLine(r);
```

A quick note on the observer pattern

The functional programming model is well suited for implementing the observer pattern. Microsoft Corporation has already created a library, christened Rx, to exploit this synergy. This library implements a subset of features that falls under the category of compositional event streams. We will be covering the relationship between the observer pattern and functional programming from the next chapter onwards.

Does FP replace GoF patterns?

There is a notion among some programmers that functional programming can help to keep us away from GoF patterns. As far as the authors of this book are concerned, it is bit of an overstatement. In this chapter, we have already seen how GoF implementations can be made simple and better using functional language idioms. But the examples in this book are mostly written using C#. If we are using F# or Haskell, there are techniques available, in the rich type system of those languages, to do away with some of the GoF patterns.

Two examples are:

- Partial function applications have made the builder pattern unnecessary for FP programming languages
- Functional pattern matching helps us to eliminate the visitor pattern

If you take a closer look at the scheme of things, the GoF pattern was a solution for the static and rigid type system of C++. After that, languages such as Java node C#, on reflection, came to the fore to simplify the implementation of GoF patterns. The FP can be treated as yet another enhancement. A dynamic language with FP support can help us implement GoF patterns better, or sometimes completely do away with patterns. But, completely replacing GoF patterns is bit of a shot in the dark!

Summary

In this chapter, you saw how imperative code (aka OOP code) can be mixed with FP constructs to write implementations of some of the GoF design patterns. Some functional programmers say that the GoF design patterns were conceived as a mechanism to overcome the limitations of an OOP in general (C++ in particular). If a language supports good FP constructs, most pattern implementations are unnecessary. According to our understanding, this view is a bit extreme and a middle path between FP and OOP seems to be a better option. In the coming days, FP idioms will become more and more popular and the progress will be a smooth transition. In the next chapter, we will delve into the nuances of functional reactive programming techniques. This is a very important paradigm where FP and events come together to provide us with frameworks such as .NET **Reactive Extensions** (**Rx**).

11
What is Reactive Programming?

By now we have seen how parallel and functional programming constructs in the .NET world help one naturally compose algorithms/business logic and model programs/data flows. These paradigms help realize a software system that has close correlation with the real world in which they exist. We have seen relevance of data structures and their role in program composition. We also saw the benefits (in terms of concurrency and parallelism) of keeping the data structures (modeled in an object-oriented way) different from the algorithms (modelled as pure function compositions) that consume them. To take this one knot further, in order to keep up with growing system complexity, there's a growing software revolution called **reactive programming**, which defines how to model applications from a behavior stand-point. In this chapter, we will try to unravel the concept through some examples, and understand how this programming paradigm becomes a natural succession, but more importantly, a unifying model for creating responsive systems. We will look at the various reactive programming constructs (including key data structures, interfaces, and operators) available in .NET **Reactive Extensions** (**Rx**). By the end of the chapter, you will understand how natural it is to model responsiveness, which becomes quite relevant in this new world of multicore, cloud, mobile, and web-scale systems.

Being reactive

To start with, let's look at the classic definition of reactive programming, and try to understand the concept brought forth by this model. This is important to undo any misconceptions that govern one's mind on this topic.

> *In computing, reactive programming is a programming paradigm that maintains a continuous interaction with their environment, but at a speed which is determined by the environment, not the program itself.*
>
> *- Gèrard Berry*

This implies that this programming model helps, or rather, has an inherent capability to propagate changes without the programmer having to explicitly wire any such logic (the conventional way, which was error prone and rendered programs inconsistent; a nightmare that still haunts some of us). This would mean that the programming model would be declarative and provide the needed constructs (including data structures and interfaces) to capture the relationship between attributes in order to ensure seamless propagation or synchronization of changes through data flows.

 The design pattern that really powers this model is observer, where the relationships between subscribers and publishers are declaratively modeled.

Let's try to understand this further via this example. In typical assignment statements (in the imperative world), relations are implicitly declared (say $c^2 = a^2 + b^2$, the Pythagorean equation that symbolizes the Pythagorean theorem), or functions (in the functional programming world) are defined explicitly, say $c = Compute\ Hypotenuse(a, b)$. On the other hand, in the reactive world, computation (value of c) is automatically done with new values of the sides (a and b). The computation is automatically triggered every time the value changes for a and b in the relation $c^2 = a^2 + b^2$. This behavior is termed as **reactive**. You could say that this is similar to event-driven programming, but there is a very distinct difference here that you need to understand.

This behavior is extremely important to model concurrent real-world systems including real-time analytics, control systems with feedback loops, electronic circuits and **printed circuit board** (PCB) design, rule engine, state machines, simulators, and so on.

Electronic spread sheets – A quintessential example

Electronic spreadsheets such as Excel software help one to input values in Cells, in a program-specific manner (for example-*A7* , *B6*, and so on). They also allow you to embed computation as a value of a cell (such as =*$A7*$B6*) using formulas. Whenever a value is changed in *A7* or *B6*, the resulting formula will be recomputed. Actually, the change is propagated to cells where there is reference to the cell which changed. This can be called a type of reactive computation. Let's see our Pythagorean triple generation in action on Excel:

	A	B	C	F
1	**a**	**b**	**c**	**Yes/No**
2	3	4	5	✓
3	3	4	4	✗
4	3	3	5	✗
5	5	12	13	✓
6	8	15	17	✓
7	7	8	9	✗
8	7	24	25	✓
9	20	21	29	✓
10	12	35	37	✓
11	23	24	25	✗
12	27	28	29	✗
13				
14				

In the preceding table, you can see that column **F** indicates (achieved with conditional formatting using icon sets) whether **a**, **b,** and **c** are Pythagorean triples or not.

The hidden columns **D** and **F** compute the values of ($a^2 + b^2$) and c^2 independently, and column F just checks for an equality in order to display a potential match. All these are done, of course, using formulas, and the changes across cells are propagated automatically.

The following screenshot illustrates this:

This example should give you an idea of how reactive programming works, and more interestingly, we will use this trivial example to illustrate a deep consequence beyond reactive programming. This spreadsheet program elegantly models the **Model-View-ViewModel** (**MVVM**) pattern, an architectural pattern heavily employed in WPF, Silverlight, and now, most of the prevalent HTML UI frameworks (JS-based). The Model in this case would be columns **A** and **B** (consider each row as entities and the columns as entity attributes). The View Model would be columns **D** and **E** (derived attributes from the model attributes). And column **F** would be the View which is bound to the View Model (and any change in View Model would be synchronized with the View; as a matter of fact, any changes in the Model would be propagated to the View Model and further down to the View).

Reactive programming model

Simply put, reactive programming is nothing but programming with asynchronous data streams. By applying various operations on stream, we can achieve different computational goals. The primary task in a reactive program is to convert the data into streams, regardless of what the source of the data is. While writing modern graphical user interface applications, we process mouse move-and-click events. Currently, most systems get a callback, and process these events as and when they happen. Most of the time, the handler does a series of filtering operations before it invokes the action methods associated with the event calls.

In this particular context, reactive programming helps us in aggregating the mouse move-and-click events into a collection, and sets filters on them before notifying the handler logic. In this way, the application/handler logic does not get executed unnecessarily.

Stream-processing model is well known, and it is very easy to encode by application developers. Pretty much anything can be converted into a stream. Such candidates include messages, logs, properties, twitter feeds, blog posts, RSS feeds, and so on. Functional programming techniques are really good at processing streams. A language like C#, with its inherent support for functional programming idioms, becomes a natural choice for writing reactive programs.

The basic idea behind reactive programming is that there are certain datatypes that represent a value over time. These datatypes (or rather data sequences) are represented as observable sequences in this programming paradigm. Computations that involve these changing (time dependent) values will, in turn, themselves have values that change over time, and would need to asynchronously receive notifications (as and when the dependent data changes). Remember the spreadsheet application discussed earlier?

Functional reactive programming

Most modern programming languages support functional programming constructs. Functional programming constructs such as Map/Reduce, Filter, Fold, and so on are good for processing streams. Programming asynchronous data streams using functional programming constructs is called functional reactive programming. This is gaining more traction among the developers these days.

The FRP programs can be classified as **push-based** and **pull-based**. The pull-based system waits for a demand to push the data streams to the requestor (or subscriber in our case). This is the classic case where the data source is actively polled for more information. This employs the iterator pattern, and `IEnumerable <T>/IEnumerator <T>` interfaces are specifically designed for such scenarios that are synchronous in nature (application can block while pulling data). On the other hand, a push-based system aggregates the events and pushes through a signal network to achieve the computation. In this case, unlike the pull-based system, data and related updates are handed to the subscriber from the source (observable sequences in this case). This asynchronous nature is achieved by not blocking the subscriber, but rather making it react to the changes. The observer pattern is put to extensive use here using the `IObservable <T>` and `IObserver<T>` interfaces (which have been introduced as part of .NET framework 4.0). As you can see, employing this push pattern is more beneficial in rich UI environments where you wouldn't want to block the main UI thread while waiting for some events. This becomes ideal, thus making reactive programs responsive.

Reactive programming principles

Reactive systems are composed of small subsystems, which have got reactive properties at the subsystems level. This is possible, because reactive applications apply sound design principles to maintain the responsiveness of their constituents.

According to the reactive manifesto, the following are the four principles of reactive programming:

- **Responsiveness**: A reactive system is supposed to respond to events in a time-bound manner. This helps in usability and utilizability of the systems. Responsive systems help us to detect anomalies very early, and can maintain good **Quality of Service (QoS)**. This is very important for systems that have **service level agreement (SLA)** and **operations level agreement (OLA)**.
- **Resilience**: Reactive systems should stay responsive even in the case of a system failure. Failures are contained in each component by careful isolation of subsystems, and making sure that failure does not get propagated to other parts. By good modularization, we can recover from failure by replacing components that fail without affecting the other modules of the system.
- **Elasticity**: Reactive systems should stay responsive under varying levels of stress due to the workloads. By effective throttling of event streams and dynamic resource management, we can write systems that can handle varying workloads.
- **Message driven**: Reactive systems rely on asynchronous messaging-based programming models to establish strict boundaries between components by maintaining loose coupling and location transparency (in the case of distributed systems). Employing explicit message-passing helps to manage load better, and to provide elasticity and explicit flow control through throttling. Non-blocking communication between components makes sure that resource management is done diligently. Moreover, system failures can be propagated as messages.

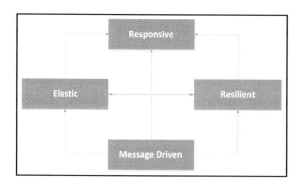

Rx from Microsoft

Microsoft brought out **software development kit (SDK)** for reactive programming, which it monikers as .NET Rx. According to them, Rx extensions is a unified library for composing asynchronous and event-based programs using observable sequences and LINQ style query operations. The key aspects of their descriptions are as follows:

- Asynchronous event streams
- Composition
- Observable sequences (streams)
- LINQ style queries

The sequences can be contents of a file, network socket, web service response, input streams, and so on. Microsoft gives a symbolic formula for Rx, that is, *Rx = Observables + LINQ + Schedulers*.

Key data structures of Rx

The Microsoft Rx SDK specifies some key data types, which a programmer can leverage to implement reactive programs. Some of the key types are as follows:

- IObservable<T>
- IObserver<T>
- Subject<T>

The signature of IObserver and IObservable is given as follows:

```
public interface IObserver<T>
{
  void OnCompleted();
  void OnError(Exception exception);
  void OnNext(T value);
}


public interface IObservable<T>
{
  IDisposable Subscribe(IObserver<T> observer);
}
```

IEnumberable/IObservable duality

The .NET framework has built-in support for the Iterator pattern (through IEnumerable<T>) and observer pattern (through IObservable<T>). If you take a closer look, there is only a subtle difference between these two patterns. IEnumerable<T> can be considered the pull-based equivalent of the push-based IObservable<T>. In fact, they are duals. When two entities exchange information, one entity's action of pull corresponds to other entity pushing the information. This duality is illustrated in the following image:

Let's understand this duality by looking at this sample code, an even number sequence generator:

```
static void Main(string[] args)
{
  int[] number_array = new int[] { 1,2,3,4,5,6,8};
  IEnumerable<int> number_sequence = number_array;
  foreach (var n in number_sequence)
    if (n % 2 == 0)
      Console.WriteLine(n);
}
```

We will write a number sequence generator to demonstrate how these data types work together in converting a pull-based program to an Rx push program. First we will write a toy implementation of IDisposable to be used later: The robustness aspect is given low priority to keep the listing terse:

```
class EmptyDisposable : IDisposable
{
  internal Action action {get;  set;}
  void IDisposable.Dispose()
  { this.action(); }
}
```

```
class EvenNumberObservable : IObservable<int>
{
  public EvenNumberObservable(IEnumerable<int> numbers)
  {
    this._numbers = numbers;
  }

  private IEnumerable<int> _numbers;

  public IDisposable Subscribe(IObserver<int> observer)
  {
    foreach(int number in _numbers)
    {
      if (number%2 == 0 )
      observer.OnNext(number);
    }
    observer.OnCompleted();

    return new EmptyDisposable { action = () => { ;  } };
  }
}

class SimpleObserver : IObserver<int>
{
  public void OnNext(int value) {  Console.WriteLine(value);}
  public void OnCompleted() { Console.WriteLine("Completed"); }
  public void OnError(Exception ex){
  Console.WriteLine("An Error Encountered");
  throw ex;
  }
}
}
```

The following code snippet invokes the preceding code:

```
static void Main(string[] args)
{
  new EvenNumberObservable(
  new[] { 1,2, 3, 4,6,7,8 })
  .Subscribe(new SimpleObserver());
  Console.ReadLine();
}
```

From this preceding example, you see how one can naturally subscribe for even numbers from an observable sequence of natural numbers. The system will automatically push (publish) the values to the observer (subscriber) when an even number is detected. The code gives explicit implementations for the key interfaces so that one can understand or speculate what really happens under the hood.

Another example would be Pythagorean triple generation from observable sequences of base, altitude, and hypotenuse. We have already seen the **functional** code for achieving this, and now, let's see the **reactive** equivalent (or should we say, a better one):

```
void Main()
{
  var result =
    from i in Observable.Range(1, 100)
    from j in Observable.Range(1, 100)
    from k in Observable.Range(1, 100)
    where k * k == i * i + j * j
    select new { a = i, b = j, c = k };

  // A Subscriber with
  // A callback (Lambda) which prints value,
  // A callback for Exception
  // A callback for Completion

  IDisposable subscription = result.Subscribe(
  x => Console.WriteLine("OnNext: {0}", x),
  ex => Console.WriteLine("OnError: {0}", ex.Message),
  () => Console.WriteLine("OnCompleted"));
}
```

Converting entities to streams (IObservable<T>)

The following constructs can be converted to a sequence source. IObservable<T> can be generated from the following:

- Events
- Delegates
- Tasks
- IEnumerable<T>
- Asynchronous programming model

Converting events into stream

We have now understood how one can convert an `IEnumerable<T>`-based pull program to an `IObservable<T>`/`IObserver<T>`-based push program. In real life, the event source is not as simple as we found in the number stream example given previously. Let us see how we can convert a `MouseMove` event into a stream with a small WinForms program:

```
static void Main()
{
  var mylabel = new Label();
  var myform = new Form { Controls = { mylabel } };

  IObservable<EventPattern<MouseEventArgs>>
  mousemove =
  Observable.
  FromEventPattern<MouseEventArgs>(myform, "MouseMove");

  mousemove.Subscribe(
    (evt)=>{mylabel.Text = evt.EventArgs.X.ToString();},
    ()=>{});

  Application.Run(myform);
}
```

Please see the following form, which displays the mouse positions:

Reduction of streams (sequences)

The whole idea of converting data to streams is to apply functional programming operators such as Reduce, Aggregate, Fold, and so on. This is quite relevant in terms of choosing the needed data (and also in an efficient way) from an enormous pile that is ever growing with respect to time:

- **Filter and partition operators**: These operations help to reduce the source sequence into a sequence of elements that we are interested in
- **Aggregation operators**: Reduce the source sequence to a sequence with a single element
- **Fold operators**: Reduce the source sequence to a single element as a scalar value

Some of the common sequence/stream operators supported by Rx/LINQ are as follows:

- `Where`: As the name implies, and for those familiar with this operator from LINQ days, it does the very purpose of filtering of sequences. If we were to rewrite our earlier example-that of extracting/filtering even numbers-it would declaratively be as simple as this:

  ```
  var evenNumbers = Observable.Range(0, 10)
  .Where(i => i % 2 == 0)
  .Subscribe(Console.WriteLine);
  ```

- In the preceding example, the input is 0, 1, 2, 3, 4, 5, 6, 7, 8, and 9, and the output will be 2, 4, 6, and 8.

- `Skip`: This helps in skipping *n* items in a sequence.
- `Take`: This helps in taking *n* items (skipping the rest) in a sequence.
- `SkipWhile`: This helps in skipping items (while a certain condition is satisfied) in a sequence. Please note that the element would be skipped until the predicate evaluates to `true`. Beyond this, all items would be returned.
- `TakeWhile`: This is the converse of `SkipWhile`, and helps in taking items (while a certain condition is satisfied) in a sequence.
- `SkipUntil`: This requires two observable sequences, and continues to skip all the values in the first sequence until any value is produced by the second sequence.
- `TakeUntil`: Again, this requires two observable sequences, and forces the first sequence to completion when the second sequence starts producing any value.
- `SkipLast`: Intelligently queues elements, skips the last *n* elements, and returns the rest.
- `TakeLast`: Returns the last *n* elements.

- `Zip`: Merges two observable sequences into one observable sequence.

Inspection of streams (sequences)

Rx provides a set of operators, which can help us to inspect the contents of a stream. Some of them are:

- `Any`: This returns an observable sequence (result), which returns one value (`True` or `False`) and completes. `True` indicates that the source sequence produced a value that caused the result sequence to produce `True`. On the other hand, the result sequence returns `False` if the source sequence completes without any values.
- `All`: This works similar to `Any` except that the results sequence returns `True` if the predicate is evaluated to `True` and `False` vice versa.
- `Contains`: This shows the same behavior as `All` except that it helps seek a specific value instead of a value that fits the predicate.
- `ElementAt`: This returns an observable sequence (result), which returns the value in the source sequence (specified by the index) and completes. It uses a 0-based index.

Aggregation of streams (sequences)

Rx provides a series of operators, which help us to aggregate the content of a stream. Some of the most important ones are as follows:

- `Count`
- `Min`, `Max`, `Average`, `Sum` (descriptive statistics)
- `MinBy`, `MaxBy`, `GroupBy` (partitioning)
- Custom aggregators and scans

Transformation of streams (sequences)

The values produced by our event source are not in the formats that we might want, and we are required to make the transformation on each element in the sequence. The most important functional transformation is bind, where we apply a function (morphism) on each element of the sequence to produce a new sequence.

In functional programming parlance, the transformations available are the following:

- Anamorphism, which transforms `T` to `IObservable<T>`:

  - `Unfold`
  - `Generate`

- Catamorphism, which transforms an `IObservable<T>` to `T`:

  - `Fold`
  - `Reduce`
  - `Accumulate`

- Bind, which transforms an `IObservable<T>` to `IObservable<T>`:

  - `Map`
  - `SelectMany`
  - `Projection`
  - `Transform`

Combining streams (sequences)

We get data from different data sources, and it is necessary to combine streams to do processing. Rx provides a series of operators, which can be grouped into the following:

- Sequential concatenation:

  - `Concat`: As the name indicates, the resulting sequence concatenates multiple input sequences without interleaving them
  - `Repeat`: Creates a sequence that emits a particular item multiple times
  - `StartWith`: Emits a specified sequence of items before beginning to emit the items from the source sequence

- Concurrent sequences:

  - `Amb`: This returns one of the sequences (from two or more source sequences), which first starts emitting an item or notification
  - `Merge`: As the name indicates, this operator combines multiple sequences into one

- `Switch`: This returns a sequence (from two or more source sequences) that emits the items emitted by the most recently emitted one of those input/source sequences

- Pairing sequences:

    - `CombineLatest`: Combines the most recently emitted items from each of the participating input sequences using a function that is provided, and emits the return value of that function
    - `Zip`: The behavior is similar to that of `CombineLatest` except that the function is applied in a strict sequence (in terms of combining items from the participating input sequences)
    - `And/Then/When`: The behavior is very similar to `Zip`, but certain intermediary data structures (namely pattern and plan objects) are used as part of combining the input sequences before emitting the resulting sequence

A philosophy for reactive programming

We started this chapter with a lot of verbose description about the reactive programming model. Then, we showed how one can convert an `IEnumerable<T>`-based sequence generator to an `IObservable<T>`/`IObserver<T>`–based push program. We also demonstrated how one can convert mouse-event data to a stream, using a toy program. The rest of the chapter was about the tools available for manipulating streams or sequences. You learned about the different genres of stream processing operators. One needs to consult the Microsoft documentation on Rx to understand the specifics of stream processors.

The basic philosophy here can be summarized as follows:

- Aggregate data into asynchronous or synchronous streams from the event source.
- Apply preprocessing methods using various operators available at the data source itself (outside the stream consumer).
- Process the resulting stream pushed from the data source at the data sink level by applying functional transformation techniques. We can compose stream operations to produce compound operations. By doing this, the whole program becomes a linear chain of functions applied on a stream. If the data stream is not mutated, there is no need for a compensating transaction logic as well.

```
try {
    outstream =  f(g(h(immutablestream)));
```

```
    }
    catch {}
```

Schematically, the preceding code snippets can be interpreted as that we can apply a series of functions on a stream to produce output stream. Since the input stream is immutable when we process at the data sink level, there is no need for a compensating transaction in the catch handler. The whole processing can be easily debugged as well.

Summary

In this chapter, you learned the conceptual underpinnings of (functional) reactive programming, and how Microsoft Rx helps you to write reactive programs using a scheduler, observable interface, and LINQ. We have avoided API documentation in this book (as that is exhaustive and redundant considering the nature of this book). We urge you to refer to the ReactiveX website (`http://reactivex.io/documentation/operators`), MSDN, interactive Rx illustrations website (`http://rxmarbles.com`), and the online book *Introduction to Rx* by Lee Campbell (`http://www.introtorx.com`) for specifics and usage examples on the various operators that we have discussed. In the following chapters, we will see detailed examples in C# and JavaScript-based functional reactive programs.

12
Reactive Programming Using .NET Rx Extensions

In the previous chapter, we saw how reactive programming shapes you up for scalability and responsiveness. We saw how these two attributes are supported in event-driven applications that enable it to readily respond to events, failures, and loads.

Now in this chapter we will:

- Take a deep dive into the Reactive Extensions (Rx) library and see how we write asynchronous and event-driven programs using observable sequences and LINQ query operators
- We will also take a detailed look at some sample use cases and their implementations with Rx to clearly understand how Observables, LINQ, and Schedulers in the .NET Framework are leveraged to create concurrent and responsive applications that can work with asynchronous data streams

By the end of this chapter, you will understand why Rx has been touted as the next big thing, and one that will become the de facto event-driven programming model, gaining traction and acceptance in various mainstream programming languages.

Streams as a way of life

As you saw in the previous chapter, the fundamental success to reactive programs is to convert events into immutable and observable streams. Program composition becomes very easy and intuitive with this format, and you can create a unifying interface using the .NET Rx extensions.

This is really important to understand, as wielding a hammer like Rx doesn't make you Thor. You don't necessarily start seeing every single implementation as a nail and drive your hammer down on it. As Uncle Ben once advised Peter aka Spiderman – "With great power comes great responsibility".

Let's understand this more by looking at the palette of options available, and making sound decisions on what can be done. Consider the following image:

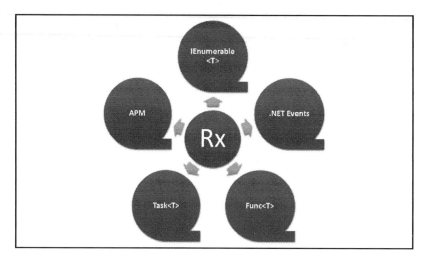

As you can see in the preceding figure, in terms of unifying the worlds, Rx brings forth bridges that help you work seamlessly across these programming models. To quickly recap what we read in `Chapter 11`, *What is Reactive Programming?*, take a look at the following table:

Factory methods	Unfold methods	Bridges
• Observable.Return	• Observable.Range	• Observable.Start
• Observable.Empty	• Observable.Interval	• Observable.FromEventPattern
• Observable.Never	• Observable.Timer	• Task.ToObservable
• Observable.Throw	• Observable.Generate	• Task<T>.ToObservable
• Observable.Create		• IEnumerable<T>.ToObservable
		• Observable.FromAsyncPattern

As reiterated earlier, we don't replace existing asynchrony. The .NET events, async methods, tasks, and so on, have their use and are perfect in their own worlds.

Rx just becomes the glue to unify these worlds, provides compositionality, and helps build bridges.

Now, let's get started on some examples that will help us understand how to put Rx to best use in our day-to-day programming. Only certain pragmatic aspects are highlighted leveraging key constructs in Rx, as complete coverage warrants another book in its own size.

Spell checker using events composition

This first example is a Windows application that integrates the previously implemented spell checker (from `Chapter 9`, *Functional Programming Techniques for Better State Management*) using Rx, and explores how this can be leveraged to suggest alternatives and corrections. Consider the following code snippet:

```
static void Main()
{
    ObservableEventsDemo();
}
```

Initialize your input from here, with some basic controls that we will need, that is, a text box (used for keyword search) and a list box that provides suggestions/corrections for a given keyword. Take a look at the following code snippet:

```
static void ObservableEventsDemo()
{
  // Input form

  var txtBoxSpellCorrect = new TextBox();
  var lstBoxSuggestions = new ListBox {
    Top = txtBoxSpellCorrect.Height + 10 };
  var frmSpellChecker = new Form { Controls = { txtBoxSpellCorrect,
    lstBoxSuggestions } };
```

Now, we will need to create a `DispatcherScheduler` that schedules units of work on the dispatcher of the current UI thread. The delegate `onInputChange` is created to clear the suggestions in the list box whenever the input keyword changes. Consider the following code snippet:

```
// Dispatcher scheduler for the UI thread

var _dispatcher = new DispatcherScheduler(
  System.Windows.Threading.Dispatcher.CurrentDispatcher);

Action<string> onInputChange = word =>
{
    lstBoxSuggestions.Items.Clear();
```

```
      Console.WriteLine("Word Changed: " + word);
};
```

We will define an observable stream/sequence on the input based by subscribing to the `TextChanged` event of the text box using the `FromEventPattern` bridge. We will further filter the input stream based on minimum characters (three, in this case) and distinct entries (helps us throttle the lookup frequency). A valid output from this input sequence will trigger the delegate that clears the list box contents and gets it ready to receive a new set of suggestions as and when they are available. Consider the following code snippet:

```
var input = Observable
    .FromEventPattern(txtBoxSpellCorrect, "TextChanged")
    .Select(evt => ((TextBox)evt.Sender).Text)
    .Timestamp().Select(evt => evt.Value)
    .Where(evt => evt.Length > 3)
    .DistinctUntilChanged()
    .Do(onInputChange);
```

This defines the second observable sequence that fetches suggestions based on the first sequence (keyword) we defined in the preceding code:

```
Func<string, IObservable<string>> matches =
    searchText => NorvigSpellCheckerModel.
        Instance.SpellCheck(searchText, 5).ToObservable<string>();
```

This is an important step where we declaratively specify to continue fetching suggestions until the keyword changes (the first observable sequence for us here). If you notice, this is done here using the `TakeUntil` operator:

```
var result = from term in input
    from words in matches(term)
    .TakeUntil(input)
    .Finally(() =>
    {
        Console.WriteLine("Disposed Lookup For: " + term);
    })
    select words;
```

We will then define delegates (onEachSuggest, onSuggestError, and onSuggestComplete) for the `Subscribe` method to receive push-based notifications, as shown in the following piece of code (onEachSuggest tend to add received suggestions to the list box as and when they are received):

```
Action<string> OnEachSuggest = word =>
{
```

```
        lstBoxSuggestions.Items.Add(word);
        Console.WriteLine("Match: " + word);
    };


    Action<Exception> OnSuggestError = ex =>
    {
        Console.WriteLine("Error: " + ex.Message);
    };


    Action OnSuggestComplete = () =>
    {
        lstBoxSuggestions.Items.Clear();
        Console.WriteLine("Suggestion Complete!!!");
    };
```

This is the final step where we will specify to observe on the dispatcher of the UI thread (it is absolutely critical for you to make the necessary UI updates) and subscribe on the default task scheduler instance (Rx will decide one for you based on the principle of least concurrency). Consider the following code snippet:

```
using (result.OnErrorResumeNext(
    Observable.Empty<string>())
    .ObserveOn(_dispatcher)
    .SubscribeOn(Scheduler.Default)
    .Subscribe(
        OnEachSuggest,
        OnSuggestError,
        OnSuggestComplete))
Application.Run(frmSpellChecker);
}
```

Let's quickly see the supporting Model code (refactored the earlier `NorvigSpellChecker` code to make it a singleton and implement the `ISpellCheckerModel` interface) as well. This interface helps in returning the results as an enumerable list, which can further be converted to an observable sequence. Lets take a look at the following code snippet:

```
public interface ISpellCheckerModel
{
    IEnumerable<string> SpellCheck(string word, int count);
}
```

This is the old code from Chapter 9, *Functional Programming Techniques for Better State Management*, based on Peter Norvig's post: http://norvig.com/spell-correct.html, modified to become a singleton. Consider the following code snippet:

```
public sealed class NorvigSpellCheckerModel : ISpellCheckerModel
{
    private static readonly Lazy<NorvigSpellCheckerModel>
    spellCheckerInstance = new Lazy<NorvigSpellCheckerModel>(() =>
      new NorvigSpellCheckerModel());
    private NorvigSpellCheckerModel()
    {
        //......... USE CODE FROM CHAPTER 9 HERE
    }

    public static NorvigSpellCheckerModel Instance
    {
        get
        {
            return spellCheckerInstance.Value;
        }
    }

    public IEnumerable<string> SpellCheck(string word, int count)
    {
        //......... USE CODE FROM CHAPTER 9 HERE
    }
}
```

Some key things to notice here are:

- The use of the FromEventPattern bridge to subscribe to the TextChanged event
- The classic use case for a Singleton (to prevent Training Model corpus creation repeatedly every time a word is looked up) to create and cache the dictionary for future use
- It will be worthwhile to take a look at the Singleton implementation that has leveraged .NET 4's Lazy<T> type for thread safety, lazy instantiation, and not resorting to the conventional double-check locking idiom, where explicit locking is used
- The use of the Where and DistinctUntilChanged operators to restrict lookup for unique four letter words and beyond

The screenshots of our spell checker in action are shown as follows:

The supporting console helps you understand the sequence of actions behind the scenes, as shown in the following screenshot:

MVVM on Rx

Now, let's convert the preceding example to see how we can apply this for a classic MVVM implementation.

MVVM is an important application development framework that has its roots with **Windows Presentation Framework (WPF)**. It is best suited for event-driven programming where you achieve clear **Separation of Concerns**, thereby facilitating parallel development (Model, View, and View Model) and testability.

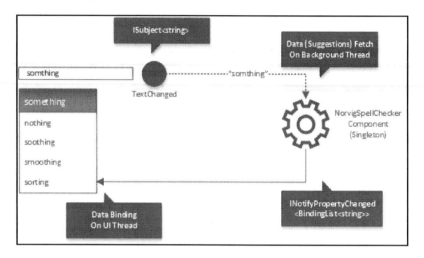

As you observe (no pun intended) in the preceding solution model, the `TextChanged` event of the text box, where the word to be looked up is entered, will indicate to the `ISubject<T>` type here, one that implements both `IObservable<T>` and `IObserver<T>` interfaces, thereby enabling you to conveniently observe and publish items to subscribers.

Ensure that you have the appropriate dependencies/packages installed via the **NuGet** package manager and referenced properly. The ones under consideration here include the following:

- `System.Reactive.Core`
- `System.Reactive.Interfaces`
- `System.Reactive.Linq`
- `System.Reactive.PlatformServices`
- `System.Reactive.Windows.Threading`

The code for the View layer is shown as follows. Take note (highlighted) of the data binding with the corresponding view model:

```
public partial class frmSpellChecker : Form
{
    private SpellCheckerViewModel _spellCheckerViewModel;
```

```
public frmSpellChecker()
{
    InitializeComponent();
    _spellCheckerViewModel = new
    SpellCheckerViewModel(NorvigSpellCheckerModel.Instance);
    //Data Binding Is Done Here
    lstBoxSuggestions.DataSource =
      _spellCheckerViewModel.Corrections;
}

private void txtBoxSpellCorrect_TextChanged(
  object sender, EventArgs e)
{
    _spellCheckerViewModel.SearchChanges(((TextBox)sender).Text);
}
}
```

As you can see, an instance of View Model is created and the Model (code in reference is the same one used for the earlier example) instance is specified. The text changes are routed to the subject in View Model through the TextChanged event. Synchronization, with respect to the data bindings, (against the suggestion list box), happens automatically through property change notifications from View Model, which happens to implement the INotifyPropertyChanged interface. The data source for the bindings is retained in the View Model. Let's take a look at the View Model now:

```
class SpellCheckerViewModel : INotifyPropertyChanged
{
    private BindingList<string> _corrections;
    private ISpellCheckerModel _spellChecker;
    private ISubject<string> _searchChanged;
    private IScheduler _dispatcher;
    public event PropertyChangedEventHandler PropertyChanged;
public BindingList<string> Corrections
{
    get
    {
        return this._corrections;
    }

    set
    {
        if (value != this._corrections)
        {
            this._corrections = value;
            NotifyPropertyChanged();
        }
```

```
        }
    }
```

Here, we will use the `CallerMemberName` attribute to avoid specifying the member name as a string argument to the called method:

```
private void NotifyPropertyChanged([CallerMemberName]
String propertyName = "")
{
    if (PropertyChanged != null)
    {
        this.PropertyChanged(this,
            new PropertyChangedEventArgs(propertyName));
    }
}

public void SearchChanges(string text)
{
    _searchChanged.OnNext(text);
}

public ISubject<string> SearchChanged
{
    get
    {
        return _searchChanged;
    }
}

public SpellCheckerViewModel(ISpellCheckerModel spellChecker)
{
    _spellChecker = spellChecker;
    _dispatcher = new DispatcherScheduler(
      System.Windows.Threading.Dispatcher.CurrentDispatcher);
    _corrections = new BindingList<string>();
    _searchChanged = new Subject<string>();
    Func<string, IObservable<string>> GetSuggestions = (searchText) =>
    {
        IsProcessing = true;
        Corrections.Clear();
        Error = null;
        return _spellChecker.SpellCheck(searchText, 5)
          .ToObservable<string>();
    };

    var searches = this.SearchChanged.Select(GetSuggestions);
```

Now, this final step provides the necessary magic in terms of:

- Providing the most recent changes in the sequence (the `Switch` operator)
- Looking up suggestions for only four letter words and above (the `Where` operator)
- Looking up suggestions only if the new value entered is different from old (the `DistinctUntilChanged` operator)
- And, finally, looking up on a background thread using the schedulers task/thread pool and returning suggestions on the UI thread's dispatcher. Take a look at the following code snippet:

```
searches.Switch()
    .Where(s => s.Length > 3)
     .DistinctUntilChanged()
     .SubscribeOn(Scheduler.Default)
     .ObserveOn(_dispatcher)
     .Subscribe(OnEachSuggest, OnSuggestError,
        OnSuggestComplete);
}
private void OnEachSuggest(string searchText)
{
     Corrections.Add(searchText);
}
}
```

This View Model clearly shows how Observables, LINQ (`Where` and `DistinctUntilChanged`), and Schedulers are put to good practical use. As highlighted in the preceding code, the lookup, which is done on a background thread, lets the observer, in this case, the data source, that is, the `BindingList<string>`, know through property change notifications; thereby, triggering automatic content refresh in the `Suggestions` list box. Another thing to note is the adept usage of the `SubscribeOn`/`ObserveOn` pair to prevent blocking of UI thread and yet update UI objects on it.

There are some key things to notice here:

- The use of `Switch` operator, in addition to the `Where` and `DistinctUntilChanged` operators, to ensure the liveliness in search in terms of showing the latest and relevant changes with respect to the sequence
- This will also serve as an example of the **Collection Pipeline** pattern, where your computation becomes a sequence of operations by taking a collection/sequence from one operation and feeding to another

It leverages immutability, comprehensions (declarative query syntax in LINQ), laziness, and parallelism to achieve this.

The screenshot of our spell checker in action is shown here:

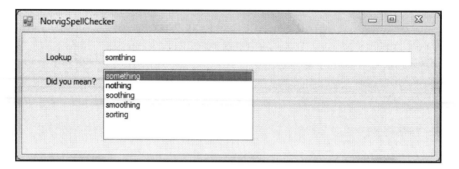

An asynchronous logger

Logging and Audit trail is an important cross-cutting or horizontal concern in the day-to-day application that we create. There are various third-party tools that we leverage; and we have seen how to write one ourselves in depth in Chapter 3, *A Logging Library*. Here, we will see how to impart reactive behavior to a custom-logging component.

We will use the same spell checker example in the preceding section and see how to integrate logging capability into the existing code base.

We will start off by initializing the log collection as a BindingList, the same way we got the corrections/suggestions initialized:

```
class SpellCheckerViewModel : INotifyPropertyChanged
{
    private BindingList<string> _logs;
    private ISubject<string> _logChanged;
    public BindingList<string> Logs
    {
        get
        {
            return this._logs;
        }

        set
        {
            if (value != this._logs)
            {
```

```
                this._logs = value;
                NotifyPropertyChanged();
            }
        }
    }
```

The following `AddToLog` method will be the generic logging method used to hand off the log text to the observer waiting on the `_logchanged` subject. You can see instrumentation code throughout the methods, shown as follows, for applicability and clarity:

```
public void AddToLog(string text)
{
    _logChanged.OnNext(text);
}

public SpellCheckerViewModel(ISpellCheckerModel spellChecker)
{
    _logs = new BindingList<string>();
    _logChanged = new Subject<string>();

    Func<string, IObservable<string>> GetSuggestions = (searchText) =>
    {
        AddToLog(string.Format("Searching for
          suggestions : {0}", searchText));
        return _spellChecker.SpellCheck(searchText, 5)
          .ToObservable<string>();
    };

    var searches = _searchChanged
        .Select(GetSuggestions)
        .Finally(() => AddToLog("Search DISPOSED!!!"));
    searches
        .Switch()
        .Where(s => s.Length > 3)
        .DistinctUntilChanged()
        .SubscribeOn(Scheduler.Default)
        .ObserveOn(_dispatcher)
        .Subscribe(OnEachSuggest, OnSuggestError, OnSuggestComplete);

    DoLogging(_logChanged);
}

private void OnEachSuggest(string searchText)
{
    AddToLog(string.Format("Suggestion Added : {0}", searchText));
}
```

```
private IObservable<string> GetSuggestions(string searchText)
{
    AddToLog(string.Format("Searching for suggestions :
      {0}", searchText));
}

private void OnEachLog(string searchText)
{
    Logs.Add(searchText);
}
```

The following `DoLogging` method sets the observer, the `OnEachLog` method in our case, to listen for log text sequences/feeds from the observable `_logChanged` based on its `onNext` method invocations via the `AddToLog` method, thus, facilitating both publication and subscription using the `_logchanged` subject:

```
private void DoLogging(IObservable<string> sequence)
{
    sequence
    .SubscribeOn(ThreadPoolScheduler.Instance)
    .ObserveOn(_dispatcher)
    .Subscribe(OnEachLog);
}
}
```

This binding list is bound to the `Listbox` specifically used in this example to view the logs. This change's property is further routed to the UI thread that senses the change in the bounded data source list in our case against the list box and forces a refresh. If you observe carefully, the logging feature is purely asynchronous and is handled by a background thread–a worker thread from thread pool in this case. Consider the following code snippet:

```
public frmSpellChecker()
{
    //Data Binding Is Done Here
    lstBoxSuggestions.DataSource = _spellCheckerViewModel.Corrections;
    lstBoxLog.DataSource = _spellCheckerViewModel.Logs;
}
```

The logs can be further persisted using the store, such as file, database, and so on, of your choice. You can also use this to clearly understand the data flow from an observer and subscriber standpoint. The modified application will look like the following:

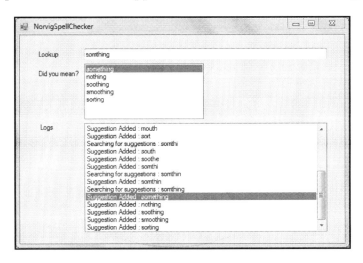

Near real-time visualizer/dashboard

Dashboards are natural candidates for viewing real-time, or near real-time, data. Reactive constructs can be very effectively utilized in realizing utility dashboards from a reporting standpoint. Let's look at an interesting scenario where election poll results are viewed on a real-time basis as and when the poll feeds come in from different states. Again, this has no resemblance to the actual polling process, but just conceptualized here in a fictitious manner that will enable learning and throw light on various interesting possibilities of leveraging reactive programming for such a reporting application. Consider the following code snippet:

```
public partial class Form1 : Form
{
    public enum Party { Republican, Democratic };
    public enum States { AZ, CA, FL, IN, NY };
    string[] xState = { "AZ", "CA", "FL", "IN", "NY" };
    double[] yRVotes = { 0, 0, 0, 0, 0 };
    double[] yDVotes = { 0, 0, 0, 0, 0 };
    Random random = new Random();
    class Vote
    {
        public Party VoteId { get; set; }
        public string State { get; set; }
```

```
    }
    public Form1()
    {
        InitializeComponent();
        chart1.Series.Clear();
        DrawSimulation(chart1);
    }
```

This is the first stage in the prototype where we start building the simulation model for data sequences/streams, in our case, votes from multiple states. Here, we are initializing a certain number of votes per state. The Take query operator is utilized here, in case you noticed:

```
    private void DrawSimulation(Chart chart1)
    {
        var azVotes = GenerateVotes<Vote>(
          () => new Vote() { VoteId = CauchyDistribution(
            random.NextDouble()), State = "Arizona" }).Take(200000);
        var caVotes = GenerateVotes<Vote>(
          () => new Vote() { VoteId = CauchyDistribution(
            random.NextDouble()), State = "California" }).Take(500000);
        var flVotes = GenerateVotes<Vote>(
          () => new Vote() { VoteId = CauchyDistribution(
            random.NextDouble()), State = "Florida" }).Take(300000);
        var inVotes = GenerateVotes<Vote>(
          () => new Vote() { VoteId = CauchyDistribution(
            random.NextDouble()), State = "Indiana" }).Take(100000);
        var nyVotes = GenerateVotes<Vote>(
          () => new Vote() { VoteId = CauchyDistribution(
            random.NextDouble()), State = "New York" }).Take(700000);
```

This is the next stage in the prototype, where we will filter democratic and republican votes from the simulation model's stream source, which is generated in the preceding code:

```
        var azDVotes = from v in azVotes.ToObservable<Vote>()
                where v.VoteId == Party.Democratic
                select v;
        var azRVotes = from v in azVotes.ToObservable<Vote>()
                where v.VoteId == Party.Republican
                select v;
        var caDVotes = from v in caVotes.ToObservable<Vote>()
                where v.VoteId == Party.Democratic
                select v;
        var caRVotes = from v in caVotes.ToObservable<Vote>()
                where v.VoteId == Party.Republican
                select v;
        var flDVotes = from v in flVotes.ToObservable<Vote>()
                where v.VoteId == Party.Democratic
```

```
        select v;
var flRVotes = from v in flVotes.ToObservable<Vote>()
        where v.VoteId == Party.Republican
        select v;
var inDVotes = from v in inVotes.ToObservable<Vote>()
        where v.VoteId == Party.Democratic
        select v;
var inRVotes = from v in inVotes.ToObservable<Vote>()
        where v.VoteId == Party.Republican
        select v;
var nyDVotes = from v in nyVotes.ToObservable<Vote>()
        where v.VoteId == Party.Democratic
        select v;
var nyRVotes = from v in nyVotes.ToObservable<Vote>()
        where v.VoteId == Party.Republican
        select v;
```

Here, we will initialize and create the data series for the X and Y axis needed by the chart component. This way the series are bound to the charting component:

```
Series democratic = new Series("Democratic");
Series republican = new Series("Republican");
chart1.Series.Add(democratic);
chart1.Series.Add(republican);
```

This is the stage where we kick-start simulation, that is, a generation of votes specified per state:

```
GetDemocraticVotes(States.AZ, azDVotes);
GetRepublicanVotes(States.AZ, azRVotes);
GetDemocraticVotes(States.CA, caDVotes);
GetRepublicanVotes(States.CA, caRVotes);
GetDemocraticVotes(States.FL, flDVotes);
GetRepublicanVotes(States.FL, flRVotes);
GetDemocraticVotes(States.IN, inDVotes);
GetRepublicanVotes(States.IN, inRVotes);
GetDemocraticVotes(States.NY, nyDVotes);
GetRepublicanVotes(States.NY, nyRVotes);
}
```

The following two helper methods, `GetDemocraticVotes` and `GetRepublicanVotes`, used as a part of kick-starting simulation ensure that the observers (the following lambda function in this case) are bound and listening for changes as and when the votes start streaming in. The filtered votes are channeled to these respective helper methods and will continuously increment the respective vote counters on a near real-time basis:

```
private void GetDemocraticVotes(States state, IObservable<Vote> votes)
{
    int stateIndex = (int)state;
    votes.SubscribeOn(Scheduler.Default)
      .ObserveOn(NewThreadScheduler.Default)
        .Subscribe(v =>
        {
            double voteCount = yDVotes[stateIndex];
            yDVotes[stateIndex] = voteCount + 1;
        });
}

private void GetRepublicanVotes(States state, IObservable<Vote> votes)
{
    int stateIndex = (int)state;
    votes.SubscribeOn(Scheduler.Default)
      .ObserveOn(NewThreadScheduler.Default)
        .Subscribe(v =>
        {
            double voteCount = yRVotes[stateIndex];
            yRVotes[stateIndex] = voteCount + 1;
        });
}
```

The following `GenerateVotes` method is the real vote generator (infinite, as you see) limited by the number specified using the Take operator, as indicated in the preceding code. This uses the generator function `CauchyDistribution` internally to generate the votes randomly and non-uniformly:

```
public IEnumerable<T> GenerateVotes<T>(Func<T> generator)
{
    while (true) yield return generator();
}

private Party CauchyDistribution(double p)
{
    return Math.Tan(Math.PI * (p - 0.5)) >= 0 ?
      Party.Democratic : Party.Republican;
}
```

This timer control helps in refreshing the chart control, which is based on the preset frequency, with values indicating votes scored by the two parties in the various states under consideration. Now, one important thing that you need to understand here is that as and when you traverse layers of subscribers and observers, you tend to introduce latency, again, based on the kind of schedulers you employ for concurrency, which makes the final output near real-time as opposed to real time not to introduce any interpretable subjectivity here. One should strive to reduce these layers and choose the right schedulers through multiple trials and calibrations to minimize these latencies and meet the required SLAs. Consider the following code snippet:

```
private void timer1_Tick(object sender, EventArgs e)
{
    chart1.Series["Republican"].Points.DataBindXY(xState, yRVotes);
    chart1.Series["Democratic"].Points.DataBindXY(xState, yDVotes);
  }
 }
}
```

As can you see, the program is divided into multiple stages, which are as follows:

- **Stage1**: A simulation model building block
- **Stage2**: Filtering votes based on `Party`
- **Stage3**: Publish to subscribers
- **Stage4**: Dashboard renderer

The near real-time dashboard will look like the following:

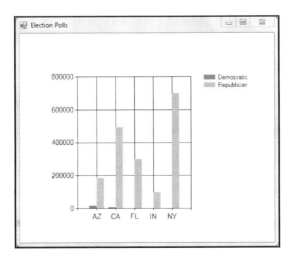

Summary

As you saw, we have gone through some interesting and pragmatic examples that illustrate the applicability of reactive programming principles. The idea is to make you aware of the possibilities and warm you up for some serious programming tasks ahead. We believe you are in a position to appreciate this paradigm now, and possibly able to relate to it as a natural way of expressing solution models in a declarative manner, which involved a lot of plumbing code earlier. The power of composability that you get in this model is quite evident. Now, in the next chapter, we will go on to explore RxJS, the reactive programming JavaScript library that helps you brace for web programming.

13
Reactive Programming Using RxJS

In the previous chapter, we saw how .NET **Reactive Extensions** (**Rx**) aided natural programming in terms of composability, scalability, and responsiveness. We saw how streams enable natural state management with respect to time. Some of the constructs were dealt with in detail as well. More importantly, we saw how reactive constructs could be integrated seamlessly into the MVVM pattern, in terms of achieving data synchronization between View and Model via the View Model layer. Now, in this chapter, we will take a deep dive into the **Reactive Extensions for JavaScript** (**RxJS**) library, and look at how to write asynchronous and event-driven programs using observable collections. We will also take a detailed look at some interesting use cases, and their implementations with RxJS, to clearly understand how the RxJS library is leveraged to create concurrent and responsive applications. This will cover the reactive spectrum of web and Windows programming and, by the end of this chapter, you will be in a position to appreciate the possibilities of JavaScript and confidently leverage RxJS by having a jump start at it. This chapter includes the following:

- A refresher on JavaScript execution context
- An analogy of RxJS with YieldJS (a custom JS framework created by the authors)
- A detailed outline on RxJS foundations and formalisms
- Detailed code samples that demonstrate RxJS in action

The JS world

It is important to recap one's understanding of some of the JavaScript world's state of affairs. The most important aspect is that the language is single-threaded and, given this, the only option left for developers to write asynchronous code is by using callbacks, promises, and events. As a developer, you should be comfortable with the functional programming aspects of JS (in addition to its innate dynamic nature), including closures, higher-order functions, anonymous functions, and extension methods (augmenting types). We also cannot discount the advancements that have been made in the language core itself, with Node.js now becoming a preferred backend for serious scalability involving async I/O. Let's have a quick peek into these core concepts before we dive into RxJS.

As we all know (we presume you do), functions are objects in JavaScript, and they are first-class citizens, which makes JS a functional programming language as well (although it is formally classified as a dynamic language). We already discussed and saw in Chapter 10, *Pattern Implementation Using Object/Functional Programming* (that too, in depth), how higher-order functions, along with closures, enable you to compose programs naturally, now that we have been thinning the OOP wall for some time (at least from Chapter 10 onwards). Well, we don't intend to imply that JS is an exception.

JS supports OOP through prototypal inheritance compared to classic inheritance in C#. This is important to understand how types can be augmented (analogous to our extension methods in C#).

Let's look at a higher-order function, which leverages callback (yet another function, which typically gets called for notification and continuation purposes):

```
function onComplete(message) {
  console.log(message);
}

function doSomething(onComplete) {
  //Do what is needed here and then trigger onComplete
  onComplete("Complete!");
}

doSomething(onComplete);
```

In the preceding code snippet, the callback (onComplete) is passed as an attribute to a function (doSomething), thus making it (doSomething) a higher-order function.

Now let's look at a Closure in action:

```
function add(x) {
  return function (y) {
    return x + y;
  };
};

var addTen = add(10);
console.log(addTen(5));    //Returns 15
console.log(add(2)(3));    //Returns 5
```

In the preceding code, `add` is a higher-order function (as it can be assigned to a variable), and x becomes a closure (lexical closure) within this function (irrespective of any nested/sub functions within). The results presented as comments against the respective statements speak for themselves. Also, see how anonymous functions (in this case, the inner function within the `add` function) are so natural in the JS realm. If you remember (from `Chapter 9`, *Functional Programming Techniques for Better State Management*), this also touches upon currying (an important concept in the functional programming world, which we've already dealt with in detail), a formalism that breaks any function with arity greater than one into a series of function evaluations (each accepting one argument at a time).

Another important concept to understand is augmenting types in JS. This provides an amazing way to impart capabilities to a type (just like the way we use extension methods in C#). Let's quickly look at the power of this, using the following example in terms of dynamically adding error-handling capability to functions (ones that don't have it) at runtime. Ever thought of that?

```
Function.prototype.throws = function () {
  var slice = Array.prototype.slice,
    args = slice.apply(arguments),
      errorMessage = args[0],
        fn = this;
  return function () {
    try {
      return fn.apply(null, args.slice(1));
    }
    catch (e) {
      console.log(errorMessage);
      //Do what is needed apart from logging
    }
  } ();
};
```

This preceding code essentially augments a function object by adding the `throws` method to its prototype object (the base object). It deftly leverages some nifty features in the JS language (including array slicing, `arguments` object, function context capture using closure, and the `apply` method used for function evaluation). We suggest you look it up in case you are unable to follow the code. The candidate function, which deliberately throws an exception and one that should gracefully exit function evaluation is as follows:

```
function errorSimulator(a, b) {
  console.log(a, b);
  return (parseInt(RxJS,10));//This statement forces an error!
}
```

The following code (line 1) can be used in place of direct function evaluation (line 2), where the program throws a runtime error (ReferenceError: RxJS is not defined) and breaks execution. What is important to note is the preservation of arity for these functions despite using the decorator. This is where you will understand the relevance of the arguments object and the `apply` method. Here, our decorator assumes the semantics – that of issuing the first argument with the error message followed by the function arguments in the exact same order! You can easily achieve this with a find and replace in your code file, can't you?

```
errorSimulator.throws("I have you!", 2, 0);  // line 1
errorSimulator(2, 0);                         // line 2
```

We guess that now you've got a handle on how things work in the JS world. It's important to know these as we move forward to explore reactive programming using RxJS.

To try out the code samples in this chapter, please ensure you have **Node.js** set up and RxJS dependencies installed through npm, as follows:

```
npm install rx
rx@4.1.0 node_modules\rx
```

Rx foundations

Although it may sound repetitive, it is so important to understand the foundations of Rx and the key design patterns that govern Rx. Being a book on patterns and idioms, it would be really gratifying to know if any interested reader would benefit from understanding the underpinnings of these keys concepts as they are realized in the host language (JS in this case) directly or via libraries.

The two key design patterns based on which Rx works are the **observer** and **iterator** patterns. Let's have a quick look at how these patterns are implemented, and then speculate or peek at a possible implementation of RxJS. This way of learning would really help in forming a deeper understanding of the core concepts. And not to hide the fact that the authors themselves have attempted to create a JS library (code-named `YieldJS` on GitHub at `http://shinexavier.github.io/YieldJS/`), which gives the rudimentary capability of RxJS despite being a pull-based implementation. However, one thing to keep in mind is that this library was never intended to be created as an RxJS clone, but to bring in the **yield** (from the C# world) capability to JS prior to ES 6.0.

 The strategy was very straightforward, since the language ES 5.0 didn't have inherent support for yield where you would want a generator object, which would continuously yield the next computed value and at the same time provide an option for forward iteration.

The preceding statement is very powerful with respect to the fact that this library would impart the following capabilities to a generator function in JS:

- Augmenting the generator function object to have forward iteration capability
- Accepting a series (unlimited) of iterator methods, which act as continuation methods to the core yielded elements
- Yielding the next valid result based on the continuous and sequenced (the very order in which it is specified during iteration) iterator function evaluations
- Supporting lazy evaluation by yielding the computed value only when requested

What do you think the authors had in mind when they set on this task of creating this library? In case you are still wondering, it was a novel attempt to create LINQ capability for sequences created by any generator object (functions, in our case) in JS. A subset of the library implementation is depicted in the following code, as this helps reason about a possible implementation of RxJS:

```
Function.prototype.getGenerator = function (setCount) {
  "use strict";
  var fnGen = this,
    numberOfElements = setCount,
    slice = Array.prototype.slice,
    gen = {},
    fnContexts = [],
    yieldIndex = -1,
    getFunctionContext = function (fnIndex, input) {
      var fnContext = fnContexts[fnIndex];
      if (fnContext === undefined) {
        fnContext = { "index": 0, "current": input, "outList": [] }
      };
```

```
        fnContexts[fnIndex] = fnContext;
      } else {
        fnContext.current = input;
        fnContext.index += 1;
      }
      return fnContext;
    },
    isYieldEmpty = function () {
      return ((yieldIndex + 1) === numberOfElements);
    },
    moveNext = function () {
      var args = arguments,
        yieldedResult = null,
        core = function () {
          var i,
            result = null,
            fn = null,
            fnCtxt = null;
          yieldIndex += 1;
          result = fnGen.apply(null, []);
          if (args.length > 0) {
            for (i = 0; i < args.length; i += 1) {
              fn = args[i];
              fnCtxt = getFunctionContext(i, result);
              result = fn.call(null, fnCtxt);
              if (result === null) {
                break;
              } else {
                fnCtxt.outList.push(result);
              }
            }
            if (result !== null) {
              gen.current = result;
            }
          } else {
            gen.current = result;
          }
          return result;
        };
      while ((yieldedResult === null) && (!isYieldEmpty())) {
        //Recursive call to find the next non-null value
        yieldedResult = core();
      }
      return (yieldedResult !== null) ? true : false;
    };
    gen.current = null;  gen.moveNext = moveNext;
    return gen;
  };
```

As highlighted in the preceding code, the key to this implementation is the state object `fnContext`, which holds information regarding every function (provided during iteration) and its evaluation details. This is critical for the continuation needed during iteration.

As you can see, the generator would be a method, `getGenerator(numberOfElements)`, which augments any generator function (by accepting the number of elements to be generated) and has the following interfaces:

- **Properties**:

    - `current`: Yields the current element during the course of a generation.

- **Methods**:

    - `moveNext`: Attempts to generate the next element based on the generator function, increments the iteration pointer, and returns `true` if successful. If unsuccessful (primarily because the iteration pointer points to the last element returned by the generator function based on the number of elements specified), it returns `false`.

From a usage standpoint, take a look at the following generic sequence generator:

```
function sequence(z) {
  "use strict";
  var y = 0;
  return function () {
    y += z;
    return y;
  };
}
```

As you can see, this accepts a seed incremental value during sequence initialization, and returns the actual function (anonymous), which can be invoked multiple times to generate the seed sequences. Another critical thing would be the accumulator (y in our case), which holds the previous item in our sequence because of its closure property. Now, let's see our generator in action:

```
var a = sequence(1).getGenerator(10);
//For generating the first 10
elements (1 through 10)
while (a.moveNext() {
  console.log(a.current);
}
```

Now, if you really look carefully, the preceding code snippet has the basic framework for creating a reactive library in terms of manipulating sequences (upon generation) to suit your needs. This is done using the iterator methods, which sort of become your LINQ operators. What really enables this are the context objects, which get created for each of the iterator functions. You will understand this when we look at some of the iterator methods shown next (ideally, the end users are just expected to write the sequence generator, and this library of iterator methods can be used for manipulating sequences in real time). Plus, the moment you understand how the context object provided during function evaluation can be used to write more iterator methods, it becomes all the more exciting and the possibilities seem endless. The context object provides the following attributes for creating various useful iterator functions:

- `index`: Gives the index of the current element in the iteration context
- `current`: Gives the current element in the iteration context
- `outList`: Gives the cumulative output collection/array till that point of iteration

The usage is as follows:

```
function square(context) {
  "use strict";
  return (context.current * context.current);
}
```

This is a very standard use of transform operators, where the `current` element in the sequence is retrieved and manipulated (squared in this case):

```
function unique(context) {
  "use strict";
  return (context.outList.indexOf(context.current) < 0) ?
  context.current : null;
}
```

In the preceding code, you clearly see how the `outList` property is leveraged for generating unique sequences! Typically, this property becomes very handy for implementing aggregation operators:

```
function filter(condition) {
  "use strict";
  return function (context) {
    return condition(context.current) ? context.current : null;
  };
}

function even(val) {
  "use strict";
```

```
        return (val % 2 === 0);
    }
```

Here is an interesting scenario, where a predicate function (even) is used in conjunction with an iterator function (filter) to filter those elements in the sequence that satisfy a certain condition:

```
function skip(count) {
    "use strict";
    return function (context) {
        return ((context.index % (count + 1)) === 0) ? context.current
        : null;
    };
}
```

And finally, here you see how the index property is leveraged for skipping certain elements in the sequence!

Now, to see the entire thing in action, look at the following example usage:

```
var a = sequence(1).getGenerator(10);
while(a.moveNext(skip(1), square)) {
    console.log(a.current);     //Yields 1, 9, 25, 49, 81
}
```

Do you get the connection now? Do you see how the two iterator methods (a filter and a transformation operator in this case) are composed elegantly in a declarative manner? One that would chain these operators during an iteration as an element in the sequence is generated. This is reactive (except that, with the iteration, you pull as opposed to the conventional push)! Don't you get it? All we need is a callback to be passed to our generator object, which would get notified any time a new element in the sequence is generated! We will leave that entirely to any interested reader (depending on whether you like to be an API producer or a consumer) to toy around with this implementation (you are free to fork it on GitHub), or directly jump to RxJS and start benefiting from it. Either way, by now, we feel you are ready and have the foundation to lock horns with RxJS!

RxJS formalism

Now, unlike YieldJS, RxJS is push-based. Here, the subscribers would automatically receive new values from the publisher. A subscriber or listener is denoted by the `observer` object, and the publisher (that pushes/publishes new values) is denoted by the `Observable` object. Just like the way we specified iterator methods (our future operators) to compose our generated sequences, we can efficiently do the same (transform, filter, and so on) for all the elements in the observable sequence.

Observables and observers

The generator becomes our observable, and the callback function, which would be interested in these sequences, becomes the observer. Having said this, creating `Observables` is pretty straightforward, as we saw in the earlier chapter with reactive extensions for .NET. The following code bares it all:

```
var client = Rx.Observable.create(function (observer) {
  observer.onNext('On Your Mark');
  observer.onNext('Get Set');
  observer.onNext('GO');
  observer.onCompleted();
});

client.subscribe(
  function onNext(x) { console.log('Next: ' + x); },
  function onError(err) { console.log('Error: ' + err); },
  function onCompleted() { console.log('Completed'); }
);
```

The client in the preceding code is the `observer`, which has the three important callbacks (highlighted), namely, `OnNext`, `OnError`, and `OnCompleted`.

As expected, this faithfully prints the following on the console:

```
Next: On Your Mark
Next: Get Set
Next: GO
Completed
```

Now let's look at some key bridges offered by RxJS when it comes to working with core language constructs.

Observables from arrays

Let's see how observables can be created from arrays using RxJS:

```
Rx.Observable
.from(['On Your Mark', 'Get Set', 'GO'])
.subscribe(
  function (x) { console.log('Next: ' + x); },
  function (err) { console.log('Error:', err); },
  function () { console.log('Completed'); }
);
```

As highlighted in the preceding code, you can see that the `from` operator does the trick here, and you get the same results as earlier!

Observables from events

Similarly, we can create observables from events using the `fromEvent` operator. The following is an observable, which displays the mouse pointer coordinates whenever the mouse crosses diagonally across the window. Since we need the DOM elements (document and window) here, we will use the **JSbin** playground for running this code:

```
var allMoves = Rx.Observable.fromEvent(document, 'mousemove')
allMoves.subscribe(function (e) {
  console.log(e.clientX, e.clientY);
});

var movesCrossingDiagonal = allMoves.filter(function (e) {
  return e.clientX === e.clientY;
});
movesCrossingDiagonal.subscribe(function (e) {
  console.log('Crossed the diagonal:', e.clientX, e.clientY);
});
```

If you observe the preceding code, you'll see that `allMoves` is the primary observable sequence, and then we derive the next `movesCrossingDiagonal` sequence from `allMoves`. All these sequences are immutable, and we just subscribe (the two subscribers are highlighted in code) to those that are of interest. We also see the use of the `filter` operator. See the following equivalent code executed in the JSbin editor:

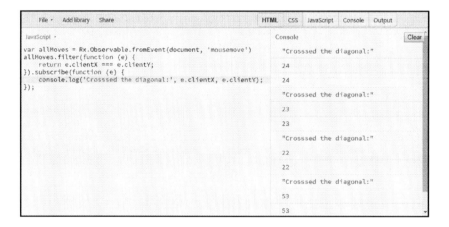

In the HTML code given in the preceding screenshot, you can see the Rx library included (you could simply do this in JSbin by using the **Add library** option shown in the web editor):

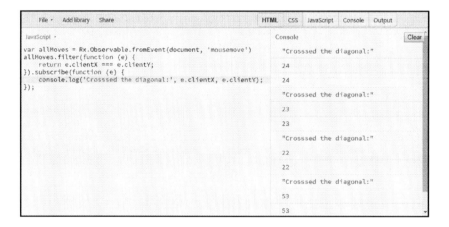

You will get these results, as seen in the preceding screenshot, the moment you move your mouse in the output window (not shown in this screenshot on account of brevity).

Observables from callbacks

Creating observables from callbacks is indispensable when it comes to asynchronous and event-driven programming, and it truly completes the final dimension of possibilities that observables have to offer:

```
// Load Node.js Filesystem module
var fs = require('fs');
// Create an Observable from the watch method
var source = Rx.Observable.fromCallback(fs.watch)('./tmp', {
encoding: 'buffer' });
// Create an Observer
var fsClient = Rx.Observer.create(
  function (changes) {
    console.log('Next: ', changes);
  },
  function (err) {
    console.log('Error: ', err);
  },
  function () {
    console.log('Completed');
  }
);
var subscription = source.subscribe(fsClient);
```

Now, let's presume you have a file named `alas.tmp` within the `tmp` folder, and you modify its contents and save it. The observer would immediately get notified of this change, as shown here:

```
Next:  [ 'change', 'alas.tmp' ]
Completed
```

Now, this preceding code, as you can see, helps you with subscribing to a file system watcher (directory watcher in this case). There's a shortcoming though! Can you spot that before we address this in the coming sections?

Observable pipeline

Remember the operator chaining we did with YieldJS a while ago? Well that's precisely what an `Observable` pipeline is. And if you remember how we trickled the state across the chaining operations (as opposed to maintaining it outside), you are in good hands. RxJS offers the same, as the `Observable` pipeline is self-contained and the state flows from one chained operator to another:

```
Rx.Observable
```

```
.from([1, 2, 3, 4, 5, 6, 7, 8])
.skip(4)
.map(function (val) { return val * val; })
.subscribe(function (value) {
  console.log('Next : ', value);
});
```

This preceding code yields the following:

```
Next : 25
Next : 36
Next : 49
Next : 64
```

Another thing to note is that this pipeline is highly efficient in terms of evaluations (or, we say, the various steps in an algorithm). In place of conventionally having three iterations/passes (per operator), we can do this operator chaining in just one iteration for all the three operators. We saw how this is clearly achieved in YieldJS. Additionally, you get the benefit of lazy evaluations as well! Be sure to check out other operators that may become handy for your day-to-day development.

Subject et al.

As we saw in the previous chapter, we have subjects (those that implement both Observer and Observable types) within RxJS as well. This makes it a powerful mediator (a proxy object to be precise) between a source and downstream subscribers/observers:

```
var subject = new Rx.Subject();
var source = Rx.Observable
.interval(1000)
.take(3);
source.subscribe(subject);
//Observer #1
var client1 = subject.subscribe(
  function (changes) {
    console.log('Client1 Next: ', changes);
  },
  function (err) {
    console.log('Client1 Error: ', err);
  },
  function () {
    console.log('Client1 Completed!');
  }
);
//Observer #2
```

```
var client2 = subject.subscribe(
  function (changes) {
    console.log('Client2 Next: ', changes);
  },
  function (err) {
    console.log('Client2 Error: ', err);
  },
  function () {
    console.log('Client2 Completed!');
  }
);
subject.onNext(5);
subject.onNext(15);
subject.onNext(20);
setTimeout(function () {
  subject.onCompleted();
  client1.dispose();
  client2.dispose();
}, 5000);
```

The following output is seen upon execution of the preceding code:

```
Client1 Next: 15
Client2 Next: 15
Client1 Next: 20
Client2 Next: 20
Client1 Next: 0
Client2 Next: 0
Client1 Next: 1
Client2 Next: 1
Client1 Next: 2
Client2 Next: 2
Client1 Completed!
Client2 Completed!
```

These are some of the specialized subjects which one could leverage based on their intent of usage:

- `AsyncSubject`: Represents the result of an asynchronous action. It can be used like a `promise` object in JS. It caches and returns only the last value, thus making it ideal for use in asynchronous operations, including AJAX calls, file I/O, and so on.

- `BehaviorSubject`: This mandates a starting value, making it ideal for initializing with placeholder values during any asynchronous operation, including AJAX calls, file I/O, and so on.

- `ReplaySubject`: Caches values (based on the buffer size specified) and re-emits those to subscribers irrespective of the time they subscribe to it.

Schedulers

As we saw earlier, schedulers are powerful tools to manage and handle concurrency. You have a lot more control in terms of the concurrency models you choose for notifications and subscriptions. You have the following three basic schedulers at your disposal:

- **Immediate**: This is de-facto for most of the operators, and is synchronous in nature
- **Default**: This is asynchronous in nature, and leverages the event loop (using `nextTick` in the case of Node.js), `setTimeout`, and so on, behind the scenes
- **Current thread**: This, again, is synchronous in nature, except that in the case of recursive operators (such as `repeat`), it enqueues executions

And we have two handy operators to help us here:

- `observeOn`
- `subscribeOn`

Both these return observable instances, but give fine-grained control on concurrency by taking in the scheduler as an attribute.

Please do check out the RxJS references for a deeper understanding of these (as coverage of these needs a chapter on its own, and that is not the true intent of this book). Now that we have looked at some of the core formalisms in RxJS, let's try to explore the world of RxJS with more examples.

RxJS samples

How can we even proceed without seeing our spell checker in action on a web page? For this, we need an ASP.NET Web API that provides the suggestions. We will reuse our earlier `NorvigSpellCheckerModel` class as-is for this:

```
using System;
using System.Collections.Generic;
using System.Linq;
using System.Net;
using System.Net.Http;
```

```
using System.Web.Http;
using SpellChecker;

namespace MvcApplication1.Controllers
{
  public class SearchContext
  {
    public string Lookup { get; set; }
    public int Count { get; set; }
  }
  public class ValuesController : ApiController
  {
    ISpellCheckerModel _spellChecker =
    NorvigSpellCheckerModel.Instance;
    // GET api/values
    public IEnumerable<string> Get([FromUri] SearchContext
    context)
    {
      return _spellChecker.SpellCheck(context.Lookup,
      context.Count);
    }
  }
}
```

In this preceding code, a `SearchContext` class has been created to pass in values for the get API! Also, a small change has been made to the `Global.asax.cs` file to accommodate JSONP responses (highlighted in the following code):

```
protected void Application_Start()
{
  AreaRegistration.RegisterAllAreas();
  WebApiConfig.Register(GlobalConfiguration.Configuration);
  FilterConfig.RegisterGlobalFilters(GlobalFilters.Filters);
  RouteConfig.RegisterRoutes(RouteTable.Routes);
  BundleConfig.RegisterBundles(BundleTable.Bundles);
  GlobalConfiguration.Configuration.Formatters.Insert(0, new
  JsonpMediaTypeFormatter());
}
```

The following utility class, which helps you with formatting needs, is needed:

```
public class JsonpMediaTypeFormatter : JsonMediaTypeFormatter
{
  private string callbackQueryParameter;

  public JsonpMediaTypeFormatter()
  {
    SupportedMediaTypes.Add(DefaultMediaType);
```

```
    SupportedMediaTypes.Add(new
    MediaTypeHeaderValue("text/javascript"));
    MediaTypeMappings.Add(new UriPathExtensionMapping("jsonp",
    DefaultMediaType));
}

public string CallbackQueryParameter
{
    get { return callbackQueryParameter ?? "callback"; }
    set { callbackQueryParameter = value; }
}

public override Task WriteToStreamAsync(Type type, object value,
Stream stream, HttpContent content, TransportContext
transportContext)
{
    string callback;

    if (IsJsonpRequest(out callback))
    {
        return Task.Factory.StartNew(() =>
        {
            var writer = new StreamWriter(stream);
            writer.Write(callback + "(");
            writer.Flush();

            base.WriteToStreamAsync(type, value, stream, content,
            transportContext).Wait();

            writer.Write(")");
            writer.Flush();
        });
    }
    else{
        return base.WriteToStreamAsync(type, value, stream, content,
        transportContext);
    }
}

private bool IsJsonpRequest(out string callback)
{
    callback = null;

    if (HttpContext.Current.Request.HttpMethod != "GET")
    return false;

    callback = HttpContext.Current.Request.QueryString
    [CallbackQueryParameter];
```

```
        return !string.IsNullOrEmpty(callback);
    }
}
```

Now let's see how we can make a responsive frontend using RxJS:

```
<h3>RxJS Samples:</h3>
<ol class="round">
  <li class="one">
<h5>Spell Checker</h5>
<script type="text/javascript" src="~/Scripts/rx.lite.js">
</script>
<script type="text/javascript" src="~/Scripts/rx.dom.js">
</script>
```

As indicated here, you would need the following two JS files:

```
<script type="text/javascript">
  var textInput;
  var throttledInput;
  var suggestions;
  var resultList;
```

The following function (`initialize`) is called as soon as the DOM is loaded:

```
function initialize() {
  textInput = document.querySelector('#textInput');
  console.log(textInput);
  throttledInput = Rx.DOM.keyup(textInput)
    .do(function (msg) {
      console.log(msg.key);
    })
    .pluck('target', 'value')
    .filter(function (text) {
      return text.length > 3;
    })
    .debounce(500)
    .distinctUntilChanged();
  suggestions = throttledInput.flatMapLatest(SpellChecker);
```

 In the preceding code, we do some throttling, and do not overload the server with requests, by doing the following:

- Transforming keyup DOM events into observable sequences
- Focusing on the value entered (the `pluck` operator here serves this purpose)

- Looking up search items which have more than three characters (using the `filter` operator)

- Slowing down user input with a timeout of 500 milliseconds (using the `debounce` operator)

- Restricting lookup for distinct values in the input stream (using the `distinctUntilChanged` operator):

```
resultList = document.getElementById('results');
suggestions.subscribe(
  function (data) {
    var results = data.response;
    clearSelector(resultList);
    for (var i = 0; i < results.length; i++) {
      resultList.appendChild(createLineItem(results[i]));
    }
  },
  function (e) {
    clearSelector(resultList);
    resultList.appendChild(createLineItem('Error: ' + e));
  }
);
}
```

This function issues the search against the web API, and gets back an observable:

```
function SpellChecker(term) {
  var url = 'http://localhost:18679/api/values/?Lookup='
  + encodeURIComponent(term) +
  '&Count=5&format=json&callback=JSONPCallback';
  return Rx.DOM.jsonpRequest(url);
}
```

The `clearSelector` and `createLineItem` functions are helper functions for DOM manipulations, which facilitate display:

```
function clearSelector(element) {
  while (element.firstChild) {
    element.removeChild(element.firstChild);
  }
}
```

```
function createLineItem(text) {
  var li = document.createElement('li');
  li.innerHTML = text;
  return li;
}
```

```
Rx.DOM.ready().subscribe(initialize);
</script>
  <input id="textInput" type="text"/>
  <ul id="results"></ul>
  </li>
</ol>
```

A sample output is shown in the following screenshot:

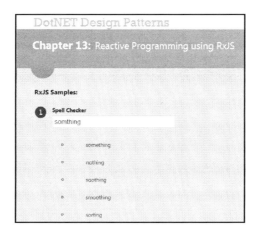

So, by now we have seen how to subscribe to observable sequences (both keyboard events and AJAX calls/responses).

The next sample we will deal with is a logical extension of what we discussed earlier. Remember we asked if you could spot a shortcoming in the file watcher sample that we discussed under observable from callbacks?

Real-time file watcher

The earlier version would terminate the observable sequence upon detecting the first change, thus impairing its ability to continuously detect changes. The solution to this fix is shown as follows:

```
var Rx = require('rx');
// Load Node.js Filesystem module
var fs = require('fs');

var disposable = Rx.Scheduler.default.scheduleRecursive(
  0,
  function (i, recurse) {
    // Create an Observable from the watch method
```

```
var source = Rx.Observable
.fromCallback(fs.watch)('./tmp', { encoding: 'buffer' });
var subscription = source.subscribe(
function (changes) {
  console.log('Next: ', i, changes);
},
function (err) {
  console.log('Error: ', err);
},
function () {
  console.log('Completed');
  ++i;
  recurse(i);
});
  }
);
```

 As you can see in the highlighted code, the fix to the earlier problem is recursive scheduling (using the `sceduleRecursive` operator) upon sequence completion (indicated using `onCompleted`) during an event detection by the file system watcher component.

The following result indicates that our fix works:

```
Next: 0 [ 'change', 'alas.tmp' ]
Completed
Next: 1 [ 'change', 'alas2.tmp' ]
Completed
Next: 2 [ 'change', 'anotherfile.tmp' ]
Completed
```

Change galore

This sample has a wider implication in various domains, especially logistics. The solution involves finding all the change sets for an amount with a given set of currency denominations:

```
// ------------------------Load RxJS module
var Rx = require('rx');
var calculateChange = function (denominations, amount) {
  'use strict';
  var changeSets = 0;
  var subject = new Rx.Subject();
  var changeSetClient = subject
      .do
      (
```

```
        function (denominationSet) {
            console.log(
                'Processing Denominations: ',
                denominationSet);
        }
    )
    .observeOn(Rx.Scheduler.default)
    .subscribe
    (
        function (denominationSet) {
            printChangeSet(denominationSet);
        },
        function (err) {
            console.log('Processing Error: ', err);
        },
        function () {
            console.log('Processing Completed!');
            changeSetClient.dispose();   //Disposal
            subject.dispose();           //Disposal
        }
    );
```

As you can see in the preceding code, here we have a global function (in order to clearly set a boundary on the global scope), which accepts the denominations (in an array) and the amount as two independent attributes. Now, what is important here is the strategy we employed to make the computation (or steps in the algorithm) asynchronous. For this, we used the default scheduler (Rx.Scheduler.default), which never blocks the event loop. In case you noticed, the resource cleanups are done in the onCompleted event:

```
//This function prints the applicable denomination sets
var printChangeSet = function (denominationSet) {
  var matchFactors = [],
    findCombinationSet = function (denominationIndex,
      cumilativeSum) {
    var transientSum = 0,
        i = 1,
        denomination = denominationSet[denominationIndex],
          factorCount = denominationSet.length;
      while (transientSum <= amount) {
        //Pretty Printing
        matchFactors[denominationIndex] = i.toString()
        + " x " + denomination.toString() + "c";
        transientSum = cumilativeSum + (denomination * i);
        if ((denominationIndex + 1) === factorCount) {
            if (transientSum === amount) {
                changeSets += 1;
                console.log(
```

```
                    changeSets + ". " + matchFactors);
            }
        } else {
            findCombinationSet(denominationIndex + 1,
                transientSum);
        }
        i += 1;
        //--------------------Pretty Printing END
    }
};
findCombinationSet(0, 0);
};
```

The `printChangeSet` function again creates a local scope, and further employs the `findCombinationSet` function to shortlist the applicable `changeSets` out of the possible currency combinations (based on the available denominations). Another important thing to note here is the tail call optimization done for the recursion involving the `findCombinationSet` function (see highlighted code) by passing accumulated transient sums, thereby eliminating call-stack growth:

```
// This function computes the possible denomination sets
var generateChangeSets = function () {
  var bitcount = denominations.length,
    mask = Math.pow(2, bitcount),
      i = 1,
      j = 0,
      k = 1,
      denominationSet = null,
      denominationSum = 0;
  while (i < mask) {
    j = 0;
    denominationSet = [];
    denominationSum = 0;
    while (j < bitcount) {
      if ((i & (k << j)) > 0) {
        denominationSet.push(denominations[j]);
        denominationSum += denominations[j];
      }
      j += 1;
    }
    if (denominationSum <= amount) {
      subject.onNext(denominationSet);
    }
    i += 1;
  }
  subject.onCompleted();
};
```

```
    generateChangeSets();
  };
```

In case you are wondering about this `generateChangeSets` function, you guessed it right. This is the JS equivalent of the C# subset generation code we saw in `Chapter 9`, *Functional Programming Techniques for Better State Management*. So, by now you would have got a hang on the algorithm employed here, which can be explained as follows:

1. Generate all possible subsets (possibly denomination combinations).
2. Try to determine possible counts per denomination.
3. If step 2 is successful, do pretty printing, as shown in the following output for `calculateChange([1, 5, 10, 25], 25)`:

```
changeSetClient Processing Denominations: [ 1 ]
changeSetClient Processing Denominations: [ 5 ]
changeSetClient Processing Denominations: [ 1, 5 ]
changeSetClient Processing Denominations: [ 10 ]
changeSetClient Processing Denominations: [ 1, 10 ]
changeSetClient Processing Denominations: [ 5, 10 ]
changeSetClient Processing Denominations: [ 1, 5, 10 ]
changeSetClient Processing Denominations: [ 25 ]
1. 25 x 1c
2. 5 x 5c
3. 5 x 1c,4 x 5c
4. 10 x 1c,3 x 5c
5. 15 x 1c,2 x 5c
6. 20 x 1c,1 x 5c
7. 5 x 1c,2 x 10c
8. 15 x 1c,1 x 10c
9. 1 x 5c,2 x 10c
10. 3 x 5c,1 x 10c
11. 5 x 1c,2 x 5c,1 x 10c
12. 10 x 1c,1 x 5c,1 x 10c
13. 1 x 25c
changeSetClient Processing Completed!
```

In case you didn't notice, the console logs appear first before the results are printed, clearly indicating that step 2 and beyond are asynchronous!

Summary

By now you must have understood how reactive programming is employed for modeling solutions the way the world exists. The principle has been applied for various mainstream programming languages, as thought leaders such as Erik Meijer found this too natural to express and compose. And we got lucky in this discovery process. We believe, as developers, you must have have started appreciating the world of functional and reactive programming beyond OOP. In the next chapter, we will be specifying, in brief, some important topics which could not be covered in the book, such as polyglot programming, **domain specific languages (DSLs)**, ontology, and AntiPatterns.

14
A Road Ahead

It has been a whirlwind journey on various topics through our book. If you have reached this point, you might have come across some new concepts, or might have had a fresh look at some things that you already knew. Broadly speaking, the theme of this book can be divided into the following four sections:

- Putting patterns into perspective (Chapter 1 and 2)
- GoF in action (Chapter 3 through 7)
- Object/functional programming (Chapter 8 to 10)
- (Functional) reactive programming (Chapter 11, 12, and 13)

Patterns are an interesting topic, and they have helped software developers to address complex business problems by providing proven and time-tested solutions. It has also improved communication between developers and their stakeholders. By learning patterns, as a developer, you get distilled knowledge and experience of those master programmers who cataloged these patterns. But there are some more topics that you should know in your journey as a developer or an architect. The authors of this book consider the following four topics of great interest to a professional (as a continuation of the topics covered in this book):

- Polyglot programming and design (multi paradigm programming)
- Domain-specific languages
- Ontology
- AntiPatterns

Polyglot programming and design

Modern applications are complex to develop as they might have the following:

- Service layer with a database for persistence (SQL or NoSQL)
- The UI code has to be responsive and calibrated for different form factor devices
- The frontend code is mostly based on some kind of **Single Page Architecture (SPA)** architecture
- In some cases, there can be desktop and mobile native frontends

A developer who has been hired for such a project should have the following skills:

- Java, C#, PHP, Ruby, or Grails for writing service layers (skills in one or more)
- For writing UI code, they should be familiar with CSS libraries and JavaScript (e.JQuery)
- For web-based responsive frontend, TypeScript/JavaScript using Angular, ReactJs, or any other JavaScript-based framework
- For writing desktop applications, the choices are C#, C++, Objective C/C++, Python, or Java
- For mobile application development (native), choices are C#, Java, or Objective C/Swift

The bottom line here is that one should be comfortable with at least more than half a dozen programming languages to be in a position to work with modern projects. If you add skills in PowerShell, Bash shell, JSP/HTML/template engines, XML, JSON, and so on, we are indeed living in a world where a person has to be really conversant in as many languages as possible.

Let us trace the evolution of this state of affairs by quickly chronicling the history of development under the PC platform. The programming landscape has changed quite a lot in the last decade. When the GoF pattern book was written, programming languages such as Java and C# had not been born. The dominant object-oriented programming language in those days, for all practical purpose was C++. Even for C++, the ANSI standards were not ratified (it happened only in 1998). Other than C++, languages such as Delphi (Object Pascal),Visual Basic, PowerBuilder, and various xBase dialects (Clipper, FoxPro, and the like) were widely used by programmers of that era. Platforms such as Microsoft Windows were just evolving. Various flavors of UNIX and MS-DOS were the primary platforms (even GNU Linux had not reached a critical mass in those times!).

Even in the early years of programming, it was realized that one cannot build solutions using a single programing language. We need to mix and match programming languages that are apt for the context. At one point in time, most numerical libraries were written in Fortran, and those libraries were interfaced with the C language for writing systems, which are numerically intensive. In the early years of programming, people used to write code in a high-level language, and interface their code with routines written in C and assembler. Thus, a programmer needs to know a high-level language, C programing language, and the syntax of the assembly language of the environment in which the program was developed and deployed. The process of developing a large system using different programming languages for writing different subsystems and composing them to create a larger system is called polyglot programming. Designing such systems, where there is a multitude of programming languages and technology stacks, is called polyglot design. To design such a system, developers should be able to think in a language-and-platform-agnostic manner.

The movement towards polyglot programming started in the early years of programming on the IBM PC platform. Polyglot programming was mostly an affair of interfacing routines written in the C programming language to a high-level language chosen for writing the system.

Polyglot programming with C/C++

When people programmed in various languages other than C/C++, there were options available for interfacing with C/C++, code packaged as DLLs or `.so` in Windows and Unix/Linux, respectively. In MS-DOS, all xBase languages offered an interface mechanism to interact with the native code written in C/C++ and Assembler/. In the Microsoft Windows platform, Visual Basic offered a mechanism to call routines written in C/C++/. Using this mechanism, people consumed a vast amount of Windows API functions provided by Microsoft. People began to program Windows using Visual Basic and Visual C++. The visual development environments such as Delphi and PowerBuilder also provided similar mechanisms to consume code written in C/C++. This can be considered as the beginning of programming systems using multiple languages, and is nowadays called Polyglot programming.

With the advent of the Java programming language, the promise of platform-neutral programming became a buzzword in the Industry. The **write once, run everywhere (WORE)** mantra came to the fore, and it did not prevent the implementers of Java to give a mechanism to interact with native code written in C/C++. The interface was called **Java Native Interface (JNI)**. Using this mechanism, people wrote wrappers around technologies such as Direct3D and OpenGL to create libraries like Java 3D. The popular computer vision system, OpenCV, is interfaced with Java software using JNI.

The .NET platform was unveiled in the year 2001, and it gave two interfaces to interface with the native code. The first one was PInvoke, a mechanism to interface with Win2/Win64 calls exported out of DLLs. Microsoft also gave a mechanism to call C++-based COM components called COM interoperability. They named it COM callable wrapper. To demonstrate the use of P/Invoke, here is a small C/C++ code snippet (compiled into a DLL) interfaced with C# code:

```cpp
#include <stdio.h>
#include <cstring>
#include <Windows.h>

using namespace std;
//A C/C++ Windows DLL which exports a Function
//ListOfSquares to be consumed from C# programming
//language. The DLL is compiled using Minimalist
//GNU for Windows (MINGW),which is freely downloadable
//
//Compile and Link
//----------------
//  gcc -c -o add_basic.o cpp_code.cpp
//  gcc -o add_basic.dll -s -shared add_basic.o -Wl,
//  --subsystem,windows
//

extern "C" __declspec(dllexport) void __stdcall
ListOfSquares(
  long (__stdcall *square_callback) (int rs) )

{
  for (int i = 0; i<10; ++i) {
    //---- Call the C# routine which handles the
    //---- integer and returns square.
    //---- This is a blocking call!

    double ret = (*square_callback)(i);
    printf("Printing from C/C++ ... %g\n", ret);
  }
}
```

We can compile the preceding code using the Visual C++ compiler or MinGW compiler (GCC under Windows) to create a DLL. We have used the MinGW 32-bit compiler to generate the Win32 DLL. The DLL can be interfaced with C# code written using Visual Studio or Mono compiler under Windows. If you know how to build a shared library (.so) under Mac OS X or GNU Linux, we can run the code on those platforms as well. The C# code can be used to invoke the DLL written previously:

```csharp
using System;
using System.Collections.Generic;
using System.Linq;
using System.Runtime.InteropServices;
using System.Text;
using System.Threading.Tasks;

namespace entrypoint
{
  class Program
  {
    //--- Now you know, a C/C++ Function Pointer
    //--- is indeed a delegate!
    public delegate long CallBack(int i);
    //--- Declare the Function Prototype of the Function
    //--- We are planning to call from C/C++
    [DllImport("D:\\DLL_FOR_DEMO\\add_basic.dll")]
    private static extern long ListOfSquares(CallBack a);

    public static long SpitConsole(int i)
    {
      Console.WriteLine("Printing from C# {0}", i * i);
      return i * i;
    }

    static void Main(string[] args)
    {
      /////////////////////////////
      // CallBack Demo
      // Will print Square from C# and C++
      ListOfSquares(SpitConsole);
    }
  }
}
```

The polyglot web programming

The **World Wide Web** (**WWW**) reached critical mass roughly in the year 1995, and the programming landscape changed all of a sudden. People who learned to program desktop systems using Windows API and X/Windows API found themselves in a position of great difficulty, forced to grapple with the complexities of the **Common Gateway Interface** (**CGI**), NSAPI, and ISAPI programming model to generate dynamic web pages. The languages of choice were Perl and TCL for CGI, and C/C++ for NSAPI/ISAPI.

The situation continued for some time, and it all changed all of a sudden when Microsoft brought out **Active Server Pages** (**ASP**) for creating dynamic web pages. Soon, Sun Microsystems came up with Java Servlet API. The Servlet API was a low-level API like C++-based ISAPI, and Sun soon brought out **JavaServer Pages** (**JSP**), a technology that embedded Java code inside markups. The JSPs were converted to Servlet code on the fly using the Java Compiler system available on the executing machine. There were technologies such as ColdFusion, which leveraged custom markups to write extensible applications, and had the capacity to interact with code written in Java. The Web programming model mandated people to learn C++, Java, Visual Basic, and ASP to write dynamic web pages. On the Microsoft platform, people began to write VBScript code interspersed with calls to COM/ActiveX objects written in C++ and Visual Basic. In fact, the emergence of web-based application delivery forced programmers to become a true polyglot.

The JavaScript evolution

The emergence of JavaScript was another thing that forced developers to learn yet another language to add a bit of interactivity to their web pages. In those times, people were mostly comfortable with statically typed languages, and found JavaScript to be a weird language. JavaScript remained in relative obscurity for a long time, until someone found out a clever way to mix JavaScript with IE ActiveX plugin. In the early years of the twenty-first century, people began to write user interfaces by embedding browser controls inside a desktop container, and used JavaScript as a glue language to interact with the ActiveX controls embedded in those pages. JavaScript picked up momentum, and people began to consider it as a first class programming language after the advent of Google's V8 engine and the Node.js platform. Another shot in the arm was the support for functional style programming using the JavaScript language, and the emergence of libraries such as JQuery, Angular, ReactJS, and the like. In the last decade, knowledge of the JavaScript programming language became essential for all programmers, whether they wrote server code or client code. JavaScript is another language that programmers were forced to learn.

Dynamic/scripting languages

The emergence of Perl, Python, PHP, Ruby, TCL, and Groovy for writing command line, GUI, and web applications forced developers to master some of them in their day-to-day job. PERL is still widely used for writing CGI applications, automation scripts, and even GUI applications (Perl/TK) all across the world. The Python programming language is the de-facto programming language for writing (or at least learning) machine learning programs because of the libraries available in that language, and they are widely used for writing web applications with some MVC frameworks.

Both Ruby on Rails and Groovy and Grails ushered in a rapid development lifecycle era to make their penetration in the start-up ecosystem. PHP is the most popular web development system in the world, and it is especially suited for writing front-facing applications. The sheer number of content management systems available with the platform is another attraction. Architecting solutions with PHP for front-facing pages, Java for Service logic, and Silverlight for frontend (for interactive parts) became popular in some circles! The popularity of the REST paradigm has made writing the server-side logic to be in whatever language one chooses to. As long as the URI is consistent, the routing system makes sure that it resolves the correct handler logic to get executed.

Emergence of functional programming

As mentioned in the first chapter, Herb Sutter's seminal article titled, *The Free Lunch Is Over*, rekindled interest in functional programming, which was mostly relegated to academic circles. The FP model was well suited for exploiting the many-core processing world. The stateless computation model of the FP helps to scale an application from a single core to dozens of cores without any additional programming effort. The emergence of Scala, F#, Clojure, Haskell (in some niche areas), and so on, and the availability of them in the JVM and CLR world made them a viable choice for writing some applications. In the Microsoft world, people began to write code in C# and F#, to bundle the code inside the same system. Learning a functional language (one or more) became absolutely essential for modern-day programmers. Another excuse to become a polyglot!

Mobile revolution

Some competence in mobile application development is necessary for every software developer in the world. Apple's iOS, Google's Android, and Microsoft's Windows Phone are the leading platforms in this arena. Unfortunately, native application development languages in these platforms are Objective C/Swift (iOS), Java (Android), and C# (Windows Phone). A .NET developer has to learn Java, Objective C, or Swift to write native applications for these platforms. If you want to avoid this, you might have to use hybrid application development with JavaScript as a programming language. Anyway, you need to be a Polyglot!

A quick note on polyglot persistence

For a long time, the **Relational database management systems** (**RDBMSs**) became the backbone of every business application ever developed. The Oracle Server, Microsoft SQL Server, MYSQL, and Postgres systems were the de-facto choice for persisting data. The emergence of the NoSQL movement gave us different types of databases suitable for distributed programs, which should scale well. They are listed as follows:

- Columnar databases
- Key/value databases
- Document databases
- Graph databases

NoSQL is a vast and varied topic, and the reader is expected to search Google to understand it, as a fair treatment of it warrants many books. So, a modern web-based application might store data in various persistence technologies available, based on the application context. A typical use case could be any one of the following:

- An RDBMS for storing transactional data
- A key/value database for storing master data (for faster lookup)
- A graph database for storing relationship between entities
- A columnar database for data that is part of analytical queries

By choosing the appropriate backend technologies, the application can ensure throughput and scalability for large-scale applications development. The process of using different persistence technologies in an application is called **polyglot persistence**. A developer should be really familiar with this paradigm along with polyglot programming.

How to become a polyglot programmer?

From a programming paradigm perspective, there are only three types of programming languages in this world, which are as follows:

- Functional languages (based on lambda calculus)
- Logic languages (based on predicate logic)
- Imperative languages (based on Turing machines)

To be a contemporary developer, one needs to master a couple of languages from each family. To be competent in FP, the language options available are F#, Clojure, and Scala. The logic programming languages are Prolog and Datalog. Learning them will help on improving design skills, especially in building hierarchical data structures. The type inference algorithm available with F#, Scala, and C# uses the unification algorithm, which forms the backbone of the Prolog language. Thus, understanding the Prolog machine model helps you to appreciate and exploit the rich type systems available with the modern programming languages. Most of the popular languages are imperative in nature, and mastering a couple of object/functional languages (such as C#, Java 8, and Scala) really helps. Once you learn a representative language from each of the aforementioned families, you have made the cognitive leap to understanding every programming language ever created or going to be created in the near future!

Domain-specific languages

A language developed for expressing solutions to problems that are specific to a domain such as finance, payroll, electronic circuit design, parser generators, input validations, and so on is called a **domain-specific language (DSL)**. Two common examples that are familiar to most programmers are **Structured Query Language (SQL)** and **regular expression (RE)**. If we were to write imperative code for retrieving data from a database, it would have been a difficult task and error prone. SQL gives you a declarative language to achieve the same objective, and it has solid mathematical foundations. While searching strings, RE helps us to give complicated patterns to match against a string. It helps to avoid writing tedious logic for searching complicated string matches.

As a concrete example of a DSL, which is quite popular in the .NET and Java world, we are pasting here a specification given to the **ANTLR** tool to write a very simple arithmetic evaluator. The tool generates a lexical analyzer and parser automatically from this specification. Please consult the ANTLR documentation to understand the semantics of the following script:

```
grammar Evaluator;

options {
  language=CSharp3;
}

@lexer::namespace{AntlrExample}
@parser::namespace{AntlrExample}
public addop
: mulop (( '+' | '-' ) mulop)*;
mulop
```

```
: INTEGER (( '*' | '/' ) INTEGER)*;
/*
  * Lexical Analysis Rules
*/

INTEGER : '0'..'9'+;
WS :  (' '|'\t'|'\r'|'\n')+ {Skip();} ;
```

The ANTLR tool will generate a lexical analyzer, a parser module, and even a tree walker to process the expression. We can write parsers for C#, Java, and even C/C++ using this tool. In the Unix and the Windows native programming world, the tool Lex (GNU Flex) and Yacc (GNU Bison) is used for the same purpose.

As another case in point, authors worked in a DSL project, which evaluated a spreadsheet for consistency. A code snippet from the turing complete DSL generated for the project is given here:

```
Boolean range_flag;
NUMERIC sum_value;

BEGIN

//--- See whether B3 cell in the CONTROL worksheet
//--- present in the Relational database
VALIDATE   LOOKUP($(CONTROL.B3),
@(EI_SEGMENT_MAPPING.EI_SEGMENT_CODE))==TRUE;

//---- The Sum of Range should be 100 or Zero
range_flag = SUM_RANGE($(HOURLY_DISTRIBUTION.C2),
$(HOURLY_DISTRIBUTION.C25))  == 100.0;
range_flag =  range_flag ||
SUM_RANGE($(HOURLY_DISTRIBUTION.C2),
$(HOURLY_DISTRIBUTION.C25)) == 0.0;

//--- If false throw exception
VALIDATE range_flag;

EXCEPTION
//----- on Exception execute this
ErrorString = "FAILED WHILE VALIDATING CONTROL Sheet Or"
ErrorString = ErroString +
" WorkSheet Error in the range C2-C25";
WRITELOG  ErrorString;
bResult = false;

END
```

The preceding code snippet was parsed using a hand-coded recursive descent parser, and an **abstract syntax tree** (**AST**) was generated. The tree was traversed in a depth-first manner to generate a .NET IL code to generate a .NET assembly (DLL). The resulting assembly was consumed as if the logic were written in C#!

The **Extensible Stylesheet Language** (**XSL**) is another domain-specific language, which is very much familiar to most programmers. A small XSL snippet is given here for the sake of completeness, and readers are expected to master this language for generating sites with variant layouts:

```
<?xml version="1.0"?>
<xsl:stylesheet xmlns:xsl="http://www.w3.org/1999/XSL/Transform"
version="1.0">
  <xsl:output method="xml"/>
  <xsl:template match="*">
    <xsl:element name="{name()}">
      <xsl:for-each select="@*">
        <xsl:element name="{name()}">
          <xsl:value-of select="."/>
        </xsl:element>
      </xsl:for-each>
      <xsl:apply-templates select="*|text()"/>
    </xsl:element>
  </xsl:template>
</xsl:stylesheet>
```

The other popular DSLs are VHDL and Verilog (Digital Hardware Description Language), CSS, and template languages available with different technology stacks, JBoss Drools, and so on.

Writing and designing one's own DSL is a very vast topic, which cannot be covered in a short chapter. Some things that one needs to take care of are as follows:

- Designing an object model, which mimics domain concerns
- Designing a linguistic abstraction and associated key words for arriving at language elements and rules for composing elements to form compound elements
- Mapping language elements to the object model created
- Deciding whether the DSL should be internal or external?
- Deciding whether the DSL should be turing complete or not

The topic is well covered by Debasish Ghosh and Martin Fowler/Rebecca Parsons in their wonderful books. Please consult the following books for a thorough understanding of the same:

- *DSLs in Action* by Debashish Ghosh (Manning)
- *Domain-Specific Languages* by Martin Fowler and Rebecca Parsons (Addison Wesley Martin Fowler signature series)

Ontology

In software engineering parlance, Ontology is the art, craft, and science of describing entities (types), attributes (properties), and relationships that exist in a particular domain of discourse. It can also be considered as a model for describing entities, attributes, their relationship, and even standard behavior. An ontology really helps to come up with a ubiquitous language (as in **Domain-Driven Design (DDD)**), where all stakeholders agree, and which eases communication. It avoids confusion while developing multi-domain software systems. An ontology defines and represents the basic terms and relations that exist in a software engineering context.

From an information processing perspective, the following points are to be noted:

- The propositional and predicate logic gives the rules of inference and formal structures to encode facts
- The ontology defines and helps to represent entities, their attributes, and the relationship between the entities in an unambiguous manner
- The computation helps to implement ontologies on a computer-it helps us go beyond the philosophical ontology (first two steps)

To write non-trivial knowledge processing systems, a software engineer should acquire skills in defining and interpreting ontologies. He should also be able to encode the ontology and its associated rules on a computer to create working computation models of the ontology in question. In software engineering, a well-defined ontology helps in the following:

- Sharing knowledge between stakeholders about problem/solutions domain using a common terminology
- Filtering the ontology to create models and meta models for application development (projections of an ontology)
- Computation using the elements defined in the ontology

There are different ways by which we can encode an ontology. All of them share common elements, which are as follows:

- Classes, types, or concepts
- Relations, roles, or properties
- Formal rules or axioms
- Instances

The W3C Semantic Web has created an XML-based language called **Web Ontology Language (OWL)** for describing ontologies in a structured manner. The OWL embeds **Resource Description Format (RDF)** tags to define standard ontologies. A transportation ontology from an IBM site goes as follows. These OWL markups specify that there are three classes:

```
<owl:Class rdf:ID="Winery"/>
<owl:Class rdf:ID="Region"/>
<owl:Class rdf:ID="ConsumableThing"/>

<owl:Class rdf:ID="PotableLiquid">
  <rdfs:subClassOf rdf:resource="#ConsumableThing" />
</owl:Class>

<owl:Class rdf:ID="Wine">
  <rdfs:subClassOf rdf:resource="&food;PotableLiquid"/>
  <rdfs:label xml:lang="en">wine</rdfs:label>
  <rdfs:label xml:lang="fr">vin</rdfs:label>
</owl:Class>

<owl:Thing rdf:ID="CentralCoastRegion" />
<owl:Thing rdf:about="#CentralCoastRegion">
  <rdf:type rdf:resource="#Region"/>
</owl:Thing>

<owl:Class rdf:ID="WineDescriptor" />
<owl:Class rdf:ID="WineColor">
  <rdfs:subClassOf rdf:resource="#WineDescriptor" />
</owl:Class>

<owl:ObjectProperty rdf:ID="hasWineDescriptor">
  <rdfs:domain rdf:resource="#Wine" />
  <rdfs:range  rdf:resource="#WineDescriptor" />
</owl:ObjectProperty>

<owl:ObjectProperty rdf:ID="hasColor">
  <rdfs:subPropertyOf rdf:resource="#hasWineDescriptor" />
  <rdfs:range rdf:resource="#WineColor" />
```

```
</owl:ObjectProperty>
```

This section was written to kindle interest in ontology for readers of this book. The DDD is a topic very closely related to ontology, and people who have written object-oriented systems can relate to them very fast. To get into the ontology-based software development method, we would like to recommend a wonderful book written by John Sowa, titled, *Knowledge Representation: Logical, Philosophical and Computational Foundations*. Chapter 2 of that book deals with ontology as applied to software engineering. Also learn about the semantic web initiative by the W3C, by visiting their site.

AntiPatterns

An AntiPattern is a solution to a problem that seems to produce gain initially, but turns out to be counterproductive eventually. As patterns are named solutions, it might not be fit for certain kind of scenarios, and end up being an AntiPattern. The context in which we apply patterns is very important. AntiPatterns occur in various scenarios of a software development life cycle. They are broadly classified into these three categories:

- Software development AntiPatterns
- Architectural AntiPatterns
- Management (process) AntiPatterns

AntiPatterns: Refactoring Software, Architectures, and Projects in Crisis by William J. Brown, Raphael C. Malveau, Hays W. McCormick III, and Thomas J. Mowbray is a seminal work on the AntiPattern.

For the sake of kick-starting the discussion, we would like to cover some of the AntiPatterns that are ubiquitous and to which the readers of this book might be able to relate in their context:

- **The Blob AntiPattern**: This often happens when people from a procedural programming language background design object-oriented systems. They create a big class, which contains most of the logic, and the associated classes are just containers of data. This AntiPattern results in making a class take a lion's share of the responsibility, while the other classes execute trivial logic. The solution is to refactor the class and distribute responsibilities.
- **The Lave Flow AntiPattern**: This is also called dead code, and is often found in systems that started out as POC, and incrementally morphed into a production system. In this transformation, a lot of code is not used or never reached.

- **Functional Decomposition AntiPattern**: An AntiPattern that emerges in scenarios where primary designers of systems come from procedural languages such as C or Fortran, and try to fit their time-tested techniques to an OOP paradigm. Even after twenty years of OOP becoming mainstream, this is a recurring pattern.

- **The Poltergeist (aka Gypsy)**: In the OOP context, sometimes, developers create classes that have a short life cycle to kick-start the processing by core classes, which have long duration. This can be eliminated by refactoring the code to include the logic of these ghost classes to the hierarchy of classes created for the solution of the problem.

- **The Golden Hammer**: This AntiPattern emerges in the context where the primary designers of the system might have a favorite technology, technique, or methodology while solving problems. The old adage, *For a person with hammer, everything appears to be a nail* clearly summarizes this mindset. The favorite tool is unleashed in a context where it might fit remotely. As anecdotal evidence, one of the author knows a person who will try to solve every problem through SNMP, where an ordinary TCP/IP program would have done the job.

- **The Dead End**: This often happens where a team might have leveraged a custom control written by an ISV to speed up the development process. While in production, the vendor might go bankrupt, or the product might not be supported by the company that acquired the vendor. By this time, the code base could get coupled with the custom control in question. Writing an isolation layer with interfaces meant for the same could avert this problem. The authors have come across dozens of such systems.

- **Resume-Driven Design**: The majority of developers, especially in the software services industry across the world, put their resume in front of the problem they are trying to solve. The presence or absence of certain buzzword technologies determines their compensation, and they use the latest technologies for situations where it is not warranted. This is so common that it is very easy to detect, as some simple scenarios will contain all the technologies currently in the hype cycle. One of the authors found himself in a situation where the code base happened to have an m framework, NoSQL database (a text file would have done the trick), a plugin architecture based on Microsoft **Managed Extensibility Framework** (**MEF**), a messaging system, and a cache manager for a system that would have taken thirty lines of a transaction-script like code. The current trend of converting projects that are running in production well to Angular 2/Typescript is another case of resume-driven design.

- **Spaghetti Code**: This is an emergent phenomena in most systems, even in systems that were well defined initially. There was a mistaken notion that Spaghetti code was found only in procedural programming code base and COBOL. In OOP systems, as the system evolves and initial developers move away, the new developers who might not have much clue about the whole system, might end up writing code in a spaghetti style. Recently, authors found a Silverlight application, which used the MVVM pattern, and that had more spaghetti style code than a mainframe COBOL program!

- **Cut and Paste Programming**: This often happens in large systems where a new developer who is given a tight deadline tries to leverage code written elsewhere to speed up his development time. The developer cuts and pastes a large block of code that implements similar functionality, and makes the necessary changes. In the process, some residual code gets executed unnecessarily in the new content. One of the authors, who worked with a large electronic CAD software, found performance issues in the code as the developers resorted to the *Cut and Paste* model development, leading to some nested loops running unnecessarily. Because of the Spaghetti code acquired over a period of time, it happened at multiple places.

- **The StovePipe System**: In most enterprises, because of the evolutionary nature of application development, software systems are integrated in an ad hoc manner. Some software might use resource tier integration (using relational databases), some might use transaction scripts (using a batch job engine) , point-to-point integration using REST/SOAP services, and applications run on multiple technology stacks through multiple messaging systems based on JMS and MSMQ protocol. Due to mergers and acquisitions, and lack of unified enterprise strategy, the whole scenario becomes a maintenance nightmare. By having an enterprise integration strategy and internal standards, we can reduce the complexity of integration.

The other popular AntiPatterns are Vendor Lock-in, Design by Committee, Warm Bodies, Architecture by Implication, Intellectual Violence, Analysis Paralysis, Smoke and Mirrors, and so on.

AntiPatterns are a topic that is as important as the patterns. While patterns give you time-trusted named solutions to common problems, AntiPatterns and their solutions avoid pitfalls in your software engineering life cycle. This topic warrants a book of its own. We have just given some brief descriptions here.

Summary

The chapter dealt with some pointers for the readers to further their study of software engineering techniques. The topics covered include polyglot programming, DSL, ontology, and AntiPatterns. We could only mention these topics briefly, as these topics require multiple books to do justice to them. There is indeed good material available on these topics in the form of YouTube videos, white papers, and books. Also try to understand more about various pattern catalogs mentioned in the first chapter of this book to have a solid foundation for architecting future systems.

Index

Y

Made in the USA
Lexington, KY
08 April 2017